Gendering Orientalism

FC 3811
B 38

To what extent did white European women contribute to the imperial cultures of the second half of the nineteenth century?

In contrast to most cultural histories of imperialism, which analyse Orientalist images of rather than by women, *Gendering Orientalism* focuses on how women themselves contributed. Drawing on the little-known work of Henriette Browne, other 'lost' women Orientalist artists and the literary works of George Eliot, the author challenges masculinist assumptions relating to the stability and homogeneity of the Orientalist gaze.

Gendering Orientalism argues that women did not have straightforward access to an implicitly male position of Western superiority. Their relationship to the shifting terms of race, nation and gender produced positions from which women writers and artists could articulate alternative representations of racial difference. In order to draw out how the meanings attributed to their words and images, as well as to the writers and artists themselves, were specifically gendered, classed and racialized, the author examines women's visual and literary Orientalism through their contemporary reception in the press.

By revealing the extent of women's involvement in the popular field of visual Orientalism and highlighting the presence of Orientalist themes and structures in the work of Browne, Eliot and Charlotte Brontë, *Gendering Orientalism* argues for a more complex understanding of women's role in imperial culture and discourse. The book should appeal to all students and lecturers in cultural studies, literature, art history, women's studies and visual anthropology.

Reina Lewis is Senior Lecturer in the Department of Cultural Studies at the University of East London.

Gender, Racism, Ethnicity
Series editors:
Kum-Kum Bhavnani, *University of California at Santa Barbara*;
Avtar Brah, *University of London*;
Gail Lewis, *The Open University*;
Ann Phoenix, *University of London*

Gender, Racism, Ethnicity is a new series whose main concern is to promote rigorous feminist analysis of the intersections between gender, racism, ethnicity, class and sexuality within the contexts of imperialism, colonialism and neo-colonialism. Intended to contribute new perspectives to current debates and to introduce fresh analysis, it will provide valuable teaching texts for undergraduates, lecturers and researchers in anthropology, women's studies, cultural studies and sociology.

Other titles in the series:

White Women, Race Matters
Ruth Frankenberg

Fear of the Dark
Lola Young

Gendering Orientalism

Race, Femininity and Representation

Reina Lewis

London and New York

First published 1996
by Routledge
11 New Fetter Lane, London EC4P 4EE

Simultaneously published in the USA and Canada
by Routledge
29 West 35th Street, New York, NY 10001

© 1996 Reina Lewis

Typeset in Times by Florencetype Ltd, Stoodleigh, Devon

Printed and bound in Great Britain by
Biddles Ltd, Guildford and Kings Lynn

British Library Cataloguing in Publication Data
A catalogue record for this book is available from the
British Library

Library of Congress Cataloguing in Publication Data
A catalogue record for this book has been requested

ISBN 0–415–12489–1 (hbk)
ISBN 0–415–12490–5 (pbk)

For my parents,
Estelle Lewis and Hilly Lewis

Contents

Plates

Plate 11 Jean-Léon Gérôme, *Slave Market*, n.d. Oil on canvas, 84.3 × 63cm. Stirling and Francine Clarke Art Institute, Williamstown, Massachusetts.

Plate 12 Henriette Browne, *Une joueuse de flûte (intérieur de harem, Constantinople, 1860), A Flute Player (Harem Interior; Constantinople, 1860)*, 1861. Oil on canvas, dimensions unknown. Photograph courtesy of the département des livres imprimés, Bibliothèque Nationale, Paris.

Plate 13 Henriette Browne, *Une visite (intérieur de harem, Constantinople, 1860), A Visit (Harem Interior; Constantinople, 1860)*, 1861. Oil on canvas, 86 × 114cm. Photograph courtesy of Sotheby's, London.

Plate 14 Alexandre Gabriel Decamps, *The Turkish School*, 1843. Materials and dimensions unknown. Amsterdams Historisch Museum – Fodor Collection.

Plate 15 John Frederick Lewis, *The Arab Scribe, Cairo*, 1852. Watercolour heightened with white, 46.3 × 60.9cm. Bridgeman Art Library.

Plate 16 John Frederick Lewis, *The Reception*, 1873. Oil on canvas, 63.5 × 72.6cm. Yale Centre for British Art, Paul Mellon Collection.

Plate 17 John Frederick Lewis, *The Siesta*, 1876. Oil on canvas, 87.5 × 109.4cm. The Tate Gallery, London.

Plate 18 Jean-Auguste-Dominique Ingres, *Bain Turq, The Turkish Bath*, 1862. Oil on canvas, 108cm diameter. Clichés des Musées Nationaux – Paris. © Photo R.M.N.

Plate 19 Jean-Jules-Antoine Lecomte de Nouy, *L'esclave blanche, The White Slave*, 1888. Oil on canvas, 146 × 118cm. Cliché Ville de Nantes – P. Jean.

Plate 20 Maria Harriet Matthias, *Crusader Castle, Gracia, Gulf of Akaba*, (detail) 1857. watercolour, 23.5 × 35cm. Courtesy of the Board of Trustees of Victoria and Albert Museum.

Plate 21 Margaret Murray Cookesley, *Nubian Girl*, 1886. Materials and dimensions unknown. Courtesy Mathaf Gallery, London.

Plate 22 Margaret Murray Cookesley, *Entertaining in the Harem*, 1894. Oil on canvas, 29 × 39cm. Photograph courtesy of Sotheby's, London.

Plate 23 Margaret Murray Cookesley, *Smoking the Pipe*, 1893. Oil on panel, 30 × 46cm. Courtesy Mathaf Gallery, London.

Acknowledgements

The research for this book was originally undertaken for a Ph.D. at Middlesex University and I must begin by thanking Francis Mulhern for being such a patient, human and, above all, encouraging director of studies. I wish also to thank Annie Coombes and Lisa Tickner for their suggestions, supervisory advice and comments. I am especially grateful to Lisa for bringing Henriette Browne to my attention. Catherine Hall and Jon Bird examined the thesis and I am thankful also for their comments. The transformation from thesis to book was assisted by three editors of this series, Avtar Brah, Ann Phoenix and Kum-Kum Bhavnani, whose readings of the manuscript were attentive, encouraging and constructive. This book has benefited hugely from the insights of all the readers above; the mistakes are, as always, all my own work.

I am grateful to the British Academy of Great Britain for awarding me the Major State Studentship that enabled me to commence my studies and to the ERASMUS scheme for granting me the monies for study abroad. Numerous libraries and librarians have assisted with queries, lost references and subject searches, in many cases being exceedingly obliging about liaising by telephone when I lived out of London. I am grateful to the staff at the libraries of Middlesex, Sussex, London (Senate House and the Moccatta Library) and Leeds universities, West Surrey College of Art and Design, the Bibliothèque Nationale, Paris, the British Library, the National Art Library at the Victoria and Albert Museum, the Witt Picture Library at the Courtauld Institute, University of London and the Institute of Historical Research, University of London.

Assistance in tracking down work by Browne and other women

Orientalists has been generously forthcoming from Phillips, London, and from Joanna Ling at Sotheby's, London; as well as Sotheby's, New York; the Tate Gallery; the Mathaf Gallery, London; Penny Thompson at the Russell-Cotes Art Gallery and Museum, Bournemouth; the Wallace Collection, London; and the Walker Art Gallery, Liverpool. I am also indebted to Kathy Gordon, at the Courtauld Institute, for sharing with me her information on the whereabouts of Browne's work. Responses to Browne's work and tips about reproductions and reviews have been generously forthcoming from Charles Newton, Briony Llewelyn, Paul Greenhalgh, Tom Gretton, John House and Mary Douglas.

Many friends have listened, sympathized, advised, fed and cheered me up on the numerous occasions that I have moaned, fixated and obsessed about the thesis and then the book. I should like to thank Annette Burfoot, Karen Adler, Katrina Rolley, Kate Stockwell, Gillian Gholam, Helen Lowe, Katie Coombes, Sally Munt, Peter Horne, Kate Sturge, Razia Aziz, Marian Fixler, Andy Darley, David Bate, Joanne Entwistle, Paula Graham and Susannah Radstone. I wish to thank Penny Hamm and friends for housing me so delightfully in Paris. My colleagues at West Surrey College of Art and Design and, more recently, at the University of East London, have been interested and encouraging as well as willing to facilitate research time, for which I am grateful. At home, I have been supported by my parents Estelle Lewis and Hilly Lewis and encouraged no end by my sisters Helena and Laura. My biggest debt of gratitude goes to Sue Hamilton who never knew the calm, sane and happy person that I seem to recall I was before I started this work and has anyway, I think, given her up as a figment of my imagination; she has provided the obsessed, anxious and driven person that I became with large measures of encouragement, love and bodily sustenance for which I shall always be thankful.

Introduction
Making connections

This is a book about a problem: a problem that crosses centuries, yet is historically specific; a problem that crosses continents, yet tells us more about one than the others; a problem that is embedded in the seemingly distant 'high' culture of the nineteenth century, yet whose dynamics are active in everyday life in the late twentieth century. This problem is the relationship between imperialism, women and culture.

Part of my reason for writing this book was to provide a historically informed and cultural perspective on specific contemporary struggles. In particular, I was concerned to help challenge the historically inscribed inequalities and patterns of discrimination that are today organized around the categories gender, race and ethnicity. Attempts by feminists and others to theorize these terms are still uneven, preliminary and tend to be ahistorical. They often lead to precisely the sort of binary oppositions – especially in debates about good feminists versus bad imperialists – that feminism has consistently disputed. One of the things that motivated me to write this book, therefore, was a nagging sense that things were more complicated than they appeared. Rather than reduce difficult situations to simple oppositions, it is one of the pressing needs of our time to understand the contradictions inherent in the relationship between these differentiating terms and our experiences of them. So, in this book I use historically informed, detailed examinations to demonstrate the inappropriateness of such totalizing explanations. Without the recognition that gender, race and subjectivity are complex, plural and contingent, it is difficult to find strategies with which to contest the present naturalization of past power relations. Thus, in order to unpick the complexities and ambiguities of women's imperial positionings in the second half of the nineteenth century, I shall explore how they were positioned simultaneously within differences of imperialism, gender, class and, in this case, in relation to discourses of creativity. Accordingly, this book explores how the three terms of its title – race, femininity, representation – are variously and variably constitutive of each other in processes of both affirmation and negation: they are words whose function is active and classificatory rather than simply descriptive.[1] Race, for example, will be presented as a term that signifies a historically variable process of racialization – the processes by which groups or individuals come to be ascribed a racial identity – and not as a word that simply denotes a given, innate, static, neutral classification. Thus, in instances where nineteenth-century sources use words such as 'Negro' unproblematically, I shall be deconstructing them to demonstrate the term's relational and contingent nature.

A number of recent historical studies have explored Western (mainly middle-class) women's experience of, and involvement in, imperialism.[2] This was for white scholars a painful but necessary journey, allowing us to begin to grapple with the multiple contradictions of a female imperial subjectivity. For Black and other scholars of colour, it marked the entry, or re-entry, of the colonial and postcolonial repressed – speaking to the iniquities of the colonial past and the continued epistemological violences of ideologies of racial and sexual difference. My focus here is on the role of white European women as cultural agents, within an analysis of the constitutive role of culture in the formation of imperial relations.[3] To do this, I use two case studies: the first examines women's contribution to the extraordinarily popular field of visual Orientalism, the other re-situates George Eliot criticism in relation to imperial discourse.

It is illustrative of traditional attitudes to women, culture and imperialism that when I started to do the research which informs this book, I did not know of any women Orientalist artists. But I was convinced that they had to exist. Everything I knew about women artists and feminist art history told me that they *must* exist, or if they did not, that the reasons for their exclusion would in themselves be revealing of the interaction between definitions of gender and nation in the second half of the nineteenth century. One of the aims of this book, therefore, is to increase our understanding of the conditions of possibility for, and reception of, women's involvement in imperial cultural production. In specific terms this allows us to see that, as I had hoped, women were involved in Orientalist cultural production and that, as I had feared, the dynamics of imperial discourse could not but enter and structure their work – even if their relationship to some racialized ideologies was self-consciously oppositional.

One of my arguments is that imperialism played a role in the very construction of professional creative opportunities for European women. The ways in which European women imagined and propelled themselves into the potentially transgressive position of cultural producer, and the ways in which their output and demeanour as creative professionals were assessed, relied on the differentiating terms of race, class and nation, as well as gender. This series of relational categories activated and was maintained by a set of hierarchical differences and value judgements that could only be imperial. It is precisely this contradiction between the opportunities to enunciate an 'against the grain' vision of imperialism thrown up by the gendered ambiguities of women's positioning within imperial discourse and the ability of dominant ideological formations to (partially but never totally) recoup their transgressive representations that forms the focus of this book.

I also want to intervene in debates about the specificity of the female gaze as part of a critical movement that has undercut the potentially unified, and paradigmatically male, colonial subject outlined in Said's *Orientalism* in 1978.[4] Thus, in contrast to many cultural histories of imperialism that analyse Orientalist images *of* women rather than representations *by* women, I will argue, first, that women did produce imperialist images and, second, that an analysis of the production and reception of representations by women will develop an understanding of the interdependence of ideologies of race and gender in the colonial discourse of the period. To this end, women's representations are read largely through their reception in the British and French critical press (specialist and general) in order to tease out the ways in which the gender-specific and author-centred criticism of the period produced a range of (often contradictory) meanings for the texts and identities for the authors.

It will be clear in what follows that I am as much interested in how things came to be talked about, written about, recorded – or even neglected and ignored – as I am in the images and representations themselves. I take the approach that representations do not have intrinsic meanings in themselves. Rather, meaning is

constructed in the interaction between the reader/viewer and the
text (simultaneously constructing meanings and identities for both
the viewer and the text). Therefore, the role of art and literary
criticism is central to this investigation. That is, I am concerned
not simply with how different forms of culture propagated imperial ideas or supported (or opposed) colonial policy, but in what
culture and the discussions about it can tell us about the heterogeneity of the imperial moment. In this I am in agreement with
Lisa Lowe's analysis that Orientalism, like any discourse, must be
regarded as multivocal and heterogeneous, a formation made
up of dissimilar and non-equivalent instances. She redefines
Orientalism as an 'uneven matrix of orientalist [sic] situations
across different cultural and historical sites' in which each
Orientalism is 'internally complex and unstable'.[5] This approach
allows us to look for evidence of counterhegemonic or subaltern
(embryonically counter hegemonic) voices that may contest and
to varying extents transform the power relations of hegemonic
discourse.[6]

In the pages that follow I argue that women's differential,
gendered access to the positionalities of imperial discourse
produced a gaze on the Orient and the Orientalized 'other' that
registered difference less pejoratively and less absolutely than was
implied by Said's original formulation. That is, the positionings
within Orientalism open to women cultural producers were always
contingent on the other shifting relational terms that structured
the presumed superiority of the Western Orientalist. I show how
women's work was read through a grid of differences that, though
it often foregrounded gender, was equally reliant on domestic
differentiations of class, religion and nation. It was, therefore, in
relation to all these differentials that the conditions of possibility
for the emergence of women's (Orientalist) cultural production
depended. Thus, we can use women's alternative 'take' on difference to throw light on the internal schisms within the fantasized
unity of the sovereign imperial subject, as it was constituted by
contemporary cultural discourse. It is my intention to highlight
the multiplicity, diversity and incommensurability of possible positionings within Orientalist discourse in order to contribute to our
understanding of how people, in this case women, came to understand themselves as part of an imperial nation: how they
understood themselves as beneficiaries of a structure of systemic
differences that, whilst it placed them as superior in the West/East

divide of colonialism (the relative privilege of the European woman traveller in the Orient), also placed them as other and inferior in the gendered divides of European art and society (women's limited opportunities for a professional art education). The book is organized around a detailed analysis of the production, reception and circulation of two very different instances of women's involvement in Orientalist cultural production: firstly, the overtly Orientalist paintings of the French artist Henriette Browne (active 1855–78), and secondly, the implicitly Orientalist depiction of Jews as the Orientalized Other in George Eliot's novel *Daniel Deronda* (1876). Although there are areas of overlap and comparability between these two Orientalist moments, they are not equivalent. Indeed, it is their very nonequivalence that offers, as Lowe puts it, an opportunity to understand the profound heterogeneity of Orientalist discourse and imperial positionings.

> French and British figurations of an oriental Other are not unified or necessarily related in meaning; they denote a plurality of referents, do not necessarily have a common style in the production of statements about their Orients, and are engendered differently by social and literary circumstances at particular moments . . . Yet, despite their essential nonequivalences, discursive means of representation overlap and are mutually implicated in one another at different moments.[7]

National differences within Europe are just one set of differences in the case of Henriette Browne and George Eliot. It is immediately obvious that these two authorial identities (neither were their 'real' names) highlight a series of other differences: different twentieth-century critical standings (who has not heard of George Eliot, who has heard of Henriette Browne?); different nineteenth-century critical statuses; different social and personal identifications; different fields of endeavour. Hidden under these contrasts, but fundamental to the pattern of this study, is the different state of the available archives.

In contrast to the wealth of readily available secondary material on George Eliot, finding out about Browne is much harder. Although she was successful and famous in her day, and was included in all the major directories of artists compiled in the early twentieth century,[8] she is little researched now and the whereabouts of much of her work is unknown. Of those that are extant, some are in private collections and unavailable for view,

others are in poor repair in gallery basements.[9] Therefore, my
work on Browne has required far more detective work and
primary research than that on George Eliot, the fruits of which
must necessarily be expressed more fully. For a study that is
concerned with the production and circulation of meanings, it is,
in a perverse way, salutary that I have scarcely had the opportunity to read too much into the images themselves: with Browne
I have never even seen the 'real thing' in some cases and, indeed,
have often been in the position of analysing responses to her work
before I had managed to track down even a black and white reproduction of the painting. Whilst not an ideal condition for study,
I have used the absence of an archive on Browne as an opportunity, not only to research her, but to introduce new material
on other (previously unknown) nineteenth-century women
painters of Orientalist subjects. The subsequent revelation of the
range and amount of women's visual Orientalism challenges
the tendency to see Orientalist art as an exclusively male field.
In following this trail it has been made abundantly clear to
me just how much critical readings of women's work did indeed
attach imperial and Orientalist concerns, enthusiasms, or fears,
to any painting that could remotely be linked with the subject
of the Orient.[10] With both Browne and George Eliot, reviews
inevitably centre on their gender. Thus, where Browne offers
an opportunity to study an obviously gendered reception of
Orientalist images, I hope that my re-reading of George Eliot will
animate Eliot scholarship by re-inserting the overt imperialism of
nineteenth-century responses to *Daniel Deronda*. This will allow
us to examine more closely the implicit role of Orientalist
discourse in the construction of the professional creative female
self and its tautological relationship to the female subject's representation of racialized differences.

As will now be evident, this book looks at both visual and
literary culture.[11] But the implications of interdisciplinarity go
further than this: in an entirely reciprocal process of intertextu-
ality these high cultural forms (as well as the 'lower' forms of
popular imperialism) contain endless traces of second-order
discourses such as ethnography and sociology. Situated within the
text, these traces link George Eliot's novels or Browne's paintings to a wider representational field. At the point of consumption,
these different cultural activities were all components of subjective experience and therefore of identification(s) for their readers

and viewers in terms of class, gender, race and nationality. Of course, reading novels and attending exhibitions are selected activities, only, and differently, available to some sections of the population.[12] The addressee or audience of the high art areas with which I am dealing was largely middle-class although, as we shall see, even different elements within the oeuvre of a single artist or writer had at different times in different parts of Europe a more diverse audience in terms of class, ethnicity and nationality.

The book aims not to linger on material that is already familiar to readers. But, since I cannot expect every reader to mirror my own particular pattern of disciplinary hybridity, I must of necessity dwell on some material that, though familiar to some readers, will be new to others. It is impossible to be expert in every area and in going for a broad scope I will no doubt have missed some nuances and offended some specialists. I hope that I will have contributed sufficient insights to the various related fields of this study to be forgiven by more singularly focused scholars, from whose research I have repeatedly benefited.

Chronologically, this study begins with Henriette Browne's first major success in France and England with the *Sisters of Charity* (Plate 1) in 1859 and ends with George Eliot's final and seriously unpopular novel *Daniel Deronda* in 1876. For a project that aims to unpick the totalizing fantasies of Western imperialism and the homogenizing tendencies of twentieth-century critiques of Orientalism, there can be no tidy boundaries, only fortuitous or gratuitous ones: not only because it is still unusual to combine the literary with the visual, but because periodization, like disciplinary boundaries, is a constructed and contested device. Different fields of enquiry set up different periodizations which frequently do not match, even where their objects of study overlap: the advent of modernism in art history (in traditional or revisionist accounts) rarely correlates with modernism in literature; French history is divided into epochs that do not match English history; postcolonial history challenges the colonialist demarcations of imperial history; women's history challenges the masculinist exclusions of his-story.[13] This project, then, can only be localized in so far as the thirty years it covers demarcate a particular series of events in the lives and work of Henriette Browne and George Eliot. It is an era, in both France and Britain, that was unmistakably (but not unchangingly) imperial, and in which Orientalism in Britain and France was becoming established as a mainstream, rather than partisan and avant-garde, area of representation. The period thus defined is, therefore, one in which we can expect to find increasing numbers of women participating in the production of imperial culture. The book does not adhere to any neat historical or thematic division and its scope is deliberately allusive and indicative rather than exhaustive or exclusive. Because of the underdeveloped state of its fields, the twin foci of the book are intended to be indicative of methodological procedures that could be used elsewhere, to reference other women's involvement in imperial culture (and to gesture forwards, for example, to women's increased involvement in visual Orientalism in the 1880s and 1890s). Thus, readers who hope to find the final word on George Eliot or the complete dossier on Henriette Browne will be disappointed. What I have tried to do is, through a detailed and attentive reading of selected works, to use them as a double focus for a series of investigations into women's participation in imperial culture.

Accordingly, Chapter 1 sets out my critical and methodological framework, covering Said's original thesis and the critical and feminist developments that ensued. The approach indicated in the chapter is demonstrated by a reading of the Orientalist gaze that Charlotte Brontë's Lucy Snowe directs at a picture of Cleopatra in *Villette* (1852). Chapter 2 is also introductory in form, attending to the possibilities of, and constraints on, women's professional cultural production. This includes an evaluation of the possible positions from which women could assume, or be ascribed, a public identity as cultural producers.

Chapters 3 and 4 focus on Henriette Browne. Chapter 3 introduces Browne's early oeuvre of portraiture, domestic narrative and religious genre pictures and analyses the critical construction of her authorial identity. The critical reception of her early images of the French religious is linked to British and French debates about female orders and, more widely, to the iconography of sequestered women. It is argued that the nexus of concerns about sexuality, power and discipline that circulates in discussions of her convent scenes, adumbrates the cluster of discourses in which her subsequent harem paintings were to signify. The second half of this chapter introduces the main themes and players of Orientalist art in Britain and France and assesses developments in the field, including new information on other women Orientalist artists. Chapter 4 analyses French and British responses to Browne's

Oriental subjects. The focus is on how the tendency to regard them as the accurate representation of a female visual privilege is alternately upheld and contested by reference to other women's accounts (written and visual) of the Orient. The relationship between Browne's work and this alternative articulation of the harem as a domestic space analogous to the European domestic is explored, including a reconsideration of twentieth-century critical theories of the female gaze.

In Chapter 5 I move into a consideration of how my conclusions about the female Orientalist gaze can re-frame the analysis of George Eliot's representation of racial difference in *Daniel Deronda*. Using Freud's concept of the uncanny I argue that the reading position produced for Gentile readers was so uncomfortable that it militated against Eliot's avowed project of challenging anti-Semitism. I also address contemporary Jewish responses to the novel in order to assess the book's role in debates over diasporic identities in an era of emerging political Zionism.

The conclusion returns to current theories of alterity and representation. It argues that an awareness of women's varied involvement in the cultures of imperialism repositions Orientalism as a diverse field of activity and representation: a flexible and heterogeneous discourse that functioned through contradiction rather than despite it, in which women's cultural activities were coded as one among a number of competing discourses.

A NOTE ON SOURCES

I have drawn extensively on art and literary criticism in the periodical press for responses to Browne's and George Eliot's work. My selection of journals is obviously partial and often, in the case of those other than the main art journals, determined largely by the availability of secondary research. I have used the main art journals in Britain and France systematically, looking at reviews for the years when Browne exhibited at the Salon, the International Exhibitions or, in Britain, at Gambart's, as well as keeping an eye on the gossip columns that offered regular updates on commissions, acquisitions and new developments. In Britain this function has been served by the *Athenaeum* and the *Art Journal*, both of which ran continuously throughout the period. In France I have concentrated on *L'Artiste*, *Gazette des beaux-arts*, and *Le Moniteur universel*, which last, though a newspaper and not a specialist art periodical, had a high profile review section and the services of Théophile Gautier who, as well as being enormously influential, was also a keen proponent of Browne. In addition to the art press I have looked at the Catholic press in France to see what they made of Browne's religious subjects (and her Orientalism) and at a women's fashion magazine, *Journal des desmoiselles*, in which Browne is featured, to see how it registers gender and art. Where a particular critic is little known but has been of significance to this book I have followed their trail to other journals to get a sense of the attitudes and allegiances they brought to their interpretation of Browne (the critic Noémi de Cadiot/Claude Vignon in the *Journal des desmoiselles* is a case in point here). In the case of more famous and more researched critics I have relied on secondary sources. As well as the periodical press I have drawn on separately published volumes of critics' work as well as making odd forays into otherwise ignored journals if they feature Browne prominently in one issue. Although most of the British and French art journals did include some literary reviews, they are not, by and large, the source for the lengthy reviews of George Eliot's work that I draw on in Chapter 5; these reviews, many of them available in secondary compilations, will be discussed fully in the chapter on George Eliot.

NOTES

1 See Cora Kaplan, 'Pandora's Box: Subjectivity, Class and Sexuality in Socialist Feminist Criticism', in Kaplan, *Sea Changes: Essays in Culture and Feminism*, London, Verso, 1986. See also Diane Roberts, *The Myth of Aunt Jemima: Representations of Race and Region*, London, Routledge, 1994.
2 See for example: Helen Callaway, *Gender, Culture and Empire: European Women in Colonial Nigeria*, Basingstoke, Macmillan, 1987; Dea Birkett, *Spinsters Abroad: Victorian Lady Explorers*, Oxford, Blackwell, 1989; Billie Melman, *Women's Orients: English Women and the Middle East, 1718–1918. Sexuality, Religion and Work*, Basingstoke, Macmillan, 1992; Vron Ware, *Beyond the Pale: White Women, Racism and History*, London, Verso, 1992; Nupur Chaudhuri and Margaret Strobel, *Western Women and Imperialism: Complicity and Resistance*, Bloomington, Indiana University Press, 1992.
3 See Chapter 1.
4 Edward W. Said, *Orientalism*, Harmondsworth, Penguin, 1978. See also Sara Mills, *Discourses of Difference: An Analysis of Women's Travel Writing and Colonialism*, London, Routledge, 1991; Jane

Miller, *Seductions: Studies in Reading and Culture*, London, Virago, 1990; Rani Kabbani, *Europe's Myths of Orient*, London, Macmillan, 1986; Melman, *Women's Orients*. For a full discussion of Said's work and responses to it see Chapter 1.

5 Lisa Lowe, *Critical Terrains. French and British Orientalisms*, Ithaca, Cornell University Press, 1991, p. 5.

6 For a detailed discussion of Gramsci's definition of subaltern classes in relation to the analysis of Orientalism and the project of writing subaltern histories see Lowe, *Critical Terrains*, ch. 1 and conclusion.

7 Lowe, *Critical Terrains*, pp. ix–4.

8 See for example entries on Browne in: Ellen Clayton, *English Female Artists*, London, Tinsley, 1876; Clara Erskine Clement, *Women in the Fine Arts. From the Seventh Century BC to the Twelfth Century AD*, New York, Houghton Mifflin, 1904; *Bryan's Dictionary of Painters and Engravers*, London, George Bell and Sons, 1903; Algernon Graves, *A Century of Loan Exhibitions*, London, Algernon Graves, 1913–15; Larousse, *Grand dictionnaire universel du XIXe siècle*, Paris, 1864–76.

See also Ulrich Thieme and Felix Becker, *Allegemeines Lexikon der Bildenden Künstler von der Antike bis zur Gegenwart*, Leipzig, Verlag von E.A. Seemann, 1907; E. Bénézit, *Dictionnaire critique et documentaire des peintres, sculpteurs, dessinateurs et graveurs de tous les temps et de tous les pays par un group d'écrivains spécialistes français et étrangers*, (1911–23) Paris, Librairie Gründ, 1976.

9 *Harem Interior: A Visit* (1861), for example, is owned by a private collector who declines to let me see the painting or have a colour reproduction; the whereabouts of its sister piece, *Flute Player*, are unknown; the *Greek Captive* (n.d.) is in the basement of the Tate Gallery, London.

10 For a good example of this see the *Athenaeum*'s review of Browne's *Rhodian Girl* that I discuss in Chapter 4.

11 For the argument that the very construction of disciplinary boundaries is itself indicative of an imperial process of classification and separation see Anita Levy, *Other Women: The Writing of Class, Race, and Gender, 1832–1898*, Princeton, Princeton University Press, 1991, p. 12.

See also Michel de Certeau, *Heterologies: Discourses on the Other*, Minneapolis, University of Minnesota Press, 1986.

12 Although developments in popular imperialism are signalled, as is the dissemination of its main texts into a wider cultural domain (via prints and the potentially extended readership of the serialized novel), this study is primarily concerned with the domain of high culture.

13 See Chaudhuri and Strobel 'Introduction', in Chaudhuri and Strobel, *Western Women and Imperialism*; Judith Newton, 'History as Usual?: Feminism and the "New Historicism"', in *Cultural Critique*, no. 9, Spring 1988.

Chapter 1

Race – femininity – representation

This book examines the work of Henriette Browne and George Eliot in order to trace how their gendered agency as cultural producers contributed to and drew on the imperial project. I am particularly concerned with the ways in which their images and texts created or reconceptualized the spaces in which a series of imperial identities for both artists and writers and their readers could be articulated. I shall argue not only that discourses of gender (by which were produced identities as masculine or feminine) were racialized and that discourses of race (by which were produced racialized and national identities) were gendered, but that the very premise on which culture was produced and interpreted in nineteenth-century France and Britain was based on the construction and exclusion of a racialized and, in this instance, Orientalized other.

The second half of the nineteenth century was a period of unprecedented colonial expansion (involving the direct conquest and domination of other countries) and increasingly imperialist foreign policy (dedicated to the extension of European influence over the globe, but without necessarily direct administrative or military intervention), in which Britain and France were established world leaders. Although the age of high imperialism is usually associated with the 'scramble for Africa' of the 1870s and 1880s, Britain and France were already by the early nineteenth century expanding their influence in those parts of the globe that were to become the imperial theatre of the late nineteenth and twentieth centuries.[1] This means that unlike the late nineteenth-century view of imperialism, which tended to paint imperial ideology as a phenomenon arising late in the century (notably in the 1860s and 1870s when it became clear that trade interests

would necessitate political control of colonized lands), we can see
pervasive structures of imperial ideology from the early part of
and throughout the nineteenth century.[2] The mid-nineteenth
century saw a change in the nature of imperial relations as the
style of the earlier mercantile period, in which a degree of acculturation by European officials and traders was encouraged, gave
way to the increased political and social intervention alongside
an emphasis on European separation from 'native' populations,
whose Eurocentric legacy we see today. This book does not
attempt a study of imperialism *per se*. I am concerned to explore
how, in certain and distinct moments, the interaction between
culture and imperialism was played out in connection to gender.
This investigation is organized by a recognition of culture's central
role in the processes by which European values and interests were
represented to Europe and extended to the colonized world.[3]
As Edward Said explains, culture was 'the vital, informing, and
invigorating counterpart to the economic and political machinery
that . . . stands at the centre of imperialism'.[4]

It is not so much that 'imperial culture' developed to promote
imperialism, but that, as a pervasive economic, social, political
and cultural formation, the imperial project could not but influence how people thought, behaved and created. As Benedict
Anderson has persuasively argued in his analysis of the development of vernacular print culture, visual and literary culture played
a crucial role in the construction of the 'imagined' national
communities in Europe that underpinned the imperial ideologies
and administrations of the eighteenth, nineteenth and twentieth
centuries.[5] Said is clear that, whilst not attaching blame to the
particular author or artist, culture in the age marked by imperialism and postcolonialism generally served to normalize imperial
power relations.[6] Although colonialism and imperialism had their
opponents (for reasons ranging from the moral to the economic),
the question of empire had an impact on all levels of British and
French domestic life, with imperialist values frequently structuring
even the terms of those who opposed it.[7] Just as the world-wide
recession of the 1990s permeates discussions about everything
from education to fashion without any of those discussions necessarily being 'about' economics, imperialism in the nineteenth
century was discussed, debated and contested as an issue of the
day, present in everyday activities and diverse forms of cultural
production – not just those that were 'obviously' imperialist.

As Daniel Bivona argues, breaking down modal boundaries (between the political and the literary) can reveal a wider domain which has the structure of both a 'culture-wide "debate" on the value and cause of imperial expansion and a cultural meta-narrative or mythology which subsumes even many of the critics of empire'.[8] Given the enormous impact of imperialism on Victorian life it is – or as Gayatri Chakravorty Spivak advocates, should be – impossible to consider any text (by man or woman) without taking imperialism into account.

> It should not be possible to read nineteenth-century British literature without remembering that imperialism, understood as England's social mission, was a crucial part of the cultural representation of England to the English. The role of literature in the production of cultural representation should not be ignored. These two obvious 'facts' continue to be disregarded in the reading of nineteenth-century British literature. This itself attests to the continuing success of the imperialist project, displaced and dispersed into more modern forms.[9]

These approaches mean, in relation to women's cultural activity, that rather than simply find the few arch-imperialist texts by women, we can analyse imperialism's role in structuring all their creative output. I am going to look at visual and literary representations of the Orient and the Orientalized other; a popular area of imagery that encapsulates the attitudes of Europe not just to its colonies but to the whole question of racial difference and which has, accordingly, been the focus of many twentieth-century critiques of imperialism. By attending to one set of representations that is obviously Orientalist (Browne's harem scenes) and another that, whilst clearly of an imperial moment, is rarely discussed as Orientalist (the representation of Jews and the division of Palestine in *Daniel Deronda*),[10] I will show the pervasiveness of women's take-up of colonial ideology and their various mediations of it.

By focusing on women as cultural producers in a field of representation generally seen as male I shall demonstrate the pervasive effects of imperial ideologies on female subjects and their particular, gendered, interpellation into imperial discourse. This does not mean that white European women were either bad racists or good revolutionaries (driven by proto-feminism to empathize with their 'sisters under the skin').[11] Instead, it allows an examination of how, as individuals growing up in an age of unprecedented imperial expansion, they were affected by and involved in colonial ideology and imperial relations. If we take the categories of race, class and gender as neither opposing oppressions nor as metaphors for each other but, as Cora Kaplan puts it, as 'reciprocally constituting each other through a kind of narrative invocation, a set of associative terms in a chain of meaning',[12] we can transform our understanding of each term by analysing its articulation with and through the other. In other words, we never only experience ourselves as female/male but also and already as Black/white – even if the whiteness of a white subject is so normative that it is often experienced as a non-event unless activated by comparison with a Black subject.[13] Thus, we can explore how discourses of femininity constrained women's access to positions of power and participation in colonialism and culture even whilst that very limitation, couched and understood in terms of gender, was also animated by imperial ideology – the gender specificities that accrued to women *qua* women were always built on their difference as *white* women.

> Applying a perspective of race, class *and* gender to historical inquiry should effectively transform interpretations based on race and class or class and gender.[14]

I shall argue that, in a period marked by heightened imperial activity and increasing female participation in the cultural sphere, the interaction of the identificatory relational terms of race and gender could produce positions from which to enunciate alternative representations of racial difference. Exploring the gender-specific discursive pressures on the production and reception of women's representation of the Orient will allow us to undercut the mastery that usually accrued to the Western viewer's position and use the tensions in women's colonial utterances to highlight the tensions in imperial subjectivity as a whole, thereby allowing a reconceptualization of the workings of power and knowledge in the domain of gender.

SAID'S ORIENTALISM AND HIS CRITICS

In 1978 Edward Said's influential book *Orientalism* offered a new way to conceptualize the history of relations between what we might commonsensically call the West and the East, or the

Occident and the Orient. Rather than accept the term as one that designates an area of neutral scholarly expertise (be it Oriental languages, literature or customs), Said argues that Orientalism was and is a discourse in which the West's knowledges about the Orient are inextricably bound up with its domination over it. Using Michel Foucault's proposition that all forms of knowledge are productive of power (constituting someone/thing as an object of knowledge is to assume power over it), Said assesses the implications of the Western construction of the Orient as an object of knowledge during the period of colonial expansion. Because he refuses to accept the innocence of knowledges about, and representations of, the Orient Said is able to consider how Orientalism's classification of the East as different and inferior legitimized Western intervention and rule.

For Said, therefore, representations of the Orient produced by Orientalism are never simple reflections of a true anterior reality, but composite images which came to define the nature of the Orient and the Oriental as irredeemably different and always inferior to the West. Orientalism establishes a set of polarities in which the Orient is characterized as irrational, exotic, erotic, despotic and heathen, thereby securing the West in contrast as rational, familiar, moral, just and Christian. Not only do these Orientalist stereotypes 'misrepresent' the Orient, they also misrepresent the Occident – obscuring in their flattering vision of European superiority the tensions along the lines of gender, class and ethnicity that ruptured the domestic scene.[15]

Eventually, Orientalism as a body of knowledge about the East produced by and for the West came to bypass Oriental sources altogether in a self-referential process of legitimation that endlessly asserted the power of the West to know, speak for and regulate the Orient better than the Orient itself.

> As a discipline representing institutionalized Western knowledge of the Orient, Orientalism thus comes to exert a three-way force, on the Orient, on the Orientalist and on the Western 'consumer' of Orientalism ... the Orient ('out there' to the East) is corrected, even penalized, for lying outside the boundaries of European society, 'our' world; the Orient is thus *'Orientalized'*; a process that not only marks the Orient as the province of the Orientalist but also forces the uninitiated Western reader to accept Orientalist codification ... as the *true*

Orient. Truth, in short, becomes a function of learned judgement, not of the material itself, which in time seems to owe
even its existence to the Orientalist.[16]

One of the problems that critics identified in *Orientalism* was the
troubling status that Said accords to the 'real' Orient: the Orient
figures as both a construction, 'the written statement is a presence to the reader by virtue of its having excluded, displaced . . .
any such *real thing* as "the Orient" ',[17] and a real thing that can
simultaneously be misrepresented by Orientalism and directly
conquered by the West.[18] As we shall see (notably in Chapter 4)
the possibility of the discursive inscription of a 'real' Orient, or
innocent experience of it, continues to haunt some scholars in
this field, although, to be fair, Said's recent work has engaged
more productively with this issue. Leaving aside for now the
question of the 'real' Orient, Orientalism emerges as a discourse
whose representation of the Orient is determined by its own
agenda (largely conceptualized in terms of the dynamics and
exigencies of colonial expansion) but whose success for the West
depended not simply on domination but on the exercise of hegemony and the development of consent – that is, that the
Orientalized Other be brought to recognize the validity of
Orientalist knowledges and abide by their implementation (be it
'better' medical training, 'proper' clothes, etc.).[19] That hegemony,
which relies on the willingness of the governed to be governed, is
conducive to a relational mode of power that can respond flexibly,
not just repressively, to unrest or resistance, is of great significance
for my analysis of Orientalism as a discourse within which a
variety of different (and differently gendered) positionalities could
be produced.

> In a quite constant way, Orientalism depends for its strategy
> on the flexible *positional* superiority, which puts the Westerner
> in a whole series of possible relationships with the Orient
> without ever losing him the relative upper hand.[20]

The 'him' of this statement is telling: for Said, in *Orientalism* at
least, Orientalism is a homogeneous discourse enunciated by a
colonial subject that is unified, intentional and irredeemably
male. Although his subsequent work, particularly *Culture and
Imperialism*, refers more clearly to the impact of discourses of
gender and references feminist scholarship, in *Orientalism* gender

occurs only as a metaphor for the negative characterization of the Orientalized Other as 'feminine' or in a single reference to a woman writer (Gertrude Bell, in which he pays no attention to the possible effects of her gendered position on her texts). Said never questions women's apparent absence as producers of Orientalist discourse or as agents within colonial power. This mirrors the traditional view that women were not involved in colonial expansion (itself a subplot of a masculinist view of history in which women, if they appear at all, are strictly marginal). In contrast, I intend to argue that women did play a part in the textual production that constituted Orientalism and, moreover, that gender, as a differentiating term, was integral to the structure of that discourse and individuals' experience of it.

To this end I am expanding, to relate to gender, Said's three-way relationship in which Orientalism exercises a force over the Orient, the Orientalist and the Western consumer of Orientalism: just as the Orient is constructed into a series of signs whose significance lies more in their relationship to the Occident's self-image than in any truth about the Orient, so has it been argued that the European paradigm of sexual difference constructs women as objects of knowledge (the 'other-within') which secure definitions of a superior masculinity rather than revealing any truth about women.[21] The question which then arises is, how can a Western woman, who is feminized as the symbolic inferior other at home (a placement that is also class-specific), exercise the classificatory gaze over the Orient that Said describes? What access does a white European woman have to the enunciative position of a white superiority that is implicitly male?

Whereas Said has tended to represent Orientalism as a discourse that is intentional and monolithic (there is, in *Orientalism*, no sense of the Orient's resistance or of internal splits – although this also is more fully explored in *Culture and Imperialism*), attention to women's role in imperial social and cultural relations, combined with an awareness of external challenges to imperial power, can resituate Western imperialism as always only one half of a power relation – contested from without and undercut from within. In addition, we are helped by the Foucauldian concept of power/knowledge that Said uses. In this, power is never willed, owned (by individuals, groups or states), unitary or monolithic, but discursive: discourse, as an ordering of knowledge, produces positionalities (enunciative modalities) into which individuals are interpellated and from which they may speak or act (as policemen, lawyers, mothers) but which are never the truth of themselves.[22] Thus, power can be seen as always productive and never simply repressive: it does not just descend from above with a string of prohibitions but, rather, through the productive force of its apparatuses, actively inscribes human agents into particular (and contradictory) subject positions. The workings and effects of power in this sense can be seen in a web (cluster) of discursive apparatuses that no one owns or ultimately controls.[23]

Since, in the Foucauldian scenario, power is a dynamic that is always bounded by resistance, a strategy of resistance could be based on an 'analytics of power' that, by asking how we come to understand ourselves in the terms of the relevant discourse, can deconstruct the operation of the forces of power and allow new forms of resistance to emerge. These new forms, rather than, for example, simply pitting women against men as the 'owners' of patriarchal power, would deconstruct the ways in which our sense of ourselves as gendered beings contributes to our oppression and could generate new alliances and resistances that were not themselves predicated on any essentialist notions of women's (or men's) nature. Although concern has been expressed that Foucault's theory of the micropolitics of power makes it almost inevitable that resistance will, despite itself, contribute to the hegemony that it seeks to undermine,[24] I still think that a discursive model is useful and politically enabling if we insist on what Lowe, after Foucault, calls the 'heterotopicality' of the discursive terrain.

> [D]iscourses are heterogeneously and irregularly composed of statements and restatements, contestations and accommodation, generated by a plurality of writing positions at any given moment ... In other words, the use of the notion of a dominant discourse is incomplete if not accompanied by a critique which explains why some positions are easily co-opted and integrated into apparently-dominant discourses, and why others are less likely to be appropriated.[25]

Thus, an analysis of the conflicts inherent in a discursive formation marked by the terms of gender and race would allow for a glimpse of points of resistance *within* the fantasized unity of Orientalist discourse. The relational and fragmented nature of discourse does not mean that it cannot appear to be unified: indeed, it is the hegemonic ability of Orientalist discourse to retain the upper hand, even whilst it accepts and incorporates challenges, that accounts for its longevity.[26] The inherent contradictions of the enunciative positionalities (both gendered and racialized) occupied by women within Orientalism can, therefore, reveal some of the fictions of the discourse and of imperial power. Women's gender specific representations do not have counter-hegemonic potential because they were all automatically anti-racists opposed to colonialism. Rather, it is the very contradictions thrown up by the assumption (then and now) that women made no contribution to, or had no active role in, imperial expansion that allowed women the positionality from which a counter-hegemonic discourse could be enunciated.

Attention to women writers and artists, therefore, does not just add to but actively reforms Said's original version: it disallows a conceptualization of discourse as intentionalist and unified by highlighting the structural role of sexual as well as racial difference in the formation of colonial subject positions; it destabilizes the fiction of authorial intent and control by highlighting the discursively produced and unresolvable contradictions in women's accounts; it insists on the impact of imperialism on the lives of women and men (colonizers and colonized); and, by so doing, disrupts the masculinism found in accounts and critiques of imperialism. On the last count, Jane Miller locates Said, like Fanon before him, as part of a trajectory of criticism that ignores women as participants in imperial power relations and as readers of Orientalist representations.

> Said [in *Orientalism*] sets out with care and delicacy the parallels and analogies developed in this field between colonial relations and sexual relations, and he shows how illuminating of the reality of the imperial adventure those parallels have been for both West and East. What he does not confront are the sexual meanings on which those illuminations depend. It is possible to feel that within his analysis it is with the distortions of male sexuality [identity and sovereignty] produced by the language of Orientalism that he is chiefly concerned . . . [something] [t]hat has often involved the theft of their women . . . The question remains: why does such an analysis not entail a concern for women's loss of political and economic status, in itself? [Women's history] does not become part of the history which is being rewritten.

In accepting the power and usefulness of an analysis like Said's there is an essential proviso ... to be made. If women are ambiguously present within the discourses of Orientalism, they are just as ambiguously present within the discourses developed to expose and oppose Orientalism. Their presence in both is as forms of coinage, exchange value offered or stolen or forbidden, tokens of men's power and wealth or lack of them. The sexual use and productiveness of women are allowed to seem equivalent to their actual presence and their consciousness. They are, finally, 'Orientalized' with Said's terms into the perceptions and the language which express, but also elaborate on, the uses men have for women within exploitative societies.[27]

In order to avoid an account that marginalizes women as agents and readers (does 'Said assume women are amongst the readers of [his] work?')[28] we must include women as agents in Orientalism without losing the complexities of their relationship to domestic discourses on both sides of the Orientalist divide. Rani Kabbani, for example, highlights the many and subtle ways with which the sexually dominated Oriental woman could resist her Western oppressor, but fails to see Western women as subjects similarly produced through the energics of imperialism. Arguing that colonialism is a discourse structured by patriarchal power relations, she points to the existence of 'notable' Victorian women travel writers only to claim that they were 'token travellers only, who were forced by various pressures to articulate the values of patriarchy'.[29] Kabbani's desire to produce women as pure agents in the face of colonial power relations leads to the problematic supposition that if women were unwilling colonialists, men must be not only self-conscious oppressors but intentionalist authors choosing (where women were 'forced') to misrepresent the other.[30] In a book with more than one version of power and authorship (intentional and discursive) some men are similarly exculpated from blame: unlike other artists who exploited the Orient, Fromentin, Matisse and Renoir, for example, were simply 'exhilarated by the Orient and were therefore considerably enriched as artists by it'.[31] That this enrichment might itself be an imperial spoil is ignored in an attempt to preserve the favoured few (and a strange few too, surely, given Renoir's arguably pornographic representations of Orientalized women?) as pure and intentional artists.

Sara Mills, in an exemplary analysis of women's travel writing, suggests that one of the reasons why their work is ignored by critics is that the fluctuating and partial allegiance to colonialism produced by women's problematic access to the superiority of a colonial position makes their work difficult to classify. Whilst attention to the gendered axis of colonial discourse may deconstruct Said's monolithic analysis by allowing for counter-hegemonic voices, it is clear that many women authors expended as much energy as their peers on creating the powerful narrative voice afforded by British colonialism. After all, nineteenth-century women who transgressed the codes of femininity to publish or exhibit art were to some extent aspiring to recognition in the terms of their culture. The contradictions of their position mean that their representations are likely simultaneously to confirm and transgress social and textual codes. For example, whilst travelling broke codes of European femininity, many women travel writers reinforced colonialist codes of white superiority and emphasized their adherence to feminine propriety of dress and decorum. The unconventionality of their occupation in terms of gender is propped up by or relies on the ideology of colonialism and white superiority in the very conceptualization of the East as a realm suitable for adventuring. A disinvestment in one set of values is counterbalanced by an overinvestment in another.

Although women writers often expressed sympathy for 'native' women or voiced criticisms of colonial administration it would, as Mills points out, be wrong to take this as a displaced feminist anger.[32] Aside from the personal conservatism of many women travellers, the proto-feminist concern for 'native' women was itself frequently structured by the same assumptions of white superiority and civilization (Indian women are oppressed by their backward menfolk and must be liberated by their more advanced white sisters) that drove imperial policy.[33]

PROBLEMS WITH 'THE DEATH OF THE AUTHOR'

Discourse theory is, as James Clifford remarks, 'unfair' to authors: it does not allow for their existence in the traditional humanist sense of the author as the origin and owner of the text's meaning.[34] In contrast to Foucault, who sees the author not as a real person but as a function of discourse, a 'means of classification' that allows us to group together those texts as the product of one author (for example, Shakespeare) and not another, Said retains a belief in 'the determining imprint of individual writers upon the otherwise anonymous collective body of texts that constitutes a discursive formation like Orientalism'.[35] For Foucault, the impossibility of the author is part and parcel of the always heterogeneous nature of discourse in which individuals may occupy multiple and contradictory positions, whereas Said's defence of the individual author affirms his conceptualization of the essentially unified nature of imperial subjectivity and colonial discourse.

When authorship and agency are seen as concepts produced by power, the political and critical implications of the anti-humanist critique of the unified sovereign subject become clear. In 'The Death of the Author' Roland Barthes counters the traditional humanist reverence for the author with the assertion that the term author does not designate a 'real' person but an entity created by readers and critics. This author is a modern figure (replacing previous modes of cultural generation that did not require a single point of origin and ownership) whose emergence is linked to the development of the modern culture industry and the capitalist valorization of the individual. Barthes replaces the primacy of the author's intent (as interpreted by critics) with the assertion that meaning is generated between the reader and the text. He transforms the activity of reading from one of decipherment (interpretation of the hidden truth) to one of disentanglement (untangling the web of structures that form the text without assigning a 'secret' or 'ultimate' meaning). Where the former closes the text by finding (creating) its one true meaning, the latter leaves it open by revealing its components but not ruling out other possible tracings.[36] The author who precedes the text, is replaced with the 'scriptor', an entity that is

> born simultaneously with the text, is in no way equipped with a being preceding or exceeding the writing, is not the subject with the book as predicate: there is no other time than that of the enunciation and every text is eternally written *here and now*.[37]

For feminists, such theories are as problematic as the critiques of imperialism I discussed earlier. Whereas the attack on the foundations of a patriarchal literary and subjective order would seem to be of benefit to feminists, its gender blindness is a problem:

although the loss of the sovereign subject that accompanied the death of the author was not such a blow to women who had never collectively 'felt burdened by too much Self, Ego, Cogito, etc.'[38] in the first place, to be told that the author was dead (just as courses in women's studies and women's literature were getting off the ground) threatened to close off the possibility of a narrative authority to which women had never really acceded. What is more, as Nancy K. Miller has observed, Barthes' insistence on the atemporality of the reader ('the reader is without history, biography, psychology'[39]) might well deny women not only the possibility of being authors but also of being (women) readers.[40]

In response to a deconstructive position that takes no referent outside the text, Nancy Miller argues for a pragmatic reinscription of the specificity of author and reader.[41] For her, signature matters – it makes a difference if a novel is signed by a woman or a man. A 'methodologically correct' position, in which 'woman' does not exist except as a product of discourse and the feminine is a mode of writing available to subjects of either gender, has no place to acknowledge the real oppression of real women (however so defined). In contrast to Peggy Kamuf's refusal to see the definition of women's literature limited to one in which 'women's writing is writing signed by women',[42] Miller illustrates the significance of signature by pointing to women's use of a male pseudonym as a 'desire to be veiled that unveils the anxiety of a genderized and sexualized body'.[43] Only female subjects are able to write not only in the 'feminine' (discursive mode) but, as Catherine Stimpson phrases it, 'of, for, to and from the "female" '.[44]

This political and strategic necessity to recognize the experiential reality of gendered identities – even as one deconstructs them – may also be a point at which to reinstate in an altered form the concept of the 'real' Orient as seen in Said's work. The necessary contradiction of reconstructing the space of the real woman/real Orient as a figure of analysis whilst simultaneously deconstructing any attempt to fix or naturalize its history or status, would be just the sort of pragmatic or 'affirmative' deconstruction advocated by Spivak in the case of subaltern historiography.[45] The liberation of meaning from author to reader offered by Barthes does not have to exclude the social. Whilst the reader as a positionality in relation to, or even formed by, each text may be a neutral space, the agents who occupy it bring with them a subjectivity (there must be a subject of sorts to perform the reading) that is formed in and through its experience of the social – a realm demarcated by differences of race, class and gender. If meaning lies in reading rather than in the text, then any text has a multiplicity of possible meanings that will be produced by each individual reader according to the subjective baggage they bring to the site of reading.[46] This is particularly important for a study of culture and imperialism, for it is not only, as Anderson argues, that the development of nationalism is indelibly linked to the cultural articulation of the imagined national community, but also, as John Tomlinson suggests, that it is in and through the processes of reading by which they are formed: imagined national communities are also interpretive communities.[47] Thus, imperial meanings are not simply inherent in texts, but are produced through the various and mediated mechanism of reading: this also means, of course, that oppositional readings may be performed on the same 'imperialist' texts by a different community of readers.[48] Foucault's theory of the author as a function of discourse allows for the retention of both the social and the subject.

> ... an author's name is not simply an element of speech (as a subject, a complement, or an element that could be replaced by a pronoun or other parts of speech) ... [it] characterizes a particular manner of existence of discourse. Discourse that possesses an author's name is not to be immediately consumed and forgotten; neither is it accorded the momentary attention given to ordinary fleeting words. Rather, its status and its manner of reception are regulated by the culture in which it circulates ...

But the subject should not be entirely abandoned. It should be reconsidered, not to restore the theme of an originating subject, but to seize its functions, its intervention in discourse, and its system of dependencies ... Rather, we should ask: under what conditions and through what forms can an entity like the subject appear in the order of discourse; what position does it occupy; what functions does it exhibit; and what rules does it follow in each type of discourse? In short, the subject (and its substitutes) must be stripped of its creative role and analysed as a complex and variable function of discourse.[49]

Thus, the form and effectivity of the author-function is reliant on the cultural, and thus necessarily social, values of the era in which it emerges and those in which it is subsequently evaluated. We can therefore locate women's cultural production within the discursively produced conditions of possibility in which they could assume the position of a writing/painting subject. This means giving attention to the restrictions on and conditions of women's access to cultural production (as I shall detail in Chapter 2) and pursuing the role of gender in the construction of the very subjectivity that the author or artist is thought to possess. As Robert Young makes clear, it should never be possible to empty the attack on the sovereign subject of its social implications, since the foundation of that very form of subjectivity, in all its innocent, transcendent universalism, is based on the construction and exclusion of an inferior other.

> As Barthes' analyses indicate, the French critique of humanism was conducted from the first as a part of a political critique of colonialism ... The anti-humanists charged that the category of the human, however exalted in its conception, was too often invoked only in order to put the male before the female, or to classify other 'races' as sub-human, and therefore not subject to the ethical prescriptions applicable to 'humanity' at large.[50]

In this instance, the deconstruction of the sovereign Western subject does not mean simply replacing a unified white male Western subject with a unified white female Western subject,[51] but using all the contradictory positions inherent in those terms to 'disentangle' the ways in which representations of an Orientalized other simultaneously undercut and contribute to imperialist ideas and policies. This involves attending to the processes of 'othering' in texts that are not obviously racist or imperialist in any simple sense of the term because as texts – received within the conventions of author-centred criticism and produced in the heyday of nineteenth-century imperialism – they cannot be considered outside of the imperialist rationale of the humanist project. Anita Levy, in her argument for an interdisciplinary focus in the study of alterity (the construction of the other), links the emergent anthropological and sociological trope of the 'other woman' as the hidden negative ('all that is "other" than normal, desirable and English') against which English domestic fiction is structured. She cites a process by which, as this monolithic figure of the other woman 'came to comprise myriad social and sexual practices, the other woman displaced other women'.[52] The form of this alterity is, as Rosemary Hennessy and Rajeswari Mohan make clear, 'continually re-articulated in terms dictated by its economic and political conditions of emergence'.[53] Thus, the textual status of the other woman in women's cultural production cannot be separated from the economic and social conditions necessary for the emergence of Western women's cultural agency; conditions which relied, among other things, on the displacement onto the feminized colonial other of forms of gendered exploitation now unacceptable at home. One of the aims of this book, then, is to trace the construction of the other woman (the feminine and feminized Oriental other) in women's texts in order to illuminate some of the gendered specificities that made up the variable conditions of emergence of the forms of alterity characteristic of Orientalism. As Deborah Cherry has pointed out, neither women cultural producers nor women consumers were a homogeneous group, so we should expect to find variety in the positionings of femininity they assume and the forms of alterity they represent.[54] In this I would support Levy's demand that we attend to the structural role of the other woman in order to 're-materialize forms of middle-class power that have since vanished into the common-sense norms of self and identity' still paramount in the twentieth-century enactment of postcolonial alterity.[55] My aim is to elaborate the contribution women made to the negotiation and naturalization of those colonialist norms.

In order to understand how imperialism figured in European women's cultural production, we first need a working hypothesis of a female writing/painting subject. We need a theory of subjectivity and agency that acknowledges the contradictions, gaps and internal splits that structure the paradoxical but necessary notion of a collective identity as women; that is not divorced from the racialized, classed and gendered experience of the social; but that can recognize the 'impermanence' of all those various social collective identities;[56] an approach that can accept the death of the author as an originating source *without* rewriting women off the cultural map by denying the importance of the historical producer.

Griselda Pollock re-inscribes the historical producer by arguing that the act of cultural production (painting) is 'in itself *a site for the inscription of sexual* [and presumably class and racial] *difference'.*[57] This thus brings into orbit the circumstances of a work's production and reception as constituents of its meaning and the identity/ies produced for its author: we cannot read a text without allowing for its productive role in the encoding of social difference. Likewise, with literary representations, as we shall see in Chapter 4, the ways in which women can represent their experience of the harem is always mediated by the form and location of their writing.[58]

In relation to the individual authors I study, I shall be using the term author/artist to refer to the originating identity constructed for the texts, whilst the term writer/painter will refer to the individual historical subject who performs those creative activities. Whilst such historical agents demonstrate relatively constant components of subjectivity over long periods of time, subjectivity is none the less produced within discursively overdetermined conditions. It is with this tension between a relatively stable individual identification and the always changing relations of discourse that this book is concerned. It is important therefore to keep in mind a sense of the authorial/artistic identity constructed for these female subjects as one that, from their first public exposure, always had a bearing on the interpretation and popularity of their work – and they knew it. So even whilst we argue for the separation of the author from the writer, it is important to acknowledge that the writer was aware of the effects of the author-function and how the author might return to the text. Barthes explains how this fiction of the author within the text is different from the paternal authority imagined to the author outside the text.

> It is not that the Author may not 'come back' in the Text, in his text, but then he does so as a 'guest'. If he is a novelist he is inscribed in the novel like one of his characters, figured in the carpet; no longer privileged, paternal, aletheological, his inscription is ludic. He becomes, as it were, a paper-author: his life is no longer the origin of his fictions but a fiction contributing to his work; there is a reversion of the work on to the life (and no longer the contrary); it is the work of Proust, of Genet, which allows their lives to be read as a text.[59]

As we shall see with Browne and George Eliot, not only was their work inevitably read as a product of their experience but changes in their work led to reconceptualizations of the nature of that experience, or life. In the case of George Eliot we know that she was acutely aware of the interface between a writer's (known) life and her fictions. With Browne, we can only speculate on the basis of representations of her in the press. Both cases indicate not only the power of public/collective readings but how writers and artists were themselves constituted as readers.

As agents socialized in an age of everyday imperialism it would have been impossible for the subjects of this study to be unaware of, or uninfluenced by, imperial discourse – even if they couched their relationship to it as oppositional. That some of the key writers of the twentieth-century feminist literary canon, like Brontë and Eliot, couched their demands for female emancipation precisely through the Orientalizing of a structural other requires even more our willingness to include the conditions and discourses of imperial difference in our analysis of the work. Attention to the role of what Spivak calls the 'other woman' ('not merely who am I? but who is the other woman? How am I naming her? How does she name me?'[60]) will open up the imperial dimensions of women's texts and allow us to locate them historically. Without this we will never be able to understand, or challenge, the structural role of racism in the history and praxis of feminism.

> ... what is at stake, for feminist individualism in the age of imperialism, is precisely the making of human beings, the constitution and 'interpellation' of the subject not only as individual but as 'individualist'. This stake is represented on two registers: childbearing and soul making. The first is domestic-society-through-sexual-reproduction cathected as 'companionate love'; the second is the imperialist project cathected as civil-society-through-social-mission. As the female individualist, not-quite/not-male, articulates herself in shifting relationship to what is at stake, the 'native female' as such (*within* discourse, *as* a signifier) is excluded from any share in this emerging norm.[61]

Although Barthes' scriptor is asocial, the instance of women's cultural production shows that even a model not reliant on the humanist concept of author cannot divorce the scriptor's activities from the social. Firstly, to perform the process of disentanglement that Barthes recommends requires an exploration of social forces that exceed the text in so far as we can detect them working structurally *in* the text. For example, the scriptor Charlotte

Brontë created simultaneously with the text *Jane Eyre* (as opposed, for example, to the author Currer Bell), cannot be understood without reference to the social experience of/exposure to colonial discourse that she (the social agent) *must* have had in order to (a) know that English citizens derived their wealth from plantation slavery in British West Indian colonies (the Eyres and the Rochesters) and (b) be able to represent the character Bertha Mason as mad and degenerate in a way that *only* makes sense within imperial discourses of race and heredity. Secondly, disentangling the possible meanings of a text requires attention to the way gender determines the social spaces in which the text can signify. That is, that the gender-specific ideologies that permeated cultural criticism of the period had substantial (though not unquestioned) impact on the types of representation women thought they could make and sell and on how they were judged. Female writing subjects, as female reading subjects, could not but variously be affected by those contemporary ideas about gender and creativity just as they were by those about nation, race, and empire.

WRITERS, READERS AND CRITICS

Historically, the reign of the Author has also been that of the Critic.[62]

The second half of the nineteenth century was an era in which the author and his or her sidekick, the critic, reigned supreme. The nineteenth century as a whole was a period of expanding access to culture (visual and literary) marked by a growth in the numbers and role of cultural critics: not only did the consumption of culture involve greater numbers than ever before, but their activities were guided by a vastly expanded periodical press. Each periodical, with its own political bent, was concerned to varying degrees with politics, economics, philosophy and culture (here interpreted in its widest sense to include music, poetry, literature, science) in an altogether more interactive and wide-ranging series of interests than we might imagine today. Although individual critics had their areas of expertise they were, in general, valued for their ability to give opinions on issues of the day within a broad political and cultural field.[63] A huge number of journals and papers were published (daily, weekly, monthly, quarterly) that, selling at a wide range of prices, were able to reach the specialist and general needs of the expanded reading public.[64] Indeed, John Klancher argues for the formative role of the periodical press in the very conception of the reading public(s); literally constructing diverse individuals into a collectively identified audience *through* their reading of, and relationship to, a periodical.[65] As well as news and entertainment, press reviews of cultural developments on all fronts were an inevitable accompaniment to cultural activities. One not only read the novels of Dickens in serial form, one also read, and discussed, reviews of each instalment.[66] Likewise, attendance at the Salon or Royal Academy occurred in the context of reading reviews in the general and (growing) art press – how else was one to make sense of the bewildering display of crowded pictures?[67] The widely read critical press contributed to the meanings ascribed to texts and the authorial identities constructed for their producers. Additionally, many reviewers or critics were themselves in the public eye as authors, artists, scientists or politicians (Disraeli, a politician who published novels, treatises and reviews, is the obvious example here), further complicating the relationship between the read and the written. And of course, all these relations were subject to variables of gender, class, race and nation.

I am going to be using contemporary criticism as indicators of the cultural codes and contemporary meanings ascribed to my 'primary' texts. As such, reviews constitute part of the social reality of the texts, contributing to how they were read and, I will argue, to how they were produced. That is, the periodical press was constitutive, rather than simply reflective, of Victorian opinion (on cultural, political and social issues).[68] This is not to say that criticism was monolithic – the meanings and values given to these texts were varied and at times hotly contested – but that as a widespread practice with an important social role (reading periodicals was part of daily family life) the ideas circulating in criticism influenced readers and therefore producers. Aside from (but bound up in) the restraints on women's training and access to cultural production, the role of the critic and the possibility of gaining (any) critical attention (which held true for all artists and writers) had a great impact on the type of work women could produce.[69] Therefore, for a study which is interdisciplinary in its objects and methods, the use of periodicals which were themselves always relational (for readers the distinctions between individual articles or issues were submerged under a general sense of the recognizable differences between titles) is instructive. It can help to focus my objects as representational practices situated at the edge of several discursive fields and contained by none, in which signification is a relational activity extending beyond the bounds of the single text. As Patricia Mainardi has demonstrated, in her study of French art criticism, critics with vastly different aesthetic and political positions used a shared critical framework and often the same terminology to discuss their very different interpretations of the same painting. She suggests, therefore, that in order to understand the 'broad dimensions of the issues which formed the field of critical discourse' we must attend to the areas of agreement – what all critics were united in believing to be the essential terms of the debate – in order to grasp the significance of their differences.[70] In my study, this approach allows us to locate the response to Browne's work within widely held, but differently registered, assumptions about gender, art and the Orient; thus, the universal assumption that Browne did see the forbidden harem can be read as symptomatic of a shared field of critical discourse within which the specific responses of individual critics will be explored.

Criticism, then, in both art and literature hints at the meanings ascribed to our texts and indicates the field in which they signified. That is, in assessing the relationship of culture and imperialism we need to see not just the meaning 'in' the text but also those around it. Thus, *The Spanish Gypsy*, which attempts a sympathetic portrait of gypsies, cannot be understood outside of the xenophobia it stirred up in its critics – feelings that are explicitly linked to contemporary identifications of class, gender and nationality. Using criticism as the sites from which were enunciated some of the possible meanings ascribed to the text can, therefore, help us position them in relation to the wider discursive field of which they all were a part.

Although Said departs from Foucault on the question of the author, I think that a parallel can be drawn between the relationality of Foucault's author-function and the political implications of relationality in Said's *Orientalism*; imagine the gendered version of Said's dynamic below:

> My principal methodological devices for studying authority here are what can be called *strategic location*, which is a way of describing the author's position in a text with regard to the

Oriental material he writes about, and *strategic formation*, which is a way of analysing the relationship between texts and the way in which groups of texts, types of texts, even textual genres, acquire mass density, and referential power among themselves and thereafter in the culture at large ... Everyone who writes about the Orient must locate himself *vis-à-vis* the Orient; translated into his text, this location includes the kind of narrative voice he adopts, the type of structure he builds, the kinds of images, themes, motifs that circulate in his text – all of which add up to deliberate ways of addressing the reader, containing the Orient, and finally, representing it or speaking on its behalf. None of this takes place in the abstract, however. Every writer on the Orient ... assumes some Oriental precedent, some previous knowledge of the Orient, to which he refers and on which he relies. Additionally, each work on the Orient *affiliates* itself with other works, with audiences, with institutions, with the Orient itself. The ensemble of relationships between works, audiences and some particular aspects of the Orient therefore constitutes an analysable formation – for example, that of philological studies, of anthologies of extracts from Oriental literature, of travel books, or Oriental fantasies – whose presence in time, in discourse, in institutions (schools, libraries, foreign services) gives it strength and authority.[71]

In the same way as all Oriental texts are positioned in relation to the Orientalist discourse that precedes them, so too are all women's texts positioned in relation to pre-existent codes of femininity, which they may simultaneously uphold and challenge. Thus, Browne's paintings were not only always related to other Orientalist paintings (Said's strategic formation), they were also always related to the work of other women artists. Critics who disputed her version of the harem often used other women's accounts to disprove them – a necessary move in a discursive formation that invested Browne's alternative accounts of the harem with truth precisely because of her gender. Men were not allowed into the harem, so Browne's allegedly truthful eyewitness account could only be counteracted with another potential – and necessarily female – eyewitness.[72]

Browne positions herself (in the choice of subjects and styles) and is positioned (in the reception and circulation of her work) in relation to both Orientalism and gender. In Chapter 3 I will consider how the respectable authorial persona constructed for Browne by the early paintings (in the traditionally feminine areas of portraiture, domestic narrative and religious genre) contributed to the success of her Orientalist subjects by maintaining an image of her as an author (classed and gendered) who could avoid being tainted with the immorality associated with the Orientalist (and particularly the harem) genre. This is not to say that these positionalities, whether strategically selected by the painter or produced by the critic, were the final determinant of meaning – that still lies in the activity of the individual reader. But a sense of the agency of the painter/writer, coupled with attention to the meanings circulated about their texts, does allow us to regard cultural production as a relational activity. Painting or writing are activities undertaken within a social field that is already suffused with meaning, and are themselves the site of the inscription of difference. As participants in relational activities determined by cultural norms, those who paint/write are also implicated as readers – an activity that for the painter, like any other reading subject, was mediated by the activities of the critic.

George Eliot is perhaps the perfect example of why the (female) writing subject can never be separated from the reading subject: she worked as a reviewer and journalist before and during the period in which she wrote fiction. Her critical writings do not reveal the hidden clues of a unified authorial intent – the review essay 'Silly Novels by Lady Novelists' should not be read as a rubric for what she intended to write herself.[73] Rather, they show signs of the internal splits of a female subject produced by the difficulty of trying to write a certain type of 'highbrow' prose without being dragged down to the level of the pot-boiler in the endless restriction of women's writing to a closed female field. The prescriptions George Eliot lays down about women's fiction show us, therefore, the processes by which she positions herself, and is herself positioned, as a reading and writing female subject.

Women constituted as subjects through discourse were therefore always consciously and unconsciously negotiating a grid of previous knowledges and representations (about the nature of women, men, the Orient, etc.). We can find in their work traces of transgressive and affirmative attitudes to these fields of representation in an often bewildering display of contradiction and conformity. (As we shall see in Chapter 2, many women artists and writers emphasized their loyalty to the ideology of separate spheres in order to compensate for the potential transgressions of their creative activities.) Browne challenges certain Orientalist codes in her depiction of the harem, but retains an allegiance to notions of proper femininity in her work and self-presentation to the press; George Eliot publishes novels which advocate a mode of self-abnegation for her female heroines but flouts propriety and conventional feminine behaviour in her personal life.

WOMEN REPRESENTING THE OTHER: VILLETTE

Sometimes the very terms of women's transgressions (as writers and readers) are derived from their position as Westerners in the Orientalist divide. For women writing subjects concerned with female emancipation the Orient often provided a valuable series of metaphors.[74] There is one such passage from Charlotte Brontë's *Villette* that has long intrigued me, not least because this passage, and the novel as a whole, is often used by feminist critics to highlight the construction of gendered subjectivities and the inherent difficulties of being a female writing subject.[75] *Villette* is a novel suffused with Orientalist references and metaphors (Polly sat 'like an odalisque' on the sofa) and filled with reference to visual spectatorship. Jane Miller quotes the following passage in her section on Orientalism: Lucy Snowe is in an art gallery looking at a painting that has all the tropes of an Orientalist odalisque;

> It represented a woman, considerably larger, I thought, than the life. I calculated that this lady, put into a scale of magnitude suitable for the reception of a commodity of bulk would infallibly turn from fourteen to sixteen stone. She was, indeed, extremely well fed: very much butcher's meat – to say nothing of bread, vegetables, and liquids – must she have consumed to attain that breadth and height, that wealth of muscle, that affluence of flesh. She lay half-reclined on a couch: why, it would be difficult to say; broad daylight blazed round her: she appeared in hearty health, strong enough to do the work of two plain cooks; she could not plead a weak spine; she ought to have been standing or at least sitting bolt upright. She had no business to lounge away the noon on a sofa. She ought likewise to have worn decent garments; a gown covering her properly, which was not the case: out of abundance of

material – seven-and-twenty yards, I should say, of drapery – she manages to make inefficient raiment. Then, for the wretched untidiness surrounding her, there could be no excuse. Pots and pans – perhaps I ought to say vases and goblets – were rolled here and there on the foreground; a perfect rubbish of flowers was mixed amongst them, and an absurd and disorderly mass of curtain upholstery smothered the couch and cumbered the floor. On referring to the catalogue, I found that this notable production bore name [*sic*] 'Cleopatra'.[76]

Jane Miller argues that for Lucy to adopt the position of white superiority that so judges the *Cleopatra* requires the assumption of a masculine positionality.

Lucy Snowe scrutinises a man-made image of female voluptuousness and adopts a man's voice (could she have done otherwise?) as she wrestles with the problems it poses for her as a woman who writes.[77]

For Jane Miller the *Cleopatra* represents a male fantasy of female sexuality (and male pleasure) that Lucy can only criticize by undertaking a 'male impersonation' and subsequently displacing onto the painting 'a life's constraints and a history of imperialism in which she is implicated'. Whilst I agree with Miller that the text projects onto the *Cleopatra* the negative aspects of an active female sexuality with which Lucy cannot be associated, I do not think that Lucy critiques the *Cleopatra* as a man. The dynamics of imperialism give Lucy the ability to criticize social norms not because she displaces them and her implications in them (onto the picture or a masculine alter ego), but because they provide a series of positional superiorities in which Lucy can claim for herself *as a woman* the authority to judge and represent that the codes of femininity and class normally deny her. The terms of Lucy's analysis are intrinsically female: evaluating the figure's stature in relation to the domestic labour (of shopping and cooking) that its maintenance would require; casting a housewifely eye over the jumble of accoutrements in the Oriental interior that to other (male) eyes might constitute the essential elements of an Orientalist fantasy of sexual fulfilment; recasting the Oriental drapes in terms of the yardage required to make clothes; asserting the Protestant work ethic over the lassitude of Oriental sexuality. To Lucy, this is not a room of inviting sexual relaxation and pleasure but an untidied (i.e., waiting to be tidied) domestic space. This is a judgement encoded in the terms of a feminine positionality that is structurally dependent on, at the same time as it is productive of, a concept of femininity that is white and Western. What Jane Miller misses out from her analysis of Lucy's judgement is that the chapter sets it from the very beginning into a context of public viewing and contested meanings which mobilizes not just gender but the classed, racialized, and nation-specific differences that structure the social. Before her long contemplation of the *Cleopatra,* Lucy's narrative voice gives us a derisive picture of the painting's status in Villette's municipal gallery.

> ... I found myself alone in a certain gallery, wherein one particular picture of pretentious size, set up in the best light, having a cordon of protection stretched before it, and a cushioned bench duly set in front for the accommodation of worshipping connoisseurs, who, having gazed themselves off their feet, might be fain to complete the business sitting: this picture, I say, seemed to consider itself the queen of the collection. [275]

The picture is put in context and given full description before its title is revealed. It is no coincidence that the subject is Cleopatra; *Villette* is a novel concerned with the quest for an 'independent self-determining female subject[ivity]'[78] that, like all the 'subject constituting'[79] proto-feminist projects of its era, relies on the axiomatics of imperialism. Lucy Snowe's *Bildungs-roman* is animated by the Orientalist construction of the Continental Roman Catholics as the inferior Orientalized other of Protestant England. Not only does Madame Beck maintain her despotic control over her charges (staff and students alike) by a regime of scopic surveillance, but Lucy explores different modes of feminine sexuality via their representation in visual culture. Despite her lowly position in the English domestic social order, once displaced onto foreign soil, Lucy, like all the impoverished younger sons who achieved rank and fortune in the colonies unimaginable at home, can assert a previously prohibited authority to judge and represent. The Roman Catholic characters are represented as essentially different and positionally inferior, characterized, as Said finds the Oriental to be, as irrational, depraved (fallen), childlike, 'different' . . . [and living] in a different but thoroughly organized world of his own, a world with its own national, cultural and epistemological boundaries and principles of internal coherence.[80]

Lucy's scopic surveillance of the Roman Catholics endlessly reiterates their difference, inferiority and threat: Catholicism is a formation of 'dreadful viciousness, sickening tyranny and black impiety'.

> Romanism pervaded every arrangement . . . each mind was being reared in slavery; but to prevent reflection from dwelling on this fact, every pretext for physical recreation was seized . . . the CHURCH strove to bring up her children robust of body, feeble in soul, fat, ruddy, hale, joyous, ignorant, unthinking, unquestioning . . . [196]

Charlotte Brontë was not the only author to substitute European for colonial differences. As Fredric Jameson points out, in the period prior to the First World War,

> the relationship of domination between First and Third World was masked and displaced by an overriding (and perhaps ideological) consciousness of imperialism as being essentially a relationship between First World powers or the holders of Empire, and this consciousness tended to repress the more basic axis of otherness, and to raise issues of colonial reality only incidentally.[81]

He argues that the tendency to mask relations of (colonial) exploitation with those of (European) rivalry was more pronounced in 'high' literature, and suggests that such substitutions be thought of as 'a strategy of representational containment, which scarcely alters the fundamental imperialist structure of colonial appropriation'.[82] In the case of *Villette* and our study, we can add that the tendency to displace imperial relations onto European differences gives the woman writer or artist the chance to avail herself of a colonial superiority that may well elude her in the colonial field itself but can be appropriated, by proxy, in the textual domain of an Orientalized Europe. In this light, read Protestant Lucy's response to the curatorial advice of M. Paul. He is shocked to find her alone in front of this painting;

'Did you come here unaccompanied?'

'No, monsieur. Dr Bretton brought me here.'

... 'And he told you to look at *that* picture?'

'By no means: I found it for myself.'

M. Paul's hair was shorn close as raven down, or I think it would have bristled on his head. Beginning now to perceive his drift, I had a certain pleasure in keeping cool, and working him up.

'Astounding insular audacity!' cried the Professor. 'Singulières femmes que ces Anglaises!'

'What is the matter, monsieur?'

'Matter! How dare you, a young person, sit coolly down, with the self-possession of a garçon, and look at *that* picture?'

'It is a very ugly picture, but I cannot at all see why I should not look at it.'

'Bon Bon! Speak no more of it. But you ought not to be here alone. . . . asseyez-vous là – là!' Setting down a chair with emphasis in a particularly dull corner, before a series of most specially dreary 'cadres' [representing four stages in the 'vie d'une femme']. [276–7]

In contrast to M. Paul's attempts to assert the fixity of gender roles (prohibiting Lucy from behaving like a boy, a garçon) the imperial ethos that gives Lucy leave to judge men's vision of female sexuality also lets her judge their judgements. She turns her attention to other people's readings of the *Cleopatra*.

A perfect crowd of spectators was by this time gathered round the Lioness, from whose vicinage I had been banished; nearly half this crowd were ladies, but M. Paul afterwards told me, these were 'des dames,' and it was quite proper for them to contemplate what no 'demoiselle' ought to glance at. I assured him plainly I could not agree in this doctrine, and did not see the sense of it; whereupon, with his usual absolutism, he merely requested my silence . . . A more despotic little man than M. Paul never filled a professor's chair, I noticed, by the way, that he looked at the picture himself quite at his ease, and for a very long while. . . .

[She asks his opinion of the Cleopatra]

. . . 'Une femme superbe – une tialle d'imperatrice, des formes de Junon, mais une personne dont je ne voudrais ni pour femme, ni pour fille, ni pour soeur. Aussi vous ne jeterez plus un seul coup d'oeil de sa côté.'[83] [278–80]

Meanwhile, the English Dr Bretton arrives and takes a turn about the room with Lucy.

> I always liked dearly to hear what he had to say about either pictures or books; because, without pretending to be a connoisseur, he always spoke his thought, and that was sure to be fresh: very often it was also just and pithy . . . I asked him what he thought of the Cleopatra (after making him laugh by telling how Professor Emmanuel had sent me to the right-about . . .)
>   'Pooh!' said he, 'My mother is a better-looking woman. I heard some French fops, yonder, designating her as "le type du voluptueux;" if so, I can only say, "le voluptueux" is little to my liking. Compare that mulatto with Ginevre!'[282]

What we see in this passage is the way that cultural consumption is demarcated by the shifting relational differences of class, gender, nationality and race. Although Lucy uses the opportunity of viewing the *Cleopatra* to pass judgement on people normally considered to be above her, she does not do this by pretending to be male, but by reframing her femininity with the signifiers of nation and class. In other words, the text uses whatever ammunition comes to hand, activating whichever set of differences will work. Lucy sides with Graham to refuse the erotic voyeurism of the *Cleopatra* on grounds not of gender but of nationality and class. Arrogating to herself the Doctor's lofty disdain, she consigns M. Paul, otherwise her ally, to the sidelines as part of the Catholic contingent along with the enraptured de Hamal.[84] But the urbanity and diffidence Graham deploys in front of the *Cleopatra* is described as 'callous' when turned on the live spectacle of female passion embodied in the performance of the actress Vashti: 'he judged her as a woman, not an artist: it was a branding judgement' [342].

Viewing is represented as a public activity subject to the power dynamics of the social; for women judgement comes from without and it is proscriptive ('Vashti was not good, I was told' [340]). But in *Villette* the text undercuts those judgements even as it represents them, displacing the authority of male interpretations and permitting a transgressive female reading.[85] The multiplicity of feminine subjectivities represented in the text (and, significantly, represented as visual images) are seen to have different meanings for those who view them, indicating that gendered identifications are contested and contingent. The transgressions of Lucy's voyeurism rely on *all* the terms of social differentiation, not just gender.

It is clear, then, that Lucy's identity is constituted through her activities as a reader and spectator and that an intervention into cultural codes is one way of challenging the positionalities open to women: Lucy does this both in her reading of culture (her knowing disbelief in cultural conventions) and her active disruption/production of the fictions that culture seeks to normalize (her disruption of the play). The contradictions of women's challenges to imperial power indicate the splits within imperial discourse and its imperial subject. In order to break up Said's monolithic Orientalist discourse, Homi Bhabha maps Said's schema of latent and manifest Orientalism onto the psychoanalytic concept of the splits between the unconscious and conscious mind. He reveals imperialism as a mode of discourse that is based on an ambivalence and anxiety, in which the colonial other is 'at once an object of desire and derision'.[86] He utilizes a Lacanian explanation of subjectivity as something that is at once formed through language (the child must learn to take up a place within a signifying system that predates it in order to join the realm of the social) and intrinsically split (the moment of recognition and splitting in the 'me/not me' of the mirror phase)[87] to decode Orientalism as a discourse, based on representation, that is driven not by a unified and intentional power but by the splits and ambivalences of the subjects who enunciate it. Bhabha takes us back to the moment of enunciation to emphasize the role of the enunciating agent (potentially in all its classed and gendered specificity – something which Bhabha, like Said, ignores), to bypass Said's reliance on the concept of the exceptional individual author (as the only one who can function outside of the constraints of Orientalism) and reveal Orientalism as an always incohesive discourse that always already contains conflictual positions.[88]

Thus, the apparent unity and homogeneity of imperial discourse attests not to the reality of imperial power (Said's problem of the real Orient) but to a motivational fantasy of unified power and control. Rather than trying to match our representations against the 'reality' of (say, women's) experience of colonialism or imperialist ideology, we can read them as traces of collective fantasies about power, control, desire and difference – channelled through the subjective particularities of the individual.[89] These fantasy traces are not simply wish fulfilment but reveal the fragmentary nature of the psychical realities engendered by the contradictions of imperial discourse. It is only with attention to the social and psychical elements of women's experience and representation of imperialism that we can explain why, for example, Charlotte Brontë's imagining of female independence relies on the subordination of other (Orientalized) female subjectivities. Fantasy, like subjectivity itself, is contradictory and unstable. It relies, as we shall see, on mechanisms of repression and displacement that may both mask and reveal the conflicting desires of the subject, and is influenced by the social realities of the subject's experience. Although the Foucauldian paradigm I have used so far would be opposed to psychoanalysis, I think that we can use psychoanalytic theory to good effect without accepting what are sometimes seen as its transhistorical and universalist claims.[90]

If we accept that subjectivity can only be produced as a fragmented and unstable structure, we can also assert that the particular splits of the subject will be in some relation to the rules and values of the society in which it is formed. Those values and codes will impact differently, to different psychic effect, on agents in different classed, gendered and racialized positions.[91] As Henriques *et al.* show in their examination of psychological practices, we cannot get away from the fact that whilst people experience their subjectivity as real, the possibilities of those subjectivities are not only historically determined but are also relational; that is, they are affected not just by some impersonal discourse, but by the relations between the individuals through whom discourse is articulated.[92] To avoid the universalizing tendencies of Lacan and the functionalist tendencies of Foucault they argue for attention to the 'motivational dynamics through which people are positioned in discourses' and the role of discourse in the production of desire.

> The content of desires, then, is neither timeless nor arbitrary, but has a historical specificity . . . It is precisely this formation of power-knowledge relations through the positioning of subjects within discursive practices [that] simultaneously produc[es] relations of desire . . .[93]

If we see desire as not only historically specific but also as a formation based in fantasy that is always relational (the unfulfillable nature of desire stems from its originatory moment – the loss of the mother, the original object – which, in turn provides the sense of absence and loss necessary to drive the infant into signification) then we can see the motivational possibilities of assuming an enunciative position in discourse – itself a placement that is relational and significatory. By theorizing the reasons why individuals take up discursive positionalities Henriques *et al.* open up a space for the recognition of how discourses are changed by the activity of the individuals who reproduce them. If desire is produced (contingent) and not innate, then it can change, and since power is relational and enunciated from relational positionalities by individual subjects, then that too can be changed. This takes us one stage further away from a mechanistic view of a unitary power. Moreover, since all subjects are the product of more than one discourse, the ascendancy of different discourses may differently complexion the relations of power and knowledge. This, in relation to our project, means that the particular contradictions we may detect in women's representations will indicate not only the limitation of, but the changes wrought by, the gender-specific access that white Western women had to the enunciative positions of colonial discourse. Thus, the representation of the Orientalized other is never one of a secure and absolute difference, although it may evidence a will to be just that. It is precisely this desire to assuage the splits and instabilities of the imperial subject that is revealed by women's problematic and partial (but not necessarily oppositional) access to colonial representation.

NOTES

1 See V.G. Kiernan, *The Lords of Human Kind: European Attitudes Towards the Outside World in the Imperial Age*, London, Weidenfeld and Nicolson, 1969; Edward W. Said, *Culture and Imperialism*, New York, Alfred A. Knopf, 1993; C.C. Eldridge, *Victorian Imperialism*, London, Hodder and Stoughton, 1978; P.J. Cain and A.G. Hopkins, *British Imperialism: Innovation and Expansion 1688–1914*, London, Longman, 1993.

2 Late nineteenth-century histories tend to depict British imperialism in three distinct phases: the 'mercantile' period up to the 1830s, the 'anti-imperialist' phase into the early 1870s, and the 'new imperial' from 1870 onwards. See Eldridge, *Victorian Imperialism*.

3 On the earlier and developing presence of ideologies of racial differ-
   ence and imperialism in European art and literature see Brian Street,
   *The Savage in Literature: The Representation of 'Primitive' Society
   in English Fiction, 1858–1920*, London, Routledge, 1975; John
   Sweetman, *The Oriental Obsession: Islamic Inspiration in British and
   American Art and Architecture 1500–1920*, Cambridge, Cambridge
   University Press, 1988; Frances Mannsaker, 'Early Attitudes to
   Empire', in B. Moore-Gilbert (ed.), *Literature and Imperialism*,
   London, Roehampton Institute of Higher Education, 1983; David
   Dabydeen (ed.), *The Black Presence in English Literature*,
   Manchester, Manchester University Press, 1985; Ania Loomba,
   Gender, Race, Renaissance Drama, Manchester, Manchester
   University Press, 1989.

4 Edward W. Said 'Yeats and Decolonization', in Terry Eagleton,
   Fredric Jameson and Edward W. Said, *Nationalism, Colonialism and
   Literature*, Minneapolis, University of Minnesota Press, 1990, p. 72.

5 Benedict Anderson, *Imagined Communities: Reflections on the
   Origins and Spread of Nationalism*, London, Verso, 1983.

6 See, for example, his analysis of Jane Austen in Said, *Culture and
   Imperialism*.

7 As Said argues, the opposition to specific imperialist or colonial
   measures was rarely accompanied by an ability to see subjected
   peoples as fully human or deserving or capable of self-government.
   See Said, 'Introduction', *Culture and Imperialism*, pp. xi–xxvii.

8 Daniel Bivona, *Desire and Contradiction: Imperial Visions and
   Domestic Debates in Victorian Literature*, Manchester, Manchester
   University Press, 1990, p. vii.

9 Gayatri Chakravorty Spivak, 'Three Women's Texts and a Critique
   of Imperialism', in *Critical Inquiry* 12, Autumn 1985, p. 243.

10 One obvious exception is Said's discussion in 'Zionism From the
   Standpoint of its Victims', in *Social Text*, vol. 1, 1978.

11 An approach adopted, for example, by Janice N. Brownfoot in 'Sisters
   Under the Skin: Imperialism and the Emancipation of Women in
   Malaya, c.1891–1941', in J.A. Mangan (ed.), *Making Imperial
   Identities: Socialization and British Imperialism*, Manchester,
   Manchester University Press, 1990.

12 Cora Kaplan, 'Pandora's Box: Subjectivity, Class and Sexuality in
   Socialist Feminist Criticism', in Kaplan, *Sea Changes: Essays in
   Culture and Feminism*, London, Verso, 1986, p. 149.

13 See Adrienne Rich on the 'thoughtlessly white' nature of white experience. Adrienne Rich, 'Towards a Politics of Location', in Rich,
   Blood, Bread and Poetry: Selected Prose 1979–1985, London, Virago,
   1987, p. 219. See also Vron Ware, *Beyond the Pale: White Women,
   Racism and History*, London, Verso, 1992.

14 Ware, *Beyond the Pale*, p. 43; (original emphasis).

15 The mid-century in Britain, for example, saw the start of organized
   feminism, with the campaigns over the Married Women's Property
   Act and the Contagious Diseases Acts; unrest in Ireland; the legacy
   of Chartism and continued agitation for parliamentary reform. See

E.J. Hobsbawm, *Industry and Empire*, Harmondsworth, Penguin, 1968.
16 Edward W. Said, *Orientalism*, Harmondsworth, Penguin, 1978, p. 67 (original emphasis).
17 Said, *Orientalism*, p. 21 (original emphasis).
18 See Lata Mani and Ruth Frankenberg, 'The Challenge of *Orientalism*', in *Economy and Society*, vol. 14, 1985; Robert Young, *White Mythologies: Writing, History and the West*, London, Routledge, 1990, ch. 7; Edward W. Said, 'Orientalism Reconsidered', in *Race and Class*, vol. 27, no. 2, 1985.
19 The obviously partial and potentially rebellious nature of 'native' conversions and capitulations to Western power will be discussed later.
20 Said, *Orientalism*, p. 7 (original emphasis).
21 See Lucy Bland, 'The Domain of the Sexual', in *Screen Education*, no. 39, 1981; Deborah Cherry and Griselda Pollock, 'Woman as Sign in Pre-Raphaelite Literature: A Study of the Representation of Elizabeth Siddall', in *Art History*, June 1984.
22 See Michel Foucault, *Power/Knowledge: Selected Interviews and Other Writings, 1972–1977 by Michel Foucault*, ed. Colin Gordon, Hemel Hempstead, Harvester Wheatsheaf, 1980, ch. 2.
23 Foucault never quite resolves the problem of how power, even if it is an 'open, more-or-less coordinated . . . cluster of relations', appears to serve the interests of particular groups. His description of how power comes to operate through a network of discursive apparatuses that move across and order the human body, is very persuasive, but as to what motivates/activates power he manages only to formulate the existence of 'strategic necessities which are not exactly interests . . .'. See 'Confessions of the Flesh', in Foucault, *Power/Knowledge*.
    On Said's use of Foucault's concept of power see Dennis Porter, '*Orientalism* and its Problems', in Francis Barker *et al.* (eds), *The Politics of Theory*, Colchester, University of Essex, 1982.
    On the possibilities of a Foucauldian analysis of power for feminist praxis (itself characterized by a diversity of localized fronts) see Biddy Martin, 'Feminism, Criticism, and Foucault', in Irene Diamond and Lee Quinby (eds), *Feminism and Foucault: Reflections on Resistance*, Boston, North Eastern University Press, 1988; Lois McNay, *Foucault and Feminism: Power, Gender and the Self*, Cambridge, Polity Press, 1992.
24 See Jonathan Arac and Harriet Ritvo 'Introduction' to Arac and Ritvo (eds), *Macropolitics of Nineteenth-Century Literature: Nationalism, Exoticism, Imperialism*, Philadelphia, University of Pennsylvania Press, 1991.
25 Lisa Lowe, 'Nationalism and Exoticism: Nineteenth-Century Others in Flaubert's *Salammbô* and *L'Éducation sentimentale*', in Arac and Ritvo, *Macropolitics*, p. 236.
    Lowe extends Foucault's binarism in which spaces are coded as either public/private, licit/illicit into a matrix of multiple sites. Thus, where Utopian/heterotopian refers to the cultural imaginings of a

reorganized society in binary terms, Lowe argues for a sense of heterotopicality as site of multiple and interpenetrative forms of othering. This allows for overlap in which 'each articulation shifts and alters the terms, conditions, and emphasized sites of the terrain'. Lisa Lowe, *Critical Terrains: French and British Orientalisms*, Ithaca, Cornell University Press, 1991, pp. 14–15.

26   On the political implications of the concept of indigenous resistance for a late twentieth-century analysis of postcolonial power relations see Vijay Mishraa and Bob Hodge, 'What is Post(-)colonialism?', in *Textual Practice*, vol. 5, no. 3, Winter 1991.

27   Jane Miller, *Seductions: Studies in Reading and Culture*, London, Virago, 1990, pp. 118–22.

28   Miller, *Seductions*, p. 121.

29   Rani Kabbani, *Europe's Myths of Orient*, London, Macmillan, 1986, p. 7.

30   See, similarly, my discussion of Melman's 'purifying' of Muslim women writers in Chapter 4.

31   Kabbani, *Europe's Myths*, p. 12.

32   Sara Mills, *Discourses of Difference: An Analysis of Women's Travel Writing and Colonialism*, London, Routledge, 1991, pp. 91–2.

33   For a good overview of feminist responses to and uses of colonial theory see Jane Haggis, 'Gendering Colonialism or Colonising Gender? Recent Women's Studies Approaches to White Women and the History of British Colonialism', in *Women's Studies International Forum*, vol. 13, nos. 1/2, 1990. See also Lata Mani, 'Multiple Mediations: Feminist Scholarship in the Age of Multinational Receptions', in *Inscriptions*, no. 5, 1989.

      On the mixed motives of British feminists in relation to India see Antoinette M. Burton, 'The White Woman's Burden: British Feminists and The Indian Woman, 1865–1915', in *Women's Studies International Forum*, vol. 13, no. 4, 1990. In contrast, Janice Brownfoot practically evacuates imperial relations to represent British women as the agents of Malay women's emancipation. Nancy Paxton usefully stresses the pleasures that imperial power offered to Western women, but marginalizes the contradictions of their position. Nancy L. Paxton, 'Feminism Under the Raj: Complicity and Resistance in the Writings of Flora Annie Steel and Annie Besant', in *Women's Studies International Forum*, vol. 13, no. 4, 1990. See also Susan L. Blake, 'A Woman's Text: What Difference does Gender Make?', in *Women's Studies International Forum*, vol. 13, no. 4, 1990.

      On the colonialist legacy in feminist analyses of Third World women see Aihwa Ong, 'Colonialism and Modernity: Feminist Re-presentations of Women in Non-Western Societies', in *Inscriptions*, vol. 3, no. 4, 1988.

34   James Clifford, *The Predicament of Culture: Twentieth Century Ethnography, Literature and Art*, London, Harvard University Press, 1988, p. 269.

35   Said, *Orientalism*, p. 23

36 Roland Barthes, 'The Death of the Author', in Barthes, *Image Music Text*, trans. Stephen Heath, London, Fontana, 1977, p. 147.

37 Barthes, 'The Death of the Author', p. 145 (original emphasis).

38 Nancy K. Miller, 'Changing the Subject: Authorship, Writing, and the Reader', in Teresa de Lauretis (ed.), *Feminist Studies/Critical Studies*, Basingstoke, Macmillan, 1986, p. 106.

39 Barthes, 'The Death of the Author', p. 148.

40 Miller, 'Changing the Subject', pp. 104–5.

41 Miller's considerations of this issue over the past fifteen years have occurred in a mainly American academic feminist context (itself in the context of French studies) and indicate the polarities and affinities between two main camps of American academic feminism, characterized as 'pragmatic' or essentialist and deconstructionist, the latter generally represented by Peggy Kamuf. See Kamuf and Miller, 'Parisian Letters: Between Feminism and Deconstruction', in Marianne Hirsch and Evelyn Fox Keller (eds), *Conflicts in Feminism*, London, Routledge, 1990.

42 Peggy Kamuf, 'Writing Like a Woman', quoted in Nancy K. Miller, 'The Text's Heroine: A Feminist Critic and her Fictions', in Hirsch and Fox Keller, *Conflicts*, p. 115.

43 The male use of a female pseudonym, such as the debate over the authorship of the *Story of O* and the *Letters of the Portuguese Nun*, reveals, 'a male (at least masculine) desire to paper over an anxiety about destination and reception: a sense of powerlessness about writing in a new genre addressed to an unknown "destinataire" '. Miller, 'The Text's Heroine', p. 116.

44 Catharine Stimpson, 'Ad/d Feminam: Woman, Literature and Society', in Edward W. Said (ed.), *Selected Papers From the English Institute*, Baltimore, 1978, quoted in Miller, 'The Text's Heroine', p. 116.

   In a study where both my subjects use pseudonyms (one masculine, one feminine) the class and gender implications of this subterfuge cannot be avoided, as will be discussed in later chapters.

45 Gayatri Chakravorty Spivak, 'Subaltern Studies: Deconstructing Historiography', in Spivak, *In Other Worlds: Essays in Cultural Politics*, London, Routledge, 1988.

46 See also Antony Easthope, *Literary Into Cultural Studies*, London, Routledge, 1991.

47 John Tomlinson, *Cultural Imperialism: A Critical Introduction*, London, Pinter, 1991.

48 See Tomlinson and James Clifford who, for example, discusses how nineteenth-century Native American objects are radically repositioned from their place within Eurocentric art and ethnographic signifying systems when read as 'newly traditionally, meaningful' by a twentieth-century Native American viewer. Clifford, *The Predicament of Culture*, pp. 246–7.

49 Michel Foucault, 'What is an Author', in *Screen*, vol. 20, no. 1, Spring 1979, pp. 19–28.

50 Young, *White Mythologies*, p. 123.

   Whilst Nancy Miller warns that instead of liberating the previously marginalized others of modernism, the end of humanist definitions of subjectivity may simply be a way to avoid reconceptualizing subjectivity in all its political implications (a critical ideology that 'celebrates or longs for a mode beyond difference'), others, like Kobena Mercer, see it as possibly empowering alternative modes of subjectivity that were disenfranchised in the modernist order. Nancy Miller, 'Changing the Subject', p. 115; Kobena Mercer, 'Welcome to the Jungle: Identity and Diversity in Postmodern Politics', in Jonathon Rutherford (ed.) *Identity: Community, Culture, Difference*, London, Lawrence and Wishart, 1990.

See also Tania Modleski, 'Feminism and the Power of Interpretation: Some Critical Readings', in de Lauretis, *Feminist Studies/ Critical Studies*; and, on the political implications of the end of the grand narratives and related criticisms of *Orientalism* see, Edward W. Said, 'Representing the Colonized: Anthropology's Interlocutors', in *Critical Inquiry*, Winter 1989.

51 On the critical and political imperatives to utilize critical theory as part of a political agenda see, Reina Lewis, 'The Death of the Author and the Resurrection of the Dyke', in Sally Munt (ed.), *New Lesbian Criticism: Literary and Cultural Readings*, Hemel Hempstead, Harvester Wheatsheaf, 1992; Richard Dyer, 'Believing in Fairies: the Author and the Homosexual', in Diana Fuss (ed.), *Inside/Out: Lesbian Theories, Gay Theories*, London, Routledge, 1991.

52 Anita Levy, *Other Women: the Writing of Class, Race and Gender, 1832–1898*, Princeton, Princeton University Press, 1991, p. 5.

53 Rosemary Hennessy and Rajeswari Mohan, 'The Construction of Woman in Three Popular Texts of Empire: Towards a Critique of Materalist Feminism', in *Textual Practice*, vol. 3, 1989, p. 328.

54 Deborah Cherry, *Painting Women: Victorian Women Artists*, London, Routledge, 1993, pp. 10–11 and p. 115.

55 Levy, *Other Women*, p. 5.

56 See Denise Riley, *'Am I That Name?' Feminism and the Category of 'Women' in History*, Basingstoke, Macmillan, 1988.

57 Pollock's argument that the socially determined spaces in which painting occurs also, to some extent, determine the spaces represented will be discussed in Chapter 4. Griselda Pollock, 'Modernity and the Spaces of Femininity', in Pollock, *Vision and Difference: Femininity, Feminism and Histories of Art*, London, Routledge, 1987, p. 82 (original emphasis, my insert).

58 For example, Oriental women writing in the West are clearly writing in relation to what they assume are the specific values of their Western readers. In the case of travel writing, Mills uses Foucault's author-function to suggest how experience is 'channelled into and negotiates with pre-existent schemas which are discursive in nature'. Mills, *Discourse of Difference*, p. 39.

59 Roland Barthes, 'From Work to Text', in Barthes, *Image Music Text*, trans. Stephen Heath, London, Fontana, 1977, p. 161.

Note that whereas in this instance Barthes uses 'work' as an oppositional term to 'text' (in which work is to author as text is to scriptor/writer) I have used it elsewhere in the body of the book in its colloquial sense.

60 Gayatri Chakravorty Spivak, 'French Feminisms in an International Frame', in Spivak, *In Other Worlds*, London, Routledge, 1988, p. 150.

61 Spivak, 'Three Women's Texts', pp. 244–5, (original emphasis). See also Chandra Mohanty, 'Under Western Eyes: Feminist Scholarship and Colonial Discourses', in *Feminist Review*, no. 30, Autumn 1988.

62 Barthes, 'The Death of the Author', p. 147.

63 See J.D. Vann and R.T. Van Arsdel (eds), *Victorian Periodicals: A Guide to Research*, vols. 1 and 2, 1989, New York, Modern Language Association of America, 1878 and 1989; John Gross, *The Rise and Fall of the Man of Letters: Aspects of English Literary Life Since 1800*, London, Weidenfeld and Nicolson, 1969; Harold Orel, *Victorian Literary Critics: George Henry Lewes, Walter Bagehot, Richard Holt Hutton, Leslie Stephen, Andrew Lang, George Saintsbury and Edmund Gosse*, London, Macmillan, 1984; R.G. Cox, 'The Reviews and Magazines', in Boris Ford (ed.), *The Pelican Guide to English Literature: From Dickens to Hardy*, vol. 6, Harmondsworth, Penguin, 1958; Christopher Kent, 'Victorian Periodicals and the Construction of Victorian Reality', in Vann and Van Arsdel, *Victorian Periodicals*, vol. 2; Walter E. Houghton, 'Periodical Literature and the Articulate Classes', in Joanne Shattock and Michael Wolff (eds), *The Victorian Periodical Press: Samplings and Soundings*, Leicester, Leicester University Press, 1982.

For a guide to the French periodic press see, Claude Bellanger, *Histoire générale de la presse française*, Paris, Universitaires de France, 1969.

64 See, Alvar Ellegard, 'The Readership of the Periodical Press in Mid-Victorian Britain. Vol. II. Directory', in *Victorian Periodicals Newsletter*, vol. 13, September 1971.

65 John P. Klancher, *The Making of English Reading Audiences, 1790–1832*, Madison, University of Wisconsin Press, 1987.

On the class make-up of and differences between the reading public (literally those who could read) and the literary public (those who could afford to buy books and periodicals and who were assumed to be their main readers or addressees) see Darko Suvin, 'The Social Addressees of Victorian Fiction: A Preliminary Enquiry', in *Literature and History*, no. 1, vol. 8, Spring 1982.

66 On the impact of serialization in terms of criticism, form, plot structure, reading habits, relationship to the other contents of the journal and economic implications for authors, see J. Don Vann, *Victorian Novels in Serial*, New York, Modern Language Association of America, 1985; Malcolm Andrews, 'A Note on Serialization', in Ian Gregor (ed.), *Reading the Victorian Novel: Detail into Form*, London, Vision Press, 1980.

67 On the development of the art press, the role of the art critic (particularly in relation to private collections and public exhibitions) and the relationship of art criticism to general review criticism see Elizabeth Gilmore Holt, *The Art of All Nations 1850–73: The*

Emerging Role of Exhibitions and Critics, Princeton, Princeton University Press, 1982; Christopher Kent, 'Periodical Critics of Drama, Music and Art 1830–1914: A Preliminary List', in *Victorian Periodicals Review*, vol. 13, nos. 1–2, Spring and Summer, 1980; and 'More Critics of Drama, Music and Art', in *Victorian Periodicals Review*, vol. 19, no. 3, Fall 1986; Helene Roberts, 'Exhibition and Review: the Periodical Press and the Victorian Art Exhibition System', in Shattock and Wolf, *The Victorian Periodical Press*; Julie F. Codell, 'Marion Henry Spielmann and the Role of the Press in the Professionalization of Artists', in *Victorian Periodicals Review*, vol. 22, no. 1, Spring 1989; Trevor Fawcett and Clive Phillpot, *The Art Press: Two Centuries of Art Magazines*, London, 1976; Joseph C. Sloane, *French Painting Between the Past and the Present: Artists, Critics and Traditions from 1848–1870*, Princeton, Princeton University Press, 1951; Leslie A. Marchand, *The Athenaeum: A Mirror of Victorian Culture*, Chapel Hill, 1941; Christopher Parsons and Martha Ward, *A Bibliography of Salon Criticism in Second Empire Paris*, Cambridge, Cambridge University Press, 1986.

68 For an overview of methodological issues in the use of the periodical press see Lyn Pykett, 'Reading the Periodical Press: Text and Context', in *Victorian Periodicals Review*, Special Issue *Theory*, vol. 22, no. 3, Fall 1989.

69 llustrating the importance of reception in the construction of meaning, Mills notes that the most striking difference between men's and women's work lay not in its style or execution, but in the way that it was circulated and judged. For example, when women travellers wrote of undertaking dangerous journeys they were accused of lying (since physical strength and courage conflicted with Victorian codes of femininity), whereas their male counterparts were not challenged. Mills, *Discourse of Difference*, p. 30 and pp. 108–23.

70 Patricia Mainardi, *Art and Politics of the Second Empire: The Universal Expositions of 1855 and 1867*, New Haven, Yale University Press, 1987, p. 68.

71 Said, *Orientalism*, p. 20.

72 In my use of women's accounts of the harem as indicators of the possible accuracy of Brown's images, I am not setting them up as another/alternative realist truth, but as an alternative regime of representation. That these accounts were published in our period and that they were evidently known to her readers and critics, points to the existence of alternative or counter-hegemonic voices within Orientalist discourse. The effort expended on denouncing her version testifies to the energy that dominant accounts expend on keeping their position.

73 See Chapter 2.

74 See also my discussion of Joyce Zonana's work on 'feminist' Orientalism in Chapter 4.

75 See, for example, Judith Newton, '*Villette*', in Newton and Deborah Rosenfelt (eds), *Feminist Criticism and Social Change*, London, Methuen, 1985; Mary Jacobus, 'The Buried Letter: Feminism and

Romanticism in *Villette'*, in Jacobus (ed.) *Women Writing and Writing about Women*, London, Croom Helm, 1979.

76 Charlotte Brontë, *Villette* (1855), Harmondsworth, 1985, pp. 275–6. All page references are to the Penguin edition and hereafter are given in brackets in the text.

77 Miller, *Seductions*, p. 109.

78 Kaplan, 'Pandora's Box'.

79 Spivak, 'Three Women's Texts', p. 249.

80 Said, *Orientalism*, p. 40.

81 Fredric Jameson, 'Modernism and Imperialism', in Eagleton *et al.*, *Nationalism*, p. 48.

82 In popular or 'lower' genres, like the adventure story, the 'more radical otherness of colonized non-Western peoples' was likely to be represented directly. Jameson, 'Modernism and Imperialism', p. 50.

83 ... 'A superb woman – an imperial figure, Junoesque, but a person I would not want in a wife, daughter or sister. You will not cast even one more glance in that direction.' Trans. Mark Lilly.

84 See Judith Newton on how the strategic disadvantaging of Paul places him in a suitably equitable position to Lucy to be her help meet and lover. With the superior Graham the only possible female positionality is that of the child-like dependence of Paulina. Newton, '*Villette*'.

85 Although, it must be noted, the scope of this transgression is limited. The derisive tone of Lucy's rejection of the *Cleopatra* and the judgement of those who admire it suggests the tension involved in denying an image (however patriarchal) of an active female sexuality. In a novel without a 'happy ending' the attempt to represent or enact an active female sexuality is problematized and unresolved. Neither the insupportable choice of images in the gallery nor the deathly Vashti in the theatre provide a sexuality to which Lucy can be reconciled.

86 Homi Bhabha, 'The Other Question', in *Screen*, no. 24, vol. 6, 1983, p. 19.

87 See Madan Sarup, *Jacques Lacan*, Hemel Hempstead, Harvester Wheatsheaf, 1992.

88 For a critique that challenges the potential innocence of Bhabha's conflicted colonial subject see Abdul R. JanMohamed, 'The Economy of Manichean Allegory: The Function of Racial Difference in Colonialist Literature', in *Critical Inquiry*, Autumn 1985.
    See also J.A. Mangan, 'Introduction', to Mangan (ed.), *Making Imperial Mentalities*.

89 On the subject's role in and relation to fantasy see J. Laplanche and J.B. Pontalis, 'Fantasy and the Origins of Sexuality', in *International Journal of Psychoanalysis*, 49, part 1, 1968.

90 See Juliet Mitchell and Jacqueline Rose, *Feminine Sexuality: Jacques Lacan and the École Freudienne*, London, Macmillan, 1982.

91 See for example Hortense Spillers' exploration of the psychoanalytic implications of the different types of kinship relations possible for enslaved Black subjects in the American plantation slavery system. Hortense J. Spillers, 'Mama's Baby, Papa's Maybe: An American Grammar Book', in *Diacritics*, vol. 17, no. 2, Summer 1987. See also

Ashis Nandy's exploration of the forms, pleasures and personal costs that colonial subjectivity produced for both colonized and colonizer in India. Ashis Nandy, *The Intimate Enemy: Loss and Recovery of Self Under Colonialism*, (1983) second edition, Delhi, Oxford University Press, 1988.

92 Julian Henriques, Wendy Hollway, Cathy Urwin, Couze Venn and Valerie Walkerdine, *Changing the Subject: Psychology, Social Regulation and Subjectivity*, London, Methuen, 1984.

93 Henriques *et al.*, *Changing the Subject*, 'Introduction to Section Three: Theorizing Subjectivity', pp. 218–223.

Chapter 2

Professional opportunities for women in art and literature

This chapter sets out the material and ideological constraints on women's cultural production in the mid- to late nineteenth century. This is an important part of the historical context. Such constraints would have affected (and been affected by, since these things were never static) the lives and work of women such as George Eliot and Henriette Browne. They worked in a period when ideas about gender variously restricted the educational opportunities open to aspiring women artists and writers, the forms and techniques they could use, the subjects they could cover and their opportunities for exhibition and publication. More than this, discourses of femininity had a determining effect on the authorial identities established for them and the meanings attributed to their work. In an era when paintings and writings tended to be received as the emissions of a specific (and typically gendered, classed and national) author, the effects of the 'critical double standard' that Elaine Showalter identified in relation to women's novels (which also holds true for women's work in the visual arts) cannot be underestimated.[1] Accordingly, one of my aims is to explore the complex and contradictory ways by which were negotiated and internalized gendered codes of behaviour and of artistic and literary production.

THE SEPARATE SPHERES: PROBLEMS OF A PROFESSIONAL IDENTITY

The nineteenth century has been characterized as a period in which the growth of the industrial bourgeoisie and the ideology of femininity led to the increasing bifurcation of men's and women's lives. The work of Catherine Hall and Leonore Davidoff has shown that whilst middle-class women were originally crucial to family businesses they were moved out of the realm of production into the domestic once the family's prosperity allowed, and subsequently required, the visible leisure of its women.[2] Conspicuous female leisure came to function as an index to the prosperity and gentility of the middle- and upper-class family. Moreover, as Levy has illustrated, it was not only the development but the *representation* of the nucleated middle-class family that was essential to the development of industrial capitalism and middle-class hegemony. She argues that novels by women and largely understood to be addressed to women ('rhetorical strategies that are also cultural strategies') functioned as educative norms that played a central role in the reproduction of the social relations required by capitalist forms of production.[3] Changes in the workplace developed alongside a sexual double standard in which men were conceptualized as sexually active beings whilst (middle-class) women were seen as naturally lacking in sexual feelings.[4] The Enlightenment valorization of Man's rationality was calibrated by social and gender divisions to produce a libidinal economy in which white Western men were able to control their natural/animal sexuality by virtue of their superior intellect and thus deserved their position of power over those lower orders (women, working classes, subject peoples) who were unable to exercise the civilizing cogito. For women, the licentious sexuality that had previously been regarded as a propensity of all women now came to function as a division between women in which the construction of middle-class women as innately chaste and asexual was countered by the attribution of a virulent, rapacious and unChristian sexuality to working-class women at home and all women in the colonies.[5]

Mary Poovey argues that the split between the public and the private rests on the ideological division between alienated and unalienated labour.[6] She extends existing work on the symbolic value of the domestic as a natural haven away from the seemingly unnatural world of commerce and work to incorporate an analysis of how the work that did occur in the domestic sphere was secured as unalienated. Domestic work was presented as the natural outcome of innate feminine qualities that, since it was unwaged and not publicly visible, was not of the same order as waged labour in the capitalist mode of production – which was represented by many as an unnatural imposition on man from which the weaker sex should be shielded. Even philosophies which valorized work as morally valuable and personally fulfilling, like the (different) ethos of Carlyle and J.S. Mill were, as Catherine Hall points out, immutably gendered – premised on the construction of a masculine middle-class power base which contrasted its definition of work, as manly and noble, to the effeminacy of aristocratic leisure.[7]

Whilst middle-class women were increasingly conceptualized as frail, leisured and in need of male protection, working-class women earned money as everything from servants and seamstresses to mineworkers. Although this made sense in terms of prevailing class identities, there was considerable anxiety that working women should not engage in manual trades (like mineworking) that might de-sex them.[8] Throughout the century opponents and advocates of women's entry into the labour market shared the assumption that jobs and professions were gender- and class-specific.[9] Even when the hardships of 'feminine' jobs, like seamstressing, were sufficiently recognized to warrant a government inquiry they were still considered preferable to more masculine, manual and visible work in heavy industry. It was common, especially in the case of middle-class women, to maintain that women's entry into waged labour relations could only be justified on account of hardship and necessity (reasons being widowhood, the unavailability of husbands or male relations' mismanagement of family finances). Like most well-known Victorian moral issues, the application of theories about women's work, though widespread, was first formulated for the middle classes themselves and only secondarily exported to the rest of the population and the empire. But, as Hennessy and Mohan make clear, the existence of imperial power relations had a more than merely symbolic importance for changes in the status of women in Europe: at different times and in different ways the possibility of the systemic exploitation of the feminized colonial other was a prerequisite for progressive developments in gender relations at home.[10]

So any woman who wanted publicly to exhibit or publish work was engaging in a process of public and remunerated labour that, in different and similar ways, contravened several codes of class- and gender-appropriate behaviour. Paradoxically, as Poovey points out, both literary and domestic work, as activities that 'seemed completely outside of the system of wages and surplus value',[11] fell into the same category of unalienated or 'creative' labour. But this attempt to maintain a rarefied space for cultural production (in this case, literature) did not mean that writers considered themselves to be like housewives or that unalienated work of the literary sort was considered suitable for women: women were not imagined to have the intellectual, philosophical or visionary qualities required for creative endeavours. Any creative energy they might possess should be more properly directed into the exercise of their innate maternal vocation. Similarly, as the debate over women's entry into art education testifies, both academic and avant-garde circles saw art as a male field . Indeed, the nineteenth century saw the start of a self-conscious artistic avant-garde and the rise of the Romantic image of the bohemian artist-hero (a sensitive, unconventional individual of personal vision who, whilst often at odds with society, could offer insights unavailable to the crowd) that was immutably male.

OPPORTUNITIES FOR WOMEN IN ART

As the middle class sought to augment their economic primacy with political and cultural capital they not only opposed themselves to previously hegemonic aristocratic cultural values (now increasingly seen as decadent and immoral) but adapted and adopted selected aristocratic traditions. As with the ethos of conspicuous leisure, it was often the bourgeoisie's women who bore the burden of signifying these developing middle-class identities. The adoption by bourgeois women of the aristocratic conventions of accomplishment art is a case in point: despite the differences between the French and English middle classes, in both countries in the first half of the nineteenth century the leisured middle-class lady was expected to be versed in the accomplishment arts practised by her aristocratic predecessor. Young ladies were routinely educated to an elementary level in the arts of painting, drawing and music, as well as sewing and other household skills. Unlike the large oil paintings of classical subjects favoured by the Royal Academy or the Salon, accomplishment art stressed drawing, copying and watercolour work in a restricted range of subjects (notably flowers, landscapes, still lives or portraits). As Charlotte Yeldham (whose detailed research I have drawn on in this chapter) has demonstrated, accomplishment skills were clearly understood to be of a minimal nature – sufficient to adorn the home, occupy leisure time, prove the family's cultural standing and provide after-dinner entertainment – but insufficient to engage in public, professional and, by implication, waged activities.[12] The one area where women were expected to demonstrate saleable skills in art was in their work as a governess, where they often had sole responsibility for the art, as well as general, education of their pupils.

But of course, many women did aspire to be artists, and many succeeded. The first obstacle facing them was the lack of proper training and the exclusive practices of the major art institutions. Art education for women in Britain and France did improve during the course of the century but was always restricted in content and availability. The worst problem for any woman wishing to pursue a professional career was lack of access to the nude model. The life class formed the centre of any serious art education, and was a prerequisite for history painting – the most prestigious academic genre.

Although the state training schools barred women students (the Royal Academy did not take women students until 1860 and the École des beaux-arts held out until 1897) there were some opportunities available even by mid-century. In Britain in the 1830s and 1840s many women who were to become successful artists (ironically often, as in the case of Eliza Bridell Fox, going on to exhibit at the Royal Academy once their career was under way) benefited from Henry Sass' School of Art in Bloomsbury (at which it is possible there was a life class). By 1848 James Matthew Leigh's General Practical School of Art was admitting women, such as Kate Greenaway, on equal terms to men (including the life class).[13] The significance of access to the live model is attested to by the efforts women made to arrange such classes for themselves: in 1848 Eliza Bridell Fox arranged a private female life class and in 1863 the Society of Female Artists (established 1857) organized a life class from the dressed model for their members.[14] Even when the Royal Academy allowed limited access to a restricted number of women students in 1860, they had to continue campaigning for entry to the life class until 1893.[15] The Slade school took women students from its establishment in 1871 and provided draped models from the first (nude study was available from 1898).[16]

As in previous eras, most women artists came from artists' families and in nineteenth-century Britain and France most were wealthy. Such art education as was available was generally too expensive to be accessible to any but the affluent. In addition to the obvious advantages of a family sympathetic to or involved in a career in art, many women from wealthy or artistic families avoided the public arena of formal education altogether by taking private lessons from successful artists who were often family friends, although, as Cherry points out, even here the daughters of the house generally received a different schooling from their brothers, being directed to lesser genres etc. The line between accomplishment and professional skills was clearly understood – Berthe Morisot's mother was warned that to allow her daughter further training would cross the line between accomplishment and a career. For lower-middle-class and working-class women the state undertook some vocational training in design – a lesser area of applied artistic activity that was compatible with gendered definitions of labour and aimed to provide women with the chance to earn a living by respectable means. The Female School of Design in Britain was opened in 1843 and initiatives to provide education in design and the applied arts continued throughout the century: like accomplishment art, it was registered as a lesser, feminine activity and thus provided no threat to male artistic supremacy.[17]

In France there were better educational opportunities for women at an elementary level but advanced opportunities for women were highly restricted. Provision for design education, based on the belief in women's innate aptitude for design, was available from 1803 at the Women's Free School of Art and Design. This included some study from life, in keeping with the greater involvement of fine art in French design, and provided a (limited) possibility of art education.[18] But higher-level art education remained largely unavailable. Although established women artists sporadically ran ateliers for women students (dating from Labille-Guyard in the 1780s) and some male artists took women students in the first half of the nineteenth century, opportunities were restricted. The École des beaux-arts was forbidden to women as was participation in the prestigious show-case for new talent, the Prix de Rome competition. Refusing women access to major commissions or reputation-enhancing awards effectively kept them out of the profession. In France the gender-specific ethos of visual representation was differently registered: whereas in England women were encouraged to paint decorative and sentimental subjects of a frivolous nature, in France this was made weightier by the stress on women's maternal role as moral educators of the family and hence nation. Women were encouraged to express their femininity by painting morally uplifting or religious subjects and by designing objects to decorate the home.[19] Education opportunities improved with the advent of the Second Empire in 1850 and more ateliers began to take women students. But the atelier system, in which master painters trained a number of students in their studio, was a male-dominated world to which women's access was still restricted, even though the number of ateliers taking women increased – not just because not all artists would teach women, but because the atelier was itself a gendered social space that was not suitable for women. Women could not respectably be present in an environment that prompted one male student after his first visit to write

> The coarseness and vulgarity of art students was something that, naturally enough, I had no idea of till then. Taunts and snubs were legion . . .[20]

Women art students went to selected ateliers, known as 'ateliers féminins', that specialized in training women. Henriette Browne went to one; the atelier of Chaplin, a popular genre painter noted for teaching women, where she would have had access to life models in women-only classes in an environment that would compromise neither her femininity nor her gentility.

This concern to balance remunerated creative labour with a public profile of genteel femininity is evident in the case of Henriette Browne – the professional name taken by Sophie Bouteiller, later Desaux, or de Saux. The artist was born in Paris in 1829, the child of her mother's second marriage to the Comte de Bouteiller (a moderately successful amateur musician hailing from an old Brittany family). Her mother, widowed young and left with insufficient funds with which to provide a proper education for her son, worked as a music teacher to supplement her income. So although Sophie Bouteiller did, in the end, enjoy affluent circumstances, as a young woman she was educated in a profession that would allow her to support herself if necessary. She studied first with Perrin in 1849 and in 1851 moved to the female art class run by Chaplin (where she was able to study from the figure). Sophie Bouteiller married Jules de Saux in 1853, the same year as her debut at the Salon under the name Henriette

Browne, a name that all sources agree was taken from a maternal ancestor.[21]

It is apparent in all the critical material on Browne that, despite the pseudonym, the details of her background and training were well known and were central to the critical construction of her artistic and social identity. These biographical details of gender and class determined Browne's access to the institutions and codes of art and influenced the critical response to her work. The adoption of a professional pseudonym reveals some of the contradictions of Sophie Bouteiller's social position. For a woman of her class to have a profession at all transgressed codes of bourgeois femininity, yet her own family's history would have revealed the precarious position of a woman unable to support herself. The clashes between definitions of artistic creativity and a classed femininity are evident in the frequent accusations of, and defences against, dilettantism in reviews of her work, whilst the contradictory combination of financial risk and classed identity was, as we shall see, central to the picture of Browne published in the feminist magazine *English Woman's Journal* in 1861.

It was unusual, however, for women artists in this period to exhibit under female pseudonyms.[22] Unlike the pseudonym 'George Eliot', 'Henriette Browne' does not conceal the gender of the artist in order to gain entry into a male field. It did not really conceal her identity either – as early as 1861 Gautier is indicating that he knows who Henriette Browne is and, it seems, he was not alone. Although many women exhibited under both maiden and married names, few used a separate name. So we are left unclear as to the function of the title Henriette Browne, since it is apparent that the artist never actually kept her identity secret and the personal details rehearsed in the press would have given her away to anyone in society. But the pseudonym, however transparent, does allow Sophie Bouteiller to create and maintain a separation between her painting and social self; a distance that obviously must have had a personal significance for her but whose function is quite different to that of the pseudonym 'George Eliot', since it had a minimal impact on the reception of her work.[23]

Browne exhibited regularly in the Salon between 1853 and 1878, winning third-class medals for painting in 1855 and 1857 and a second-class in 1871. From 1866 she was awarded the distinction of exhibiting *hors concours*, that is, without having to compete in the annual Salon selection procedure. She was known as an engraver as well as a painter and obtained a third-class medal for engraving in 1863. Browne met with immediate success in her career; after her first Salon she sent five paintings to the Paris Exposition Universelle in 1855, all of which sold, one (*L'École des pauvres*) achieving the distinction of purchase by the Emperor Napoleon. Her work continued to sell well and claim high prices in both France and Britain throughout her career.

The frequent references to her studies with Chaplin tend to place her within a line of painters of charming but inconsequential genre pieces, assisting in the (re)categorization of her early religious scenes as feminine genre paintings. (In France religious subjects were a well-developed traditional genre that appears to have been open to women artists, since several are named in reviews, but not one in which Browne counted.) But that does not mean that her pictures were simply neutral. If they are able to be uncontentious it is due to the way that certain meanings are foregrounded from the range of associations available in what was a volatile area of representation. Further, their crossover from religion to feminine genre painting and their pleasing and traditional qualities means that they could also be related to what Tamar Garb, writing about the turn of the century, identifies as *l'art féminin*, a womanly art concerned with tradition and moral continuity which reflects woman's role as guardian of the nation.[24]

Marriage to the Comte de Saux (d. 1879), secretary to Count Waleski, would have brought Sophie Bouteiller into diplomatic circles. Waleski, the illegitimate son of Napoleon I, acted as diplomat for Louis Napoleon and the de Saux were associated with him during the Second Empire in which his power was at its greatest. In addition to diplomacy, Waleski was also known as a writer and moved in intellectual circles. This, coupled with the aristocratic heritage of the Bouteiller and de Saux families, placed Browne in a powerful conservative and intellectual milieu, guaranteeing contact with patrons, critics, dealers and other key figures of the literary and artistic world. It also involved travel. By 1860 she had visited Holland and Italy, made a fortnight's trip to Constantinople and journeyed to Morocco in 1865 and Egypt and Syria in 1868–9.[25]

Once women managed to find themselves some form of art education their practice was continually affected by the discursive pressures of femininity. Gendered ideas of art were mapped onto, if not internal to, the European Academies' division of visual art into a series of hierarchical genres that, running from history painting down through portraiture, genre (scenes of daily life), still life and landscape, relegated women (untrained in the nude or classics) to minor fields of endeavour. In the nineteenth century subject and technique were morally weighted issues for all artists, but for women the codes of artistic activity were comparable to the strict codes of behaviour in which they had been tutored since childhood. Women, within the areas of representation open to them, were encouraged to paint in a manner that could be read as suitably feminine according to the prevailing codes of femininity: subjects should be respectable and performed in a manner that could be traced back to innate feminine qualities such as delicacy, intuition, compassion. Although men also specialized in genre it had come, particularly in France, to be associated with the feminine qualities of sensibility and simplicity. By the time Browne was painting it was customary to read the sentimental qualities of genre pictures as a sign of the (often female) artist's own morality and compassion. Cherry notes that the tendency to read women's work in relation to stereotypes of femininity emerged most clearly in the 1850s – at precisely the moment when women were 'increasingly numerous and visible as professional artists'.[26] As we shall see in the next chapter, Browne's initial practice of portraiture, domestic narrative painting and scenes of the French religious (of the domestic, not the grand historico-classical, type) fell precisely within the remit of feminine art. Portraiture, which several leading women artists concerned themselves with almost exclusively, did offer a crossover from accomplishment art of which 'taking a likeness' was an essential component. Portraiture, unlike classical subjects, required no specific education and could be seen as eminently suitable for women who were believed to be endowed with innate qualities of intuition and sympathy. Browne was acclaimed as a portrait painter throughout her career but never specialized in portraiture to the exclusion of other areas of representation.

If women produced art that echoed their perceived social and moral role, it compensated for the transgression of their artistic activities. Likewise, as Whitney Chadwick has pointed out, women whose progressive professional endeavours might lead us to presume that they were personally radical, often emphasized their allegiance to the ideology of the separate spheres – precisely because it deflected attention from their potentially de-sexing cultural activities.

The ways in which women achieved success in the art world depended on both the relationship of their work to existing or developing codes, styles and conventions of art and the form of their particular authorial and professional identity. Different conditions of production facilitated the conditions of possibility for different forms of success. So, for example, in contrast to Browne's respectable, ladylike persona and initially feminine subjects could be ranged her compatriot Rosa Bonheur who challenged codes of femininity and art in both subject and life-style but still managed to be a very successful artist. Bonheur (unmarried and living with a female companion) rose to phenom-enal fame as an animal painter with canvases that, like her most famous picture *The Horse Fair* (1855, Plate 3), celebrated the passion and beauty of the untamed beast and were a far cry from the saccharine domestic pets expected from a lady's brush.[27] Bonheur had the advantage of a supportive artistic family. But the success of her work (sufficient to compensate for her notori-ously unconventional lifestyle) must be understood in the context of the changes in and increased critical status of the representa-tion of animals brought about by the development of Romanticism. But this professional success did not mean that Bonheur's personal life ceased to be a matter of public con-cern, and in Chapter 3 I shall be examining the different ways in which Bonheur and Browne's personal and social identities were negotiated in the critical representation of themselves and their work.

In Britain in this period we see the meteoric rise of the battle artist Lady Elizabeth Thompson Butler. She managed to make inroads into the male preserve of history painting in the 1870s without compromising her classed and gendered identity – even though her subject was the previously male-dominated field of battle art. Butler, who was wealthy, well behaved and well connected, managed to enter the realm of history painting as a woman artist with works that were understood to be intrinsically feminine. This was made possible by a social climate ready to re-evaluate the depiction of war and an art world ready to extend the definition of history painting to include contemporary events (see Plate 4). The bourgeoisie's growing influence in the art world and increasing power in the military (via the army reforms of the

1870s) meant that her humanizing studies of war met with enormous success.[28] Her narratives managed simultaneously to valorize the common soldier, endorse middle-class criticisms of the aristocracy's uncaring and inept military administration and uphold the values of colonial expansion, and could still be accommodated within notions of feminine compassion. Like Browne's intervention into the male field of Orientalism, Butler's battle painting was sufficiently consistent with codes of femininity to allow her to be incorporated as a lady artist without the sort of scandal that attended Bonheur. But, as we shall see, Browne's successful entry into Orientalism depended not only on it being a popular area of representation in which she was offering something new, but also on her existing reputation as a respectable lady artist – which could mitigate the potential immoralities of the subsequent Orientalist subjects.

The amount of women's work on display in public exhibitions in Britain rose during the course of the century (most notably after 1875) but never accounted for more than 14 per cent at any of the major venues (the Royal Academy, the British Institute and the Society of British Artists).[29] Apart from the all-women exhibitions of the Society of Female Artists there were a few private galleries that specialized in exhibiting women's work: the Dudley Gallery (from 1848), the Grosvenor Gallery (from 1877) and Gambart's French Gallery where Bonheur and Browne were represented.[30] But women were still refused entry to the majority of artists' exhibiting societies, which limited their access to important professional forums. If women's work was not seen, it was not reviewed and their reputation floundered. (The role of the Society of Female Artists should not be underestimated here. Despite the mixed quality of their exhibitions – and it was clear to most that this only proved the detrimental effects of women's limited education – the Society did manage to keep the issue of women's art in the public eye and received considerable and sympathetic press attention.)[31] In France the situation was reversed. Women showed more work at the start of the century and less during the Second Empire when their contributions to public exhibitions decreased from an average of 11–13.3 per cent to one of 4.9–8.9 per cent.[32]

Henriette Browne had a successful career by any standards. Though not as revered as Bonheur (the first woman to be awarded the Legion d'Honneur, in 1894), her work, regularly on display at the major public exhibitions in England and France (the Salon, the Royal Academy and the International Exhibitions), received substantial critical attention and acclaim. In the late 1860s Browne and Bonheur were the only women to be given honorary member-ship (and hence exhibiting rights) of the New Watercolour Society in Britain which, though it allowed a few women to join as ordinary members, never honoured any British women in such a way.[33] In France Browne was one of four women allowed to hold associative membership (*sociétaires*, or *membres fondateurs*) of the Societé nationale des beaux-arts in 1862.

Her reputation in Britain was helped enormously by her early and continued association with Ernst Gambart's French Gallery which was the premier showcase for contemporary continental art in Britain. It was under his auspices that she first showed in Britain when he brought paintings from her debut Salon to London in 1856, although her reputation did not take off until the exhibi-tion of the famous *Sisters of Charity* in 1859 (Plate 1).[34] Gambart's gallery in Pall Mall was at the forefront of the move away from the Old Masters and towards contemporary art in the mid-century.[35] Although at first he had difficulty selling contemporary French work in Britain, by the late 1850s Browne's work would have been seen in a popular venue by an audience sympathetic to modern continental art. In 1861 her Orientalist works on display at Gambart's (after their initial exhibition at the Salon) would be seen in conjunction with the great masters of French Orientalism, Gérôme and Fromentine. Visits to his French Gallery became a regular part of the London Season and thus on the itinerary of the buying public. Although women accounted for a very small proportion of artists shown at his gallery, they included some of the leading French and British women artists of the day (Browne, Bonheur, Barbara Leigh Smith Bodichon, Eliza Bridell Fox).[36] He also represented several of the British Pre-Raphaelite circle (Holman Hunt, Millais and Rossetti) and the phenomenally popular Alma-Tadema.

The demands of the growing market of middle-class art buyers played a large part in the increasing interest in modern art. They wished to acquire the genteel ring of cultural capital associated with High Art but were not, in the first generation, products of the Grand Tour and therefore tended not to have a predilection for the Old Masters (many of which in circulation in the 1840s had turned out to be fakes). Dianne Sachko Macleod presents the middle-class penchant for contemporary art and domestic genre scenes as not simply a lack of education or an inability to appreciate the Old Masters, but a sign of their growing confidence and influence in the cultural sphere.[37] The middle classes, who now sought a cultural authority to augment their economic power, exerted increasing influence on the art market and the growing national art collections. These important new patrons instigated new patterns of patronage and taste and were guided in this by a new art press, such as the *Athenaeum* and the *Art Journal*, aimed at the middle classes. Although, as Phillip Hook and Mark Poltimore argue, genre was a characteristic taste of the developing international art market that served the middle classes throughout Europe (and also in the colonies), we must not forget that the shared enthusiasm for art of an emotive nature and domestic detail was experienced alongside a series of perceived national differences in artists and audiences. As we shall see Browne's work, whether displayed at Gambart's or the International Exhibitions, was always treated as a specifically French, as well as gendered, phenomenon.

The large market for genre subjects and small canvases (suitable for the middle-class drawing room rather than vast aristocratic halls) opened up the market for, and raised the prestige of, areas of representation traditionally associated with women artists. Additionally, avant-garde moves to treat contemporary subjects with the weight of history painting shocked the Academy but had wide-reaching effects for the choice of subjects in the second half of the century. The French Independents' response to Baudelaire's call for the painting of modern life (1852) gave artistic credibility to the representation of modern urban life and increased status to the experience of the domestic sphere removing it from a previous categorization as feminine and trivial. Although gendered codes of behaviour severely restricted women's participation in avant-garde artistic circles and, as Griselda Pollock has shown, in the modern subjects considered suitable for women to view and paint, the fashion for these new subjects did mean that in both the avant-garde and the Academy women were able to participate more fully in high-prestige areas of representation.[38] More than this, the 'triumph of genre' influenced other subjects, couching everything from history painting to classical or Oriental subjects in the tropes of sentiment, domesticity and embourgeoisiment that characterized genre, thereby creating opportunities for precisely the sort of feminine intervention into generic codes with which Butler and, as we shall see, Browne were so successful.

OPPORTUNITIES FOR WOMEN IN LITERATURE

If the nineteenth century was a period in which women artists struggled to break down the existing exclusions of the art world, women writers faced the opposite problem:[39] contrary to the traditional twentieth-century feminist view that the nineteenth century was a period of expanded and successful activity for the woman writer,[40] Gaye Tuchman argues that their situation worsened as the century wore on.[41] Women writers faced not only the maintenance of the *status quo* but the development of new forms of exclusion as the novel made the transition from a low form of popular entertainment, suitable only for ill-educated girls and women, to a serious and high-prestige area of literature suitable to be read and written by men. Women *were* publishing in substantial numbers and, although the anxiety that prompted nearly every periodical in the mid-century to carry an article on the phenomenon of the lady novelist outweighed women's actual share of the market, writing for publication did offer a better return on labour than other wage-earning opportunities open to middle-class women.[42] (Novelists of either gender were overwhelmingly recruited from the upper or middle classes.) Tuchman argues that as the status of the novel, its writer and reader began to change, men moved into novel writing so effectively that by the early twentieth century women had lost what, in 1859, had been a 50 per cent share of the fiction market.[43]

Although the novel as we recognize it today had been developing since the early eighteenth century, it did not come to be considered as high literature until later in the nineteenth century.[44] In the first half of the nineteenth century high literature consisted of poetry and non-fiction – areas largely prohibited to women because they lacked a classical education. The novel, typified by the sensationalist three volume 'triple-decker' that sustained the circulating libraries with their largely female readership, was seen as a low form of literature suitable only for women writer's petty literary skills of observation and romance. In the 1870s, as novel writing rose in prestige, literary critics began to detect and encourage a version of the realist novel that, rather than being simply a realistic description of life, was of a philosophical nature, a superior 'manly' form of fiction that concerned itself with abstract concepts and intellectual issues – qualities usually held to be absent from women's work. Although George Eliot was one of the few women who made, and contributed to, this transition to the modern novel, her work was always judged in relation to her gender. Like many women writers of what Showalter calls the 'feminine stage', she emphasized her allegiance to the ideology of separate spheres and dominant literary values.[45] Just as in visual art, the prevalent critical double standard praised women's literature for displaying qualities that endorsed their femininity (such as sentiment, refinement, tact, observation, high moral tone and knowledge of the female character) and criticized it for lacking precisely those attributes that women were not supposed to have (intellectual training, originality, abstract intelligence and knowledge of male character). Men's work, on the other hand, was found to display the valued qualities of 'power, breadth, distinctness, clarity, learning, abstract intelligence, shrewdness, experience, humor [sic], knowledge of everyone's character and open mindedness'.[46]

Not only were women's novels judged differently from men's, but their ability to pursue and further a literary career was hampered by prevailing codes governing feminine behaviour. Tuchman emphasizes that the critical double standard was mirrored by a double standard in the publishing industry that consistently offered women less advantageous terms. Women, who were seen as delicate creatures intended to be separate from the alienating world of work and commerce, were unable or unwilling to argue for better contracts or negotiate aggressively with publishers. Like women artists, women novelists found the institutions of the increasingly professionalized literary world largely closed to them[47] just as the restricted social spaces available to bourgeois women largely prohibited them from access to, or effective cultivation of, the social and business networks that provided such useful patronage for their male peers. Women did not enjoy an equal share of the proliferating jobs in the literature industry that accompanied the rising status of fiction. They were underrepresented as reviewers, critics, editors and publishers' readers, positions that were financially and professionally rewarding. Although the new opportunities offered by the feminist presses and periodicals in the 1860s and 1870s[48] ameliorated the situation somewhat, when George Eliot started her career writing was still a transgressive and potentially compromising activity.[49]

Women's access to literary pursuits was always double edged. On one hand, writing was an activity that required little by way of space, equipment or special education and so was relatively easy to do (the *English Woman's Journal* was convinced that this was why women had succeeded far more in literature than in art),[50] but on the other, to publish for money transgressed all the codes of the separate spheres. Like careers in art or design, women frequently claimed that writing was undertaken in response to dire need, rather than out of personal ambition and often emphasized that writing did not compromise their 'normal' femininity and family responsibilities.[51] They de-emphasized the labour involved, presenting novel writing as a natural outpouring of feminine emotion, thus camouflaging the deviancy of their literary activities and devaluing the creative labour involved. In an era when creativity was increasingly seen as a male prerogative, this vision of unmediated, unskilled transposition found considerable favour and upheld the vision of the leisured lady.

Women writers were inevitably compared to other women and by the 1860s it was customary to range George Eliot and Charlotte Brontë as the two poles against which women were judged. Both Brontë and George Eliot tacitly acknowledged the existence of the critical double standard by beginning their fiction careers with male pseudonyms, although the commonality of this experience was, as we shall see, undercut by important differences between them. Marian Evans/George Eliot was already widely published in the conventionally anonymous field of periodical criticism and did not take the pseudonym George Eliot until she began to publish fiction. The tenacity of gendered judgements of literary merit, subject and technique is attested to not only by the terrific debate about the gender of the mysterious authors of *Jane Eyre* (1847) and *Adam Bede* (1859) but by the prompt re-interpretation of both novels as *women's novels* once their author's gender was known. Readers of *Jane Eyre* could not believe that a woman had written such a daring and innovative novel with its indelicate heroine and convincingly passionate hero whilst the quality, insight and convincing male and female characters of *Adam Bede* confounded George Eliot's readers. Although some thought they detected a woman's hand, most readers assumed a male writer and deliberated whether he was a member of the clergy and, if so, of what age, rank and denomination. When George Eliot and her publisher decided to reveal her gender in 1860 the public were shocked and critics instantly reinterpreted the novel in relation to its female point of origin – scenes which previously had been seen as realistic representations of clerical and country experience were now judged on their suitability for the female author's presumed presence.

Like women artists, women writers were faced with restrictions about subject and technique. In fiction, as in visual art, women's limited experience and socialized behaviour led to a preponderance of novels with domestic settings and an emphasis on the romantic and personal that corroborated the prevalent view of women as small-minded emotional creatures.[52] Although some critics did recognize that women were forced to specialize in such subjects because of limited opportunities rather than natural aptitude, very few suggested that the social causes should be changed.[53] The very language that women could use was restricted: strong language or indelicate subjects brought censure (as was the case with the 'damn' of *Jane Eyre* and the 'vein of perilous voluptuousness' in *Adam Bede*).[54]

Like many women who succeeded in gaining access to the professional literary world, George Eliot often subscribed to dominant ideas about the inferiority of women's writing. Her 1856 essay 'Silly Novels by Lady Novelists' was sympathetic about the restrictions inflicted on women by poor education but poured scorn on the 'mind-and-millinery' fripperies associated with the lady novelist, maintaining that such pulp would not advance the cause of women's education or women's literature.[55] She argued against those who believed that clemency in judgement was an act of charity towards the poor, if not destitute, women driven to writing from desperate circumstances by revealing that most novels emanated from women in 'lofty and fashionable society' whose only experience of poverty was in their 'poverty of brains'. Her demand was that women's fiction be taken seriously and judged by the same standards as men's.[56] In this she was not alone. Other women who aspired to critical success and professional standing often felt it necessary to disassociate themselves from the failings of lesser women writers and prove their allegiance to dominant literary and social standards:[57] the popular novelist Dinah Murlock Craik warned women against overestimating a minor talent;[58] and Geraldine Jewsbury (who secured work as a publisher's reader for Bentley's) frequently upheld the gendered ideas of the critical double standard in her reviews and recommendations.[59]

Such contradictions abound in the lives and works of women writers and artists in the 1850s–60s. The internalization of dominant values exists alongside, may even be a necessary component of, their potentially radical acts as authors and professionals. George Eliot who was not only a novelist – she was also a poet, literary critic, editor, translator and essayist – was in many ways typical of her era. Despite the transgressions of her professional life and her personal relationships (notably the adulterous liaison with Lewes) she was conservative in her manner and restrained in her support for the feminist politics of her friend Barbara Bodichon.[60] Unlike the transgressive romance of Brontë's novels, the transgressions of George Eliot's private life were not mirrored in her fiction which, though it explored the fate of women in contemporary society, advocated a cult of fulfilment through renunciation.[61]

Just like the contradictions and complexities we experience in our lives today, nineteenth-century women writers and artists, along with their audiences, struggled to make sense of the contradictions inherent in women's cultural production. It is not that all publishers tried to swindle women writers, or that they laboured under a protectionist code of chivalry, but that as agents formed within a society structured by divisions of gender and class, it was impossible for them to ignore prevalent concepts of identity in their dealings with each other. That these notions of identity were formulated across structural divisions of not just class and gender, but also race and nation can be seen in the changing responses to Browne's and George Eliot's work.

By the time *Daniel Deronda* was published the author George Eliot was known to be a woman and had become one of the foremost literary figures of her day. Unlike Browne, who though popular in her day is obscure now, George Eliot has been the subject of massive investigation in the late twentieth century.[62]

Her status as a female literary figure was, and is, complicated by her notoriety as Marian Evans – the adulterous partner of the philosopher, publisher and writer George Henry Lewes. The methodological problems of differentiating between George Eliot the authorial persona confirmed by nineteenth- and twentieth-century criticism, Marian Evans the anonymous writer and editor of articles and reviews, and the historical individual Mary Ann or Marian Evans (or Marian Lewes as she chose to be addressed) who wrote the letters, diaries and notebooks that make up the George Eliot archive has been elucidated elsewhere (notably by Gillian Beer).[63] In this instance, I shall use George Eliot to refer to the author of the novels and the journalism (which after Cross' *Life* in 1885 was read into the corpus of George Eliot's published work). I shall reserve Marian Evans for references to the historical personage attested to by the letters and diaries, which will be introduced in so far as they are read into the construction of the author George Eliot. Thus, my use of the two terms Marian Evans and George Eliot should signal the book's movement between a biographical and a discursive subject. For example, the letter from Marian Evans to Harriet Beecher Stowe[64] which is frequently used to prove Marian Evans' own hatred of prejudice, can also be read in light of how critics have used it to construct not only Marian Evans but also George Eliot as the agent of that tolerance. I shall follow the conventions of George Eliot scholarship and include letters written by George Henry Lewes which it is usual to presume are representative of their shared opinions.

Daniel Deronda was George Eliot's last novel in a literary career that encompassed journalism, translation, editing, poetry and fiction. Before she began to write and publish fiction at the age of thirty-six (*Scenes of Clerical Life*, 1858), George Eliot had established herself in journalism through her work (as a contributor and editor) for the *Westminster Review*. This liberal intellectual journal was concerned with literature, politics, art, philosophy and the developing social sciences, with which *Daniel Deronda* was to be so associated. She also translated the German humanist critics of Christianity, Strauss and Feuerbach in 1846 and 1854. So she had built a considerable literary reputation for critique and commentary before venturing into fiction. But although Marian Evans was regularly in print, her name was not: like all journalism her contributions to the *Westminster Review* were anonymous and her identity would only have been known to the small coterie of intellectuals associated with the magazine. The name George Eliot first appears as the author of the novel *Scenes of Clerical Life* in 1858 and again with *Adam Bede* in 1859. There is the question of why – when so many women writers published under their own names – Marian Evans chose a male pseudonym? Gillian Beer provides three possible avenues of explanation here: firstly, a desire to create an authorial persona that would not be tainted by the controversy surrounding Marian Evans; secondly, the need for an authorial identity that would not publicly impact on her journalistic career if the novels failed; and thirdly, a desire to write from a space that would not be judged as female.[65] Evidence for this last is provided by George Eliot's demand that serious women writers be read and judged on the basis of their work not their gender. Even after George Eliot had been revealed as a woman and the possibility of a male narrator was past, Marian Evans continued to publish under her chosen authorial name (although her journalism would have remained anonymous to most of her readers). By the time *Daniel Deronda* was published, nearly twenty years after *Adam Bede*, George Eliot was recognized as a famous female author and debate centred more on the novel's relation to her oeuvre than on her gender, as had been the case with her earlier fiction.[66]

NATION, EMPIRE AND CULTURE

The imperial project might have been supported by an ideology that saw all Europeans as superior to all colonized peoples, but it also brought Europeans into competition with each other for the new lands and markets of the colonies and for cultural supremacy. Thus, we find that the critical press in the second half of the nineteenth century is characterized by the attempt to define national cultural characteristics (the Dutch excel at still life, the French at history painting) that parallels the ethnographic division of the world into clearly demarcated types. It is this widespread imperial ideology, and the tensions within it (for national and imperial identities were always only precariously maintained in the face of external challenges and internal contradictions)[67] that, I shall argue, structures the work and reception of Browne and George Eliot. Their audiences were familiar with imperial concepts whether related to Orientalist paintings (which were so numerous as to be commonplace), Orientalist references and analogies in literature or the increasingly common first-hand experience of travel in North Africa or the Near East.[68]

One important cultural contribution to the dissemination of imperial ideology was the series of International Exhibitions that punctuated the nineteenth century. Although these were purportedly a chance for the leading nations to enjoy amicable cultural exchange they were, in fact, the site of intense national rivalry with governments sinking vast sums into their country's display.[69] Sensationalist exhibitions (of technical developments or 'native villages') and reduced entry fees attracted a wider audience than the annual art exhibitions at the Royal Academy or Salon. This provided an opportunity to develop not only an awareness of the benefits of empire (which opponents thought too costly or immoral) but also a sense of national (and imperial) identity that would overide the internal schisms of class, gender, politics and ethnicity. The fine art pavilions were selected by each nation to show the best of their art and Browne frequently represented France: showing five paintings at the Exposition Universelle in 1855; eight in 1867; and one at the British International Exhibition in 1872. As Paul Greenhalgh has shown, the International Exhibitions were integral to the presentation of colonies as part of the national heritage and resources: from the display of imperial produce in the French National Exhibition in the Champs Elysées in 1839 to the British Great Exhibition in 1851 it became usual to organize display around the presentation of imperial wealth and acquisitions.[70] Thus, Browne's paintings of both domestic and Oriental subjects were viewed in spaces imbued with imperial ideology that were significant events in the formation of a sense of national culture and imperial pride for vast sectors of the population.[71]

The battle for cultural supremacy that split the imperial nations of Europe can be seen most clearly in the belief that there were discernible national schools of art and patterns of taste. For example, no matter how widespread the taste for genre, critics could still detect national differences. This is the *Art Journal* in 1862.

> The French paint *genre* with more point and play of intellect, the English with greater breadth of sympathy: the French with more vivacity and cleverness, the English with more sobriety and decorum. . . . [The English school has] now seldom to complain of intentional coarseness: Hogarth's works would, in this day, be intolerable. We are, in like manner, preserved from the *double entendre* in which the French rejoice. Virtue is respected: vice . . . has a moral tagged on to it . . .[72]

Lynda Nead has identified this as a trajectory of art criticism that attempted to harness the newly elevated status of genre to the national reputation by claiming it as an area of British excellence.

(A possible balm to the ego of a nation that could not deny that
the French continued to excel at history painting.) Thus, Britain's
talent at and taste for genre figure as proof of both the nation's
moral standards and artistic skill. Contrasted to British taste for
decodable moral narratives executed in a clear realist style, the
French treatment of genre reveals their moral as well as stylistic
ambiguities. The alleged French tendency to innuendo is not
restricted to their treatment of genre subjects. It is highlighted
again in the *Art Journal*'s review of the French Orientalist Jean
Louis Gérôme in 1866. Gérôme, whose highly finished and glossy
eroticism was extremely successful in France and Britain, nonetheless provided a problem for his viewers. His salacious scenes were
difficult to align with their vision of art's moral and educative
purpose.[73] This is the *Art Journal* on his painting *Phryne* in 1866
(Plate 5).[74]

> It might ... have been possible for Gérôme to have touched
> on such a history with discretion; but then he would have lost
> the point and purpose... it can scarcely, indeed, be a matter
> of surprise that a French artist should be expressly French in
> his treatment; cleverness of innuendo, a certain semblance of
> decorum preserved in the midst of sentiment dubious, such is
> the cunning subterfuge which has made French novelists,
> dramatists and painters notorious.[75]

Note again how the charges of immorality are seen as signs
of a peculiarly national indecency that extends to the whole of
French culture. Considering that Gérôme was very successful
it is surprising that reviews betray such profound discomfort. Of
course, as Linda Nochlin has pointed out, part of Gérôme's appeal
is precisely that he shocks and titilates at the same time[76] but
I think that there is also something about Gérôme's work that
pushes it to the limits of acceptability, particularly for his British
reviewers.[77] Whilst French art critics question his choice of subject
but admire his skill,[78] there is something about the way Gérôme's
combination of subject choice and glossy realism so substantially
discomforts the British press that suggests that his work transgresses not only propriety (almost beyond the range of artistic
licence) but also the boundaries of what they consider to be British
national taste and sensibility. This national code of art and interpretation makes a pleasure in viewing for the British critic
differently problematic.

It is difficult to imagine a woman artist emerging unscathed from such attacks as were levelled at Gérôme. In British reviews of Browne's work, discourses of gender mediate the construction of a nation-specific analysis so that although her work is criticized for displaying 'French faults' which may even be defined as 'cowardly', the accusations are restricted to comments on the poor tone and 'slurred' detail – a far cry from the indecencies attributed to Gérôme.[79] Accordingly, the following two chapters explore how Browne's early work was seen as specifically French and Catholic within the structural differentiations of European nationalism, and how her Orientalist subjects figured as generically European within the discursive divide between Occident and Orient.

NOTES

1 Elaine Showalter, *A Literature of Their Own: From Charlotte Brontë to Doris Lessing*, (1978) second edition, London, Virago, 1982.
2 Leonore Davidoff and Catherine Hall, *Family Fortunes: Men and Women of the English Middle Class 1780–1850*, London, Hutchinson, 1987.
3 Anita Levy, *Other Women: The Writing of Class, Race and Gender, 1832–1898*, Princeton, Princeton University Press, 1991, p. 9.
4 See Lucy Bland, 'The Domain of the Sexual', in *Screen Education*, no. 39, 1981.
5 On the differentiated ways in which the sexuality of colonized women was constructed in relation to Europeans and to colonized men see Rosemary Hennessy and Rajeswari Mohan, 'The Construction of Woman in Three Popular Texts of Empire: Towards a Critique of Materialist Feminism', in *Textual Practice* vol. 3, 1989, pp. 338–352.
6 Mary Poovey, *Uneven Developments: The Ideological Work of Gender in Mid-Victorian England*, London, Virago, 1989.
7 See Catherine Hall, 'The Economy of Intellectual Prestige: Thomas Carlyle, John Stuart Mill, and the Case of Governor Eyre', in *Cultural Critique*, no. 12, Spring 1989.
8 See, for example, Sally Alexander, 'Women's Work in Nineteenth Century London: a Study of the Years 1820–50', in Juliet Mitchell and Ann Oakley (eds) *The Rights and Wrongs of Women*, Harmondsworth, Penguin, 1983; Liz Stanley (ed.) 'Introduction' to *The Diaries of Hannah Cullwick: Victorian Maidservant*, London, Virago, 1983; Leonore Davidoff, 'Class and Gender in Victorian England: The Diaries of Arthur Munby and Hannah Cullwick', in *Feminist Studies*, 1979.
9 Poovey, *Uneven Developments*, p. 159
10 See Hennessy and Mohan, 'The Construction of Woman', p. 332.

11 Poovey, *Uneven Developments*, p. 156.
12 The advent of accomplishment arts in the middle classes was not without criticism. Hannah Moore as early as 1789 was bewailing the rise of accomplishment in art and design and the subsequent loss of a previous, more functional, level of art training. The practice continued to receive criticism throughout the nineteenth century, especially after the aristocracy lost interest in the 1840s and accomplishment became an exclusively middle-class enthusiasm. See Charlotte Yeldham, *Women Artists in Nineteenth-Century France and England: Their Art Education, Exhibition Opportunities and Membership of Exhibiting Societies and Academies, with an Assessment of the Subject Matter of their Work and Summary Biographies*, New York, Garland, 1984, pp. 8–34.
13 Yeldham, *Women Artists*, pp. 20–1.
14 Although opportunities for women to study from the live model were available from the 1840s, it seems that they were little known and insufficient for demand. Comments and reviews through the mid-century reiterate that the unavailability of study from life impeded women's careers. The *Art Journal* wrote sympathetically of this in 1858 and even the feminist *English Woman's Journal* knew of only one that year. The *Art Journal* 1858 p. 143, in Yeldham, *Women Artists*, p. 24; 'On the Adoption of Professional Life by Women', The *English Woman's Journal*, 1858.
15 Yeldham, *Women Artists*, p. 31.
16 Yeldham, *Women Artists*, p. 33.
17 Though men in the design field did complain that women were taking their jobs. See Yeldham, *Women Artists*, p. 13.
18 This varied from school to school: the Paris School under Rosa Bonheur in the 1850s was very artistic in orientation and compared favourably to provision in England.
19 Yeldham, *Women Artists*, p. 174.
20 Alfred de Curzon on Drolling's studio, in Alfred Boime, *The Academy and French Painting in the Nineteenth Century*, London, Phaidon, 1971, p. 53.
21 Chris Petteys, *Dictionary of Women Artists. An International Dictionary of Women Artists Born Before 1900*, Boston, G.K. Hall, 1985; John Dennison Champlin, *Cyclopedia of Painters and Paintings*, London, Bernard Quaritch, 1888; *Bryan's Dictionary of Painters and Engravers*, London, George Bell and Sons, 1903; Clara Erskin Clement, *Women in the Fine Arts. From the 7th Century BC to the Twentieth Century AD*, New York, Houghton Mifflin, 1904.
22 Personal conversation with Briony Llewelyn.
23 Although 'Henriette Browne' could not produce the preferential treatment instigated by a male pseudonym, it would be misleading to imagine that it had no impact at all. The common references to the title's pseudonymous status and to the figure that hid behind it, seem to have activated a set of class associations that may possibly have reinforced the impression of the artist's gentility and thus affected the interpretation of her work.

Note that although I follow Gillian Beer in always referring to George Eliot by the full pseudonym (to avoid naturalizing this constructed title), I do shorten Henriette Browne to Browne, allowing it to function syntactically as a real name. This is because Henriette Browne is the title generally used to designate both the painter and the artist of the corpus of works.

24 Tamar Garb, ' "L'Art Féminin": The Formation of a Critical Category in Late Nineteenth-Century France', in *Art History*, vol. 12, no. 1, March 1989.

25 See Yeldham, *Women Artists*, pp. 347–9. Champlin records that she 'has sketched in the East and North Africa'.

26 Deborah Cherry, *Painting Women: Victorian Women Artists*, London, Routleldge, 1993, p. 66.

27 See also Whitney Chadwick, *Women, Art and Society*, London, Thames and Hudson, 1990; Alfred Boime, 'The Case of Rosa Bonheur: Why Should a Woman Want to be More Like a Man?', in *Art History*, vol. 4, no. 4, December 1981.

28 See J.W.M. Hichberger, *Images of the Army: The Military in British Art, 1815–1914*, Manchester, Manchester University Press, 1988; Paul Usherwood and Jenny Spencer-Smith, *Lady Butler: Battle Artist 1846–1933*, London, National Army Museum, 1987.

29 Figures from 1800–75 rose from 5.5 to 10.5 per cent at the Royal Academy, from 3.1 to 11.4 per cent at the British Institution and from 5.9 to 14 per cent at the Society of British Artists. Yeldham, p. 63.

30 See Pamela Gerrish Nunn, *Victorian Women Artists*, London, The Women's Press, 1987, ch. 3.

31 The Society initially showed work by professional and amateur women artists, prepared to brave the inevitable criticisms, even from their supporters, of the 'preponderance of children and flowers'. Its widely known reputation gained support from professional women around Europe, including Browne who exhibited with the Society on one occasion. In 1872 the name changed to the Society of Lady Artists and displayed only professional work, although it subsequently reverted to the earlier name and policy. In France the equivalent l'Union de femmes peintres et sculpteurs was not established until 1881 and promalgated a belief in an innately female art. Yeldham, *Women Artists*, pp. 88–105 and Garb.

32 Yeldham, *Women Artists*, p. 65.

33 Nunn, *Victorian Women Artists*, pp. 99–100.

34 See Jeremy Maas, *Gambart. Prince of the Victorian Art World*, London, Barrie and Jenkins, 1975.

35 Gambart sold both paintings and prints and it was through print sales that he first familiarized the British public with modern continental artists. His reputation as a print dealer was established by the late 1840s and stood him in good stead as his picture trade and status in the art world increased. Prints in the nineteenth century formed a growing part of the art trade. Copyright was sold independently of the painting although often a patron would purchase both. Apart from making potentially vast sums from the copyright for the owner

and printer, print ciculations of a large run were invaluable in establishing an artist's reputation and ensuring success. The international print trade meant that not only were cheap reproductions available to large sections of the British population (also via the illustrated press) but that popular paintings travelled the world, and most certainly the colonies.

36 Cherry maintains, however, that despite representing several female artists, Gambart 'tokenized' them and reserved his best efforts for male clients. Cherry, *Painting Women*, p. 98.

37 Dianne Sachko Macleod, 'Art Collecting and Victorian Middle-Class Taste', in *Art History*, vol. 10, no. 3, September 1987, pp. 328–50.

38 Griselda Pollock 'Modernity and the Spaces of Femininity', in Pollock *Vision and Difference: Feminity, Feminism and Histories of Art*, London, Routledge, 1987. Tamar Garb highlights how subject alone could not secure a picture's moral meaning. Women Impressionists, who painted apparently 'feminine' subjects, provided a problem of moral meaning depending on how one read the political implications of the Impressionist technique. This was seen as both innately suitable for women (being decorative and frivolous) or as radical and hence unsuitable (its fragmented surface being incompatible with the unambiguous moral meanings expected from art). Garb, ' "L'Art Féminin" ', p. 43.

39 This section is concerned only with women writers in Britain.

40 For an overview of developments in twenthieth-century feminist literary criticism see Toril Moi, *Sexual/Textual Politics: Feminist Literary Theory*, London, Methuen, 1985.

41 Gaye Tuchman with Nina E. Fortin, *Edging Women Out: Victorian Novelists, Publishers and Social Change*, London, Routledge, 1989.

42 Women could earn more from the publication of a novel that might have taken a year to write than from the annual salary of a governess or the income derived from fancy work. Showalter, *Literature*, p. 48.

43 Tuchman (using records of the publishing house Macmillan) defines a three-stage process by which women were edged out of the novel: the invasion period of 1840–79, where most novelists were women and women were more likely to have their manuscripts accepted than men; the period of redefinition, 1880–99, in which men of letters redefined 'good' novels as those with a form of realism that tackled great philosophical questions, where men and women were equally likely to have their manuscripts accepted (though she does not define which men she thinks were considered to be successful practitioners of this new style); and lastly, the period of institutionalization 1901–17, in which men confirmed their hold of the high culture novel and were more likely to have manuscripts accepted.

44 See Ian Watt, *The Rise of the Novel: Studies in Defoe, Richardson and Fielding*, London, (1957) The Hogarth Press, 1993.

45 Showalter divides women's literature into three phases: the feminine phase, from 1840 to the death of George Eliot in 1880, in which women emphasized their allegiance to the ideology of the separate spheres and wrote literature that tended to emulate dominant/male

literary values; the feminist stage, 1880–1920, characterized by a literature of protest; and the female phase, from 1920, notable for the quest for authentic forms of literature to represent the female experience. Showalter, *Literature*, p. 13.

46 Showalter, *Literature*, p. 90.

47 One indication of both the increased status and professionalization of novel writing and the exclusion of women from high-prestige literature is that women were not eligible for entry to the Society of Authors – a body dedicated to the protection of authors' interests founded in the late 1880s.

48 On the feminist press see David Doughan and Denise Sanchez, *Feminist Periodicals: 1855–1984*, Brighton, Harvester Wheatsheaf, 1987.

49 As an indication of the unrespectability of being a novelist Tuchman cites the 1865 census where only 8.7 per cent of all persons who listed themselves as authors were women as compared to the 23.9 per cent of those who identified themselves as painters or sculptors or the 17.1 per cent of musicians who were women. (Was it harder to remain anonymous as a visual artist than as a writer?) This is balanced against the teaching profession where 72.5 per cent were women and stage performers where women accounted for 40.5 per cent. Tuchman, pp. 51–2.

50 Writing on professional opportunities for women, the *English Woman's Journal* was convinced that women could more easily achieve professional standards in literature than in art:

> . . . it is infinitely more difficult to draw passably well than to write passably well, and for this simple reason, that our ordinary education furnishes us with the main instruments of literature, while the *méchanique* of art is a study unconnected with any other. . . . The Art Student has, therefore, to acquire a whole technical language . . . [and] demands space, freedom, quietness, and unbroken hours . . . It is possible to write fine things at a desk in the corner of the kitchen . . . but it is not possible to paint without a studio, or some sort of separation from the noise and bustle of the external world.
>
> (The *English Woman's Journal*, 1858, pp. 4–5)

51 Showalter, *Literature*, pp. 55–85.

52 Showalter, *Literature*, pp. 79–80.

53 George Henry Lewes (1852) detected a correlation between women's domestic orientation and their literary tendency to excel at the observation of detail and the representation of pathos whilst failing in the masculine skills of plot construction; Richard Holt Hutton (1858) suggested that the differences in men's and women's writing could be traced to the differences in their education and resultant habits of intellectual discipline. G.H. Lewes, 'The Lady Novelists', in *Westminister Review*, 1852 and R.H. Hutton, 'Novels by the Authoress of *John Halifax*', in *North Britain Review*, 1858, both in Showalter, *Literature*, pp. 84–8.

54 Quoted in Showalter, *Literature*, p. 25.
55 George Eliot, 'Silly Novels by Lady Novelists', in *Westminister Review*, October, 1856, in Thomas Pinney, *Essays of George Eliot*, London, Routledge, 1968.
56 J. Russell Perkin notes that although George Eliot did herself rely on the money she earned from her writing, her connections in the literary world allowed her to command larger sums than many women who were never able to get off the treadmill of writing pot-boilers to order. He compares the £10,000 she was offered for *Romola* against the few hundred generally offered to such well-known novelists as Julia Pardoe (author of *Beauties of the Bosphorous*) for the copyright of their work. J. Russell Perkin, *A Reception-History of George Eliot's Fiction*, Ann Arbor, Mich., UMI Research Press, 1990, p. 27.
57 Just as in art, women were involved in literary pursuits on an amateur level although their place in George Eliot's debate is not clear. Tuchman defines the 'hobbyist' writer as one who published less than eight novels (based on definitions of occupation in the *Dictionary of National Biography*) though Showalter does not maintain such rigid distinctions. Tuchman's point, that amateurs tended to have a different agenda from that of professional writers, is credible and explains the tension between the two groups. Amateurs, who were less likely to be involved in literary debates, often wrote the type of fiction they would like to read rather than that which would gain symbolic capital in the cultural elite. Tuchman's identification of eight publications as the benchmark appears to indicate a high level of amateur literary activity, the social implications of which I can only at present speculate about for women who wished to write without entering the public/waged domain of professional literature.
58 Showalter, *Literature*, p. 45.
59 Tuchman, *Edging Women Out*, p. 184.
60 Gillian Beer suggests that George Eliot's refusal to give public support to feminist causes also arose from a fear that public association with the name of one notorious for her adulterous liaison would bring disrepute on the cause she advocated. Gillian Beer, *George Eliot*, Brighton, Harvester Wheatsheaf, 1986, ch. 1.
61 Showalter, for whom George Eliot's conservatism is a disappointment, points out that by the 1860s (i.e. before *Daniel Deronda*) many of her fellow women writers preferred the image of the passionate but tragic Brontë produced by Mrs Gaskell's biography to the austere and superior sybilline intellectualism of George Eliot. Showalter, *Literature*, pp. 107–9.
    On George Eliot's female friendships and relationships see also Pam Johnson, 'Edith Simcox and Heterosexism in Biography: A Lesbian-Feminist Exploration', in Lesbian History Group, *Not a Passing Phase: Reclaiming Lesbians in History 1840–1985*, London, The Women's Press, 1989.
62 Eliot's reputation declined after her death, and her work languished in relative obscurity for the first few years of the twentieth century until she was rescued by Virginia Woolf in 1919 and subsequently

immortalized in the literary canon by F.R. Leavis' *Great Tradition* in 1948 (Leavis of course wished to edit out the Jewish parts and republish *Daniel Deronda* as the 'Gwendolen Harleth Story'). Apart from Leavis' notable aberration, twentieth-century critics have tended to integrate *Daniel Deronda*'s scientific themes into their analysis, whether in relation to scientific philosophy, structuralism, psychoanalysis, Judaic scholarship and historiography or feminism. There are, of course, a number of competing interpretations in all these fields, notably in feminist literary criticism which has placed Eliot on a series of (often conflicting) pedestals since the 1970s.

Virginia Woolf, 'George Eliot', in *The Times Literary Supplement*, 20 November, 1919, pp. 657–8; F.R. Leavis, *The Great Tradition*, (1948) Harmondsworth, Penguin, 1980.

On *Daniel Deronda* and science see Sally Shuttleworth, *George Eliot and Nineteenth-Century Science: The Make-Believe of a Beginning*, Cambridge, Cambridge University Press, 1984; Suzanne Graver, *George Eliot and Community: A Study of Social Theory and Fictional Form*, Berkeley, University of California Press, 1984; Peter Allan Dale, *In Pursuit of a Scientific Culture: Science, Art and Society in the Victorian Age*, Madison, University of Wisconsin Press, 1989.

For an overview and example of deconstructive readings see J. Russel Perkin, *Reception-History*; George Levine, 'Determinism and Responsibility in the Works of George Eliot', in *PMLA*, vol. 77, 1962; Peter Dale, 'Symbolic Representation and the Means of Revolution in *Daniel Deronda*', in *Victorian Newsletter*, no. 59, Spring 1981; Mary Wilson Carpenter, 'The Apocrypha of the Old Testament: *Daniel Deronda* and the Interpretation of Interpretation', in *PMLA*, vol. 99, 1984; Cynthia Chase, 'The Decomposition of Elephants: Double Reading *Daniel Deronda*', in *PMLA*, vol. 93, 1978.

On feminist readings see, for example, Elaine Showalter, 'The Greening of Sister George', in *Nineteenth-Century Fiction*, no. 35, 1980; Carol A. Martin, 'George Eliot: A Feminist Critic', in *Victorian Newsletter*, no. 65, Spring, 1984; Elaine Showalter, 'Looking Forward: American Feminists, Victorian Sages', in *Victorian Newsletter*, no. 65, Spring 1984; Jacqueline Rose, 'George Eliot and the Spectacle of the Woman', in Rose, *Sexuality in the Field of Vision*, London, Verso, 1986.

63 See Beer, *George Eliot*.

64 See Chapter 5.

65 Beer, *George Eliot*, p. 10.

66 David Carroll notes that the intellectual rigour and thwarted romance of *Daniel Deronda* fed into a critical reassessment of George Eliot's career in the 1870s and 1880s which, especially after Cross' *Life*, tended towards a view of her oeuvre (including the journalism alongside the novels) that stressed the continuity of her moral and philosophical outlook, rather than the sense of disjunction that met the overt scientificity of *Daniel Deronda* on its publication.

David Carroll (ed.), *George Eliot; The Critical Heritage*, London, Routledge, 1971.

67 See also Benedict Anderson, *Imagined Communities: Reflections on the Origin and Spread of Nationalism*, (1983) second edition, London, Verso, 1991, chs. 4–8.

68 See Chapter 3.

69 They were also the source of intense internal machinations over selection, precedence and so on. Of particular significance in France was that the Expositions, unlike the Salon which showed only commissioned work (and therefore was bound to reflect aristocratic and Church taste), exhibited non-commissioned work. This led to fears that it cheapened the artist and reduced the display to a marketplace in which the vulgarities of middle-class taste would hold sway. See Patricia Mainardi, *Art and Politics of the Second Empire: The Universal Expositions of 1855 and 1867*, New Haven, Yale University Press, 1987, part 1.

70 Paul Greenhalgh, *Ephemeral Vistas: The Expositions Universelles, Great Exhibitions and World's Fairs, 1851–1939*, Manchester, Manchester University Press, 1988, ch. 3.

71 Schneider quotes ten million visitors to the Paris Exposition Universelle in 1878. William H. Schneider, *An Empire for the Masses: The French Popular Image of Africa, 1870–1900*, Westport, Conn., Greenwood Press, 1982, p. 8.

The relationship of the fine art exhibits to the display of material culture from home or the colonies is difficult to ascertain but, although the fine art pavilions were probably less popular with working-class visitors, we cannot assume that their audience was homogeneously middle class. The availability of cheap prints and the fact that exhibition guides, aimed at all pockets, included details of the fine art pavilions indicates that the fine art displays were probably visited by a more socially mixed audience than that which attended the Royal Academy if not the Salon. (One British observer at the Salon noted that its audience was far more mixed than the Royal Academy and bewailed that British artists has not such an opportunity to 'be published', i.e. reach a wide audience.)

See Phillip G. Hamerton, 'The Salon of 1863', in *Fine Arts Quarterly Review*, October 1863, in Elizabeth Gilmore Holt, *The Art of All Nations 1850–73: The Emerging Role of Exhibition and Critic*, Princeton, Princeton University Press, 1982.

72 The *Art Journal* 1862, p. 150, in Lynda Nead, *Myths of Sexuality: Representations of Women in Victorian Britain*, Oxford, Blackwell, 1988, p. 57 (original emphasis).

73 Gérôme will occur again in this book as a yardstick against which to measure Browne's work and its reception, since he was, and arguably is, taken to be the paradigmatic French Orientalist.

74 Phryne was accused of profaning the Eleusinian Mysteries but acquitted by the judges on account of her beauty, which she is seen displaying naked to them in the chamber.

75 The *Art Journal*, June, 1866, p. 194.

76 See also his *Slave Market*, n.d., Plate 13.

77 Linda Nochlin, 'The Imaginary Orient', in *Art in America*, May, 1983.

See also Olivier Richon, 'Representation, the Harem and the Despot', in *Block*, no. 10, 1985.

78 As Mainardi elucidates, this is as much to do with the genre-ization of history painting that critics of all political persuasions detected in *Phryne* as it is with moral issues. Mainardi, *Art and Politics*, p. 162.

79 The *Athenaeum*, August 1857, p. 213. See Chapter 3 for full analysis of this review.

Gender, genre and nation
Henriette Browne, the making of a woman Orientalist artist

Henriette Browne was an artist who painted a lot of things, but
the subjects for which she was most famous were convents and
harems. It might seem odd that a book concerned with Orientalism
devotes space to images of nuns, but I think that the only way to
understand the meanings given to Browne's images of the harem
is to relate them to the meanings associated with the image of
the artist herself. The particularities of this authorial persona were
constructed in response to her first major paintings in 1859
and 1860. These paintings were of nuns. The reaction to early
pictures like *The Sisters of Charity* (Plate 1) and *The Convent
Dispensary* (Plate 2) delineates the class-, gender- and nation-
specific persona of the artist and focuses on her representation
of female labour, sexuality and space. The critical construction of
Browne as a naturalistic artist with a reputation for working from
observable fact that stems from these early works was central to
the subsequent reception of her Orientalist subjects. Because these
powers of observation were also registered as feminine – tied to
gendered ideas of intuition, compassion and perception – it was
possible for critics both to emphasize the verisimilitude of her
representations of the harem and to undermine these claims on
account of her susceptibility, as a woman, to the effects of the
harem.

Therefore, this chapter begins with an examination of Browne's
early work and the construction of her authorial identity seen in
two early profiles that were instrumental in establishing the particularities of her British reputation (in the *English Woman's Journal*,
1860, and by Charles Kingsley in the *Fine Arts Quarterly Review*,
1863). Next, it outlines the field of Orientalist art in Britain
and France in order to discuss how a respectable lady artist, for

such is how Browne came to be seen, could intervene in an area notorious for its sexual suggestiveness and dubious morality. The chapter concludes with a brief analysis of the work of other women Orientalist artists. This demonstrates the heterogeneity of visual Orientalism and indicates the range of gendered approaches in relation to which Browne's work was received.

THE RECEPTION OF BROWNE'S RELIGIOUS WORKS IN BRITAIN AND FRANCE

Browne's early oeuvre consisted of portraiture, domestic genre scenes (in both contemporary urban and picturesque rural settings) and representations of the French *religieuse*. (This mixture of subjects continued throughout her career.) Her pictures of nuns gained the most critical attention, but their critical status in Britain and France was quite different. In France they were significant in establishing her as a woman artist and paved the way for her later fame as an Orientalist. But they were not seen as controversial or significant within the genre of religious painting (despite the central role of images of religion in aesthetic and political debates). In Britain they were exceedingly popular and well received despite the widespread anti-Romanism expressed during the Anglo-Catholic Revival and the associated controversy over female nursing orders in the 1850s and 1860s. Indeed, the British interest in her religious subjects and portraiture eclipsed the far more moderate interest expressed in her Orientalist works.

The Sisters of Charity was shown in London at the French Gallery in 1859 after its success at that year's Paris Salon. Its unusual provenance made it something of a *cause célèbre* and guaranteed that it would get press coverage. (The painting had been purchased for a lottery by the French government at 20,000 francs and was won by the holder of a single ticket who immediately sold it on. When the second owner went bankrupt the picture was bought by Gambart, owner of the French Gallery, who was already in possession of the copyright.)

The British reviews of this early and apparently unproblematically womanly painting illustrate the grid of gender, class, religious and national values within which all of Browne's paintings were to signify. The *Athenaeum* begins by describing Browne as 'a lady almost as clever as Rosa Bonheur, but in a gentler and more tender way', before likening her also to Angelica Kauffman and asking, 'are they ['ladies'] now going to beat us in our own cold intellectual Kingdom?'[1] This ostensibly facetious question attempts to dismiss as ridiculous the inroads women were making as cultural practitioners – fears about which were out of all proportion to women's still meagre share of the market. One of the few sources to comment on her anglicized pseudonym, the *Athenaeum* makes attempts to claim Browne as British, 'we believe, [she is] of English or Irish extraction', before going on to read her work as laden with feminine and French characteristics.[2]

> The picture, if a little less thin and timid, would be almost perfect as an expression of Christian charity and religious sentiment . . . what delicacy of colour and feeling for textural variety! Story there is none to tell: it is merely a little fevered child wrapped in a blanket, lying on the lap of a Sister of Mercy; while another (with a face painted hard and flat) mixes medicine . . . The French faults of low tone and slurred detail are here; but what beauties, what careful yet unpedantic drawing. What delicious love for the languid child is visible in the thoughtful eyes of the Sister of Mercy – a real face too, not a keepsake one, or a stone one – a rosy warm face, glowing with a woman's love for children and looking so blossom like, pretty and innocent and good between the stiff snowy wings of the starched linen head-dress. Surely Corporal Trim's Béguine was such a loving motherly creature as this Sister, with her sober Puritan gown, apron and rosary. The details are, of course, kept back in the usual cowardly French way, for fear of detracting from the faces . . . the child's frock is naturally arranged, but not with English feeling – but let that go.[3]

Frenchness in this instance is constructed as operating at the level of technique, rather than in the choice and treatment of subject, as was the case with the same issue's criticism of Gérôme which I looked at earlier. But, whether the body of the critique rests on subject or style, the tone is uniformly xenophobic. What poses as a technical discussion is overwhelmingly moral: it is Frenchness that is being criticized as much as the artist's skill. Note that the faults decried as typically French are cowardice, low tone and a slurring of detail, all defects that it is imputed are part of the French national character. The review of Browne cannot avoid playing on the national difference it perceives in her art. But, with respect to the aristocratic Browne as a gendered and classed subject, the negative moral terms used here are not loaded with the ideas of sexual transgression that are attached to Gérôme. The complimentary use of terms like careful, delicate, gentle and tender secures the painting as the product of a feminine brush and suggests that being timid and a 'little lacking in decision' is hardly surprising in the work of a young woman.

Both the *Athenaeum* and the *Art Journal* (which I shall come to shortly) refer to the painting and its female subjects as Sisters of Mercy rather than as Sisters of Charity, as it was exhibited and known in France (*Les soeurs de charité*). Although such liberties with translation or title were not uncommon (the painting appears to have been variously exhibited in Britain under either title and is referred to by both names in the British press) the confusion over which order the sisters are from is hard to explain. Both orders, and presumably the differences between them, were known in Britain. Although the Sisters of Charity were the most prominent internationally it seems likely that the Sisters of Mercy were the most familiar in Britain, not only for their high profile as nurses in the Crimean War, but also as the name of orders based in Britain; an Irish Catholic order of the Sisters of Mercy was established in London in 1839 and one of the first British Anglican nursing orders, founded in 1848, was called the Sisters of Mercy of Devonport.[4]

The *Art Journal* of 1859, like the *Athenaeum*, detects evidence of a French style but treats it far less judgementally.

> The beauty of the picture is its captivating simplicity: the dispositions are most effective, without appearing in the slightest degree artificial. The painting of the face of the seated figure is a masterpiece of Art; presented under the amplitude of the linen head-dress, the features are lighted by reflection, and the lighting and the brilliant transparency of the face are triumphs of a character that are very rarely accomplished . . . The smaller pictures [*The Hospital Laboratory*, *The Toilet*, *The Muse* and *The Portrait*] are painted on a fine ticken, of which the sharp threaded texture plays an important part in assisting the painter to that indefinite and facile manner that is a characteristic of the French school.[5]

The canvas which started Browne's reputation in Britain is identified as a masterpiece – literally, the large significant painting proffered by an aspiring artist to denote their arrival on the academic art scene. Although Browne is identified as an artist of the French School the technical discussion about canvas and the notice that she was a pupil of Chaplin seem to present this as a simple matter of genealogy and training rather than as a moral indictment. Note also that the spectacular head-dress of the sisters is picked out for mention, presumably as one of the simple and un-artificial details that so delight the reviewer. Attention to the sisters' head-dress, as we shall see, serves to mark both the representation's authenticity and signify the Catholic order's picturesque exoticism.

Both journals appear to have no difficulty in ascribing to the sisters, women outside of familial relations, the motherly emotions considered innate in bourgeois women. This surety about the sisters' femininity is surprising considering that pictures of nuns and nursing were not necessarily safe and uncontentious subjects in the anti-Papist climate of Britain in the 1850s. Although a familiar issue since the Crimean War, Browne's paintings of nuns were shown in a period of raging debate about nursing, medicine and religion prompted by the Anglo-Catholic Revival's espousal of religious orders for women in Britain and proto-feminist demands for the professionalization of waged work for women.[6]

The popular John Bull image of an anti-Papist Protestant Britain falls apart in the face of the struggle for the national religious imagination that marks this period. The Orientalist divide that posed a heathen Islamic Orient against a superior Christian Europe struggled to maintain the idea of a united Europe in the face of religious differences between European nations and internal schisms within the religious life of each nation. In Britain the nineteenth century is marked by the gradual emancipation and growing power of religions outside of the Church of England and rancour within the Anglican Church – the most pertinent of which, in this instance, was the Anglo-Catholic Revival.

Dating to the Oxford Movement of the 1830s, the Catholic Revival marked a movement among certain groups in the High Anglican Church to reclaim those elements of the early Church that they considered to be Protestantism's true Reformation heritage. The apostolic tradition that they sought to rekindle was often grafted onto a nostalgia for the era of the medieval Church which they, like Disraeli's Young England group, saw as a time of powerful popular religion, an undivided Church and a socially responsible hierarchy of gentry and clergy. With a mission to reach

the increasingly urban parishes of industrial Britain the Revivalists
stressed both ritual and sacrament and, through poor work and
the nursing orders, the holistic role of the priest and piety in the
lives of the masses.

In a power/knowledge relation typical of Orientalism, scholars
of the Anglo-Catholic Revival looked to the current Eastern
Churches for a solution to their domestic crisis of faith. Extending
their research parameters to include the modern and classical
East, they produced the Oriental Church as an object of study
for the West. For Anglo-Catholics striving to recreate an authen-
tically classic Catholic Church, the modern Eastern Churches
could be extrapolated from their living moment and reconstituted
as an unmediated expression of patristic religion, the embodiment
of the original Church before the advent of Roman Catholicism.
The Oriental Church figures as simultaneously contemporary and
archaic, its contemporaneity being significant only as an example
of its lack of progress. In this instance, the anachronistic culture
that the West so frequently found and deplored in the Orient
(as a sign of barbarity and lack of progress) is valorized as a
commitment to true Christian principles that the West has left
behind. Just as the Jews, as we shall see, in *Daniel Deronda* are
presented as an ancient religion and society whose thriving
example may illuminate and galvanize the degenerating English,
the Eastern Churches are produced as a possible solution for the
crisis within British Protestantism. But note that the way the East
is seen as providing a way forward rests on its apparent isolation
from history, the freeze-frame that presents the nineteenth-century
Oriental Church as an uninterrupted, unchanging slice of the
first four centuries of the Christian era. The way forward suggested by the Eastern Church is in fact a way back to an earlier
era, couched in terms of a return to former (proto-European)
glory.

Formed in the 1840s, the female orders developed their nursing
role from the 1850s. For all that nursing or nunning were conceptualized in relation to women's innate femininity, submission
and selfless devotion, they were also seen as a threat to women's
divine role as wife and mother, and a Catholic incursion into
British life. Nursing was developing as both a respectable job
for working women and a high-profile philanthropic activity for
leisured women.[7] Ostensibly the nuns were able to avoid the
anxieties about class and sexual probity that surrounded lay nurses

since, as brides of Christ, they were symbolically declassed and morally beyond question.[8] But the evidence that numerous women did find the cloisters an attractive alternative to the bourgeois Christian family threatened the very basis of femininity. Recruitment to the 'Puseyite nunneries' was explained away as brainwashing, a dilettante fad for socially sanctioned displays of fashionable and fake piety, and art and literature that appeared to condone the conventual life faced critics ready to pounce on any sign of popery.[9] Typical of the mockery faced by the convents are these two extracts, one from *Punch*'s 'Convent of the Belgravians' (1850) and the other from Charles Kingsley's novel *Yeast* (1860):

> ... Absolute seclusion will by no means be enforced; indeed it will be incumbent on the Nuns to appear in society, in order to display the beauty of sanctity ... At the same time, they will renounce the world, in the Belgravian sense ...[10]
> ... the thought of menial service towards the poor, however distasteful to her, came in quite prettily to fill up the little ideal of a life of romantic asceticism and mystic contemplation, which gave the true charm in her eyes to her wild project.[11]

It is evident, then, that Browne's pictures of French Catholic nursing nuns on display in Britain in 1860 were highly unlikely to be seen as neutral: so how did they come to be so popular? A look at the reception of other representations of nuns in Britain may help us to understand how Browne's were positioned. Nuns were a popular theme in the mid-century; Susan Casteras finds an increase in the frequency of images of nuns and novices in visual art and literature that parallels the development of the Anglican sisterhoods.[12] But not everyone depicted nuns with the same contemporaneity as Browne. The early Pre-Raphaelite Brotherhood, for example, who were known to have Revivalist connections, painted nuns that were Biblical or medievalist rather than ostensibly contemporary.[13] Their style and subject choice outraged the aesthetic and religious sensibilities of their critics who saw the New Medievalists' emphasis on early (and definitely Catholic) masters as an anti-Protestant aesthetic. Targets for such treatment included Charles Collins' *Convent Thoughts* (1851, Plate 6) which had too many Romanist and Tractarian tendencies even for Ruskin, the Pre-Raphaelites' great champion.[14] In contrast, Millais' *The Vale of Rest* (RA 1859, Plate 7) managed to be sufficiently gloomy about convent life to avoid charges of popery (one nun is seen digging what many reviewers took to be her own grave) and sufficiently gracious in its style to avoid charges of medievalist ugliness without giving up the romantic interest in the old Church.[15]

There was, as well, a market for visual representations of nuns and novices that were clearly opposed to the female orders. Like their literary equivalents, prints and paintings in this camp portrayed convents as the misguided destination of lovelorn maidens: Alfred Elmore's Royal Academy canvas *The Novice* from 1852 (Plate 8) shows a fashionably buxom maiden entombed in a convent gazing wistfully out of the window awaiting rescue. Where Browne pictures nuns as busy middle-aged women, the convent's opponents favoured languishing (beautiful) novices and postulants whose probationary status left open the possibility that they might change their mind.[16] What is surprising, then, given this level of xenophobia and anti-Catholic feeling – both the *Athenaeum* and the *Art Journal* responded favourably to the anti-conventual sentiments of Elmore's painting[17] – is that nothing negative is made of the Catholicity of Browne's nuns. It is clear that they were recognized as being from a French Catholic nursing order, despite the confusion over their affiliation, but they are nonetheless read as perfect expressions of Christian humility and devotion. Where, as we shall see, the *English Woman's Journal* marks them as other in terms of their Catholicism, the art press is astoundingly neutral in its reading of Browne's nuns, reserving its national slurs for the failures of her French painting technique – a transmogrification of a religious dispute into aesthetics that, for all its prejudice, has nothing like the venom directed at British supporters of Anglican female orders. Susan Casteras suggests that British artists tended to represent nuns as vaguely Catholic or medieval in order to share in the heightened interest in the subject aroused by the controversies over the Anglo-Catholic Revival without being damaged by accusations of Tractarianism.[18] In this light, the specifically French Catholic significations of Browne's pictures, though suppressed by the *Athenaeum* and the *Art Journal*, start to function as markers of a difference that, rather than being threatening signs of a Roman incursion, are precisely what make a pleasure in the painting possible. The routine dis-approval of Catholicism is projected onto a nationally inflected critique of Browne's style which establishes the pictures' foreignness sufficiently to re-present them to a British gaze. Conversely, in the *English Woman's Journal* and Kingsley reviews, where discourses of national schools of art are more marginal, the signification of otherness returns to the subject, rather than style, of the painting and the nuns themselves re-surface as a trope of difference and alienness.

In France, as well as the traditional market for religious subjects, nuns and religiosity, along with the peasantry, took on a new currency in the mid-century debate over naturalism, associated with the new realism and radical subject choice of Courbet and the Independents (Impressionists). As Linda Nochlin suggests, the construction of a new type of religious painting in this period rested on the representation of the religious life of peasants whose relationship to religion was understood as fundamental to their significance for the nation: whether they figured as radical revolutionaries or steadfast serfs, religion and religiosity were clues to their collective identity and political affiliations.[19] Structurally the peasantry are propelled into the place of the Orient in the schematic Occident/Orient divide: they are both irredeemably different and similar, acting as a key site for the production of meanings that always relate back to the dominant discourses of urbanity and nation just as all 'truths' about the Orient can be seen to function in relation to the Occident.[20]

Whereas in France there was a clearly understood difference between the academic painters of peasants (Hébert, Frere, Dagnan-Bouveret) and the avant-garde (Courbet, Millet, Breton), British critics often mix together the different types of peasant painter. British commentators minimize the differences between, for example, Millet and Breton's extollation of rural labour and Hébert's picturesque poverty in order to present a group of artists as generically French. Thus, Browne, who does not figure in the French art press as a significant figure in either the battle over realist technique or peasant subjects, is often cited amongst a group of French naturalist painters in the British press. Despite her detailed and naturalistic style, and although much of her early oeuvre included scenes of the peasantry and religion (for example the poor rural children in *The Catechism*, Salon 1857, Plate 9), she has more in common with an older tradition of domestic genre painting than with Courbet's attempt to put rural labour on the the map of history painting. The *Art Journal* in 1862 identifies her as a naturalist and in 1868 reviews her in a group of other naturalist painters including Breton, Millet, Hébert and Frere, claiming that 'no apology can be needed for so doing, seeing that she paints not the smallest accessory without placing nature before her eyes'.[21]

In France images of religion and the peasantry were central to debate over the nation's morals and the Church's changing political role. (The Second Empire had initially appeared to promise an increase in Church and Papal power under Louis Napoleon: until his plans for a Papal Confederation failed in 1859.)[22] Although the British tended to remark on *The Sisters of Charity*'s strong moral message, the French Catholic press do not include Browne among their lists of notable religious painters in their 1859 Salon (although a number of other women artists are mentioned).[23] This omission of *The Sisters of Charity*, a moral subject which clearly did attract public attention, is surprising. It is obviously considered to be neither on the first rung of religious painting nor a danger to the faithful (there was much concern over the visual pleasures offered by 'profane' paintings).

The French art press make little of the painting's moral subject either. Browne merits attention mainly as the female producer of a work that has caught the public eye and the painting's themes are often only glancingly referenced. For example, in the honourable mention given to Browne in *L'Artiste* (1859), gender is obviously a key reason for notice.

> Her portrait of M. de G. is treated with a hand of a delicate and nearly virile touch. Madame Browne is, I do believe, the most gifted and clever women artist that we have at the moment. *The Sisters of Charity*, in which the work is less apparent than in the portrait, holds the first rung in what we call today light painting [la peinture claire]. The sick child who figures in the picture is of fair and masterly execution.[24]

The oscillation between masculine and feminine qualities in her technique (delicate and virile, fair and masterly) and the desire to secure her as a woman artist clearly take precedence over any discussion of the painting's moral content. Théophile Gautier, writing in *Le Moniteur universel*, offers a gendered reading of both artist and content.

> We will not give away the real name which is hidden by the anglicized pseudonym of Henriette Browne; a modesty

resistant to success doubtless has reasons which must be respected. *The Sisters of Charity* has caught the public's fickle attention. A young sister, whose charming figure is illuminated by the white sheen of her large winged head-dress, holds on her knees, a sick young child ... An older religious stands near a table strewn with phials and pharmaceutical ingredients, preparing a medicine for the poor baby, all morose and worried on the young religious' lap: because in the end a sister of charity is not totally a mother. She will also be of service to another child who is in her charge ... The figures in the painting are of natural grandeur ...[25]

The prominence Gautier gives to Browne's anonymity amplifies both the secret of her real identity and the gender of the artist. His arch tone indicates that her real identity is no secret to him and hints that she is a public personage of some status.[26] The review simultaneously describes the nuns in the terminology of femininity and places them outside of it; their innate spark of maternal feeling is, in fact, prohibited by their holy vows. One of the problems presented by this canvas is that it lends itself to being read as the feminine work of a woman artist at the same time as it raises questions about the nature of women's work and their relationship to the labour market. In Britain, where most nuns were middle class, such displays of maternal solicitude could be incorporated into the idea that it was only middle-class women who were naturally inclined to the higher points of good mothering. This, whilst not minimizing the orders' threat to gender roles, at least allowed treasured ideas of class difference to remain intact. In France, where the clergy (male and female) were recruited from lower social orders and where nursing orders were more established, the concept of the sisters as hired help (one who will serve many children) was less contentious, but the interplay between the duplicate demands of family and religion continued.

In *Journal des desmoiselles*, Noémie Cadiot, writing under the male pseudonym of Claude Vignon, is overtly concerned with the gender of the artist, making only passing reference to the moral value of the paintings.

[Henriette Browne] is well enough despite inevitably mixed praise, this year her critical success has been less than her public success. It is said, that when a woman joins the crowd and distinguishes herself, she must pay for her success; while the public, the real public, the one that goes to the Salon in search of a pleasurable time among admirable subjects, stops in front of madame [*sic*] Browne's pictures, the artists and judges aim acerbic praise at her, slip a barb in the guise of a caress, drawing parallels between her and certain prickly rejects [artistes hérrissés et refusés], giving her the worst of it by insinuation.[27]

The main thrust of her argument is the gender inequality of Browne's reception. She asserts the validity of Browne's claim to fame by constructing an alternative 'popular' public whose taste is held to be more discerning than that of the august jury and art world. The construction of this other public introduces another protagonist into the diatribes commonly levelled at the Salon jury by reviewers. In this case the public serves to justify Vignon's estimation of Browne, whose works are only signalled and not discussed in detail. The reader is invited to identify with this appeal to a popular public, who see the Salon as a source of entertainment and edification, just as her young lady readers might regard *Journal des desmoiselles*.

The readership of *Journal des desmoiselles* was young, unmarried women who could afford to subscribe to what must have been a costly journal whose contents indicate an affluent female, but not (proto-)feminist, bourgeois readership.[28] Many of the named contributors are female, some like Claude Vignon are male pseudonyms and others are definitely male. Being neither an art journal nor a political paper, *Journal des desmoiselles* readers will not be expected to have a personal stake in the machinations of the art world – what is assumed to concern them is the treatment of a woman, not the internal disputes of the Academy. In contrast, Vignon's 1861 Salon review for *Le Correspondent* – a more intellectual review journal of current affairs, philosophy and art – adopts a serious tone, dwelling on aesthetic debates in the assumption that these readers are familiar with the Salon and its concerns.

It is possible therefore, that the discussion of discrimination against Browne in *Journal des desmoiselles* can be accounted for as a way of capturing the young readers' interest. Few critics considered Browne's gender to be immaterial: reviews in vastly different locations reference it one way or another and also criticize the inequality of the Salon judging (see the *Art Journal* review discussed in Chapter 4). Vignon is able to take the judges to task in 1859 on the grounds of popular support for Browne, posing the diatribe as a general rally against injustice and self-interest rather than as a political demand for equality. As we shall see, her own reading of Browne's Orientalist paintings relies on a specifically gendered author, so we must not interpret this 1859 review as a demand for the abolition of gender as a criteria of critical judgement but rather as a demand, couched in the prevailing terms of gender, for a fair judgement of the reviewer's favoured artists.

MAKING A NAME: THE ESTABLISHMENT OF BROWNE'S ARTISTIC IDENTITY IN BRITAIN

The themes set up by these initial reviews of *The Sisters of Charity* were consolidated in the early 1860s by two reviews of Browne which crystallized, for the British reader, the definition of the artist and her ocuvre. A long profile of Browne in the *English Woman's Journal* in 1860 enhanced her reputation and established her as a paradigmatically ladylike artist prior to the potentially risqué subjects of the Orientalist paintings,[29] and Charles Kingsley's review of *The Sisters of Charity*, on the occasion of its second showing at Gambart's in 1863, provided what was to become an influential interpretation of the artist and her work. (It is Kingsley that Mrs Clement quotes in 1904.)

The *English Woman's Journal*, associated with the Bodichon/Boucheret feminist set of Langham Place, was a campaigning periodical that included profiles of prominent and creative women and female figures of the day alongside reports on women's legal status, education and employment opportunities, married women's property, female emigration, charity work and poetry and fiction.[30] The article on Browne, by an author known only as A.B., sets out a portrait of Browne as a professional artist.[31] But, at the same time as it relies on her gentility in its portrayal of her as the perfect working wife and mother, it is haunted by the spectre of her equally genteel mother brought into pecuniary hardship and stresses the importance of women's ability to be financially independent. For a journal that assumes a mainly middle- and upper-class readership (the poor occur only as the recipients of middle-class philanthropy) the spectre of the impoverished aristocrat was one of the staple real-life nightmares that the supporters of women's financial independence relied upon to make their case. Browne's story thus serves as both a success story and a warning.

> ... this excellent mother ... never lost sight of the importance to women, even in comparatively easy circumstances, of possessing some honourable and certain means of making money ... such a reverse she naturally regarded as most improbable in her daughter's case; but taught by her own experience, she regarded it in principle as a positive duty for every woman, no matter what may be her position or prospects, to be prepared for such a possible contingency.[32]

The review, which begins by stressing Browne's impeccable lineage, gentility and present position as wife of a well-known diplomat, is faced with the problem of insisting on the artist's talent and diligence without compromising her as perfect wife, mother, hostess and, above all, lady. At this point in the narrative we begin to see the contradictions inherent in the *English Woman's Journal*'s (classed) feminist reworking of discourses of labour and art. Whilst the first insists on the necessity of women's financial independence and ability to earn a living, the second wants to secure a status for art that is beyond the alienation of wage labour. It is here that the class status of the subject Browne takes a narrative ascendancy over a feminist discourse supporting the respectability of (certain kinds of) labour. Aristocratic connections and wealth serve to free the artist from any taint of financial motivation: Browne is a woman trained in a profession, but one who fortunately has no need of its wages. At this stage the counter-claims of an art discourse intervene again to demand a defence of the artist's professionalism against the gendered charges of dilettantism and fashionable dabbling that she so frequently faced.

> Cultivating painting from the pure and simple love of art, apart from the ordinary incentives of ambition and pecuniary gain ... [Henriette Browne is] of a remarkably modest and retiring disposition, devoted to her family and her home, and prizing the sympathy of friends far more than the applause of strangers, she has scrupulously kept her personality in the background ...[33]

Browne is represented as holding herself aloof from the 'stormy precincts' of the art world and as leading, apart from her painting, 'the ordinary life of a woman of this nineteenth century in the

higher walks of social existence'. The contradiction of the position artist/woman, or more correctly artist/lady, is evident in the
detailed portrait of Browne that follows. Having made a case for
her absolute and unremarkable normality, the writer now tries to
weld onto this a female version of the artist/genius persona and
begins by listing the artist's manifold talents: 'she [is] *au fait* at
every species of cutting out and sewing; . . . but she is also a fair
upholsterer, fully equal to the task of putting up curtains, covering
chairs and sofas, . . . and has a knack at all sorts of domestic
carpentering'.[34]

Note that the description of her prodigous skills is, in the case
of a female practitioner, carefully associated with the domestic.
Unlike the popular image of the male artist, Browne's plethora
of skills and excess of creative energy lead her to home improvement, not to a diversification into other activities rated as serious
art. Indeed, in the review her venture into the realm of art is
characterized by the same 'complete and orderly practicality' that
she adopts in the domestic.

> Having devoted the morning to superintending her household
> affairs . . . she makes her toilet for the walk or visits of the
> afternoon, and proceeds . . . to her *atelier* . . . She there takes
> off her bonnet, puts on a pair of gloves which lie ready beside
> her easel, and works at a picture for a couple of hours, without
> even turning up her sleeves or putting on the least bit of an
> apron. And so neat and methodical is she in all she does, that
> to this day she has never dropped a particle of paint, never
> made the slightest speck or smear, on any part of her dress
> while painting. About four o'clock . . . the artist lays aside her
> palette, wipes her brushes, exchanges her painting-gloves
> (without which she never touches a brush) for a pair of spot-
> less kid, resumes her bonnet, and goes off to take a walk, pay
> visits . . .[35]

The review's approval of Browne's scrupulous attention to the
details of dress signals the heightened importance of these
markers of class, and thus respectability, in the face of her possibly
demeaning manual activities as a professional painter. By exhibiting and selling her work Browne clearly refuses the status of
accomplishment artist but must still hold herself above the taints
of the art market. This is where these details of personal appearance (the gloves, the bonnet)[36] come in as signs of her femininity

that minimize, or compensate for, her deviation from the ladylike model of art as a leisure pursuit.[37]

The significance of this obsessive detailing of dress and personal habit is illustrated by the lengths to which the *English Woman's Journal* went in 1858 to try to present as similarly respectable and feminine the transgressive persona and activities of Rosa Bonheur. Bonheur, unlike the eminently respectable Browne, never married but travelled and worked with her companion Nathalie Micas.

Further, she was notorious for wearing men's clothing during sketching visits to horse fairs and cattle markets.[38] The *English Woman's Journal* tries to take the sting out of Bonheur's transgressive dress and lifestyle by justifying both as signs of her dedication to her art. Her approach to both leisure- and work-wear is described as utilitarian.

> [Bonheur has] a compact, shapely figure ... true artist's hands, small delicate, nervous; and extremely pretty little feet. She dresses very plainly ... [in] a close fitting jacket and a skirt of simple material ... She wears none of the usual articles of feminine adornment; not from contempt of them, but simply because the elegant trifles so dear to womankind are so utterly foreign to her thoughts and occupations, that even to put them on, would be, to her, a forced and unnatural proceeding. When at her easel, she wears a sort of round pinafore or blouse of grey linen, that envelops her from the neck to the feet.[39]

This picture of a woman in overalls is very different from that of Browne working neatly in her afternoon dress. Bonheur's male attire at the cattle market is rationalized as a necessary 'precaution' against the 'annoyances' that would have been directed at a woman. Despite the reviewer's sympathies for Bonheur, the difficulties of her cross-dressing and disregard for appearance produce confusions in the text. It is essential that it secure her as beautiful in some way – her 'pretty little feet' – despite the trouble to which this leads when trying to tiptoe round the transvestism of her public persona and secure the respectability of Bonheur's household; 'Living solely for her art, she has gladly resigned the care of her outward existence to an old and devoted friend Madame Micas, a widow lady'.[40] Whereas Browne is presented as prioritizing home over art, Bonheur's refusal of household responsibilities moves her part way into a symbolically male space in keeping with the new model of the single-minded existential artist. The convoluted logic deployed to somehow present Bonheur within dominant definitions of the feminine highlights how relatively unproblematic was Browne's gender identity. Compare the description of Bonheur's attire with this glowing report of Browne's grasp of the intricacies of female fashion.

> The same natural and unstudied simplicity which forms so striking a feature of this lady's character, distinguishes her personal appearance, and gives a peculiar *cachet* even to her style of dress. She never wears a mixture either of materials or of colours; and whether her dress be of velvet, or of muslin, it is always of the same material and the same hue throughout ... she is always conspicuous above all others for a certain undefinable grace and harmony of appearance which are too often wanting in costlier and more elaborate toilets.[41]

This vision of elegant loveliness is important in the *English Woman's Journal* not only for the glow it throws on Browne's aristocratic femininity, but also because by emphasizing the responsibility of her taste and judgement it pre-empts challenges over her rather dubious conduct in the affair of the nun's habit for *The Sisters of Charity*.

Browne, whose principle of painting only from observation was well known, encountered enormous difficulties in obtaining permission to study the order's habit (it being out of the question that a real sister might pose for her). After spending over a year in negotiations, she was 'permitted to have the use – at her own house, for a few days only – of the complete costume of a Sister of Charity, to put upon a lay figure [mannequin] which she had had prepared expressly for that occasion'.[42] A.B.'s account of the artist's persistence in this matter ostensibly shows Browne's dedication as an artist, but the incidentals of the story reveal the writer's anti-Catholic feelings and the extent to which Browne's aristocratic position is used to forgive and even applaud her subsequent conduct. The nuns themselves are patronizingly represented as worthy but needlessly superstitious: '[they have] an invincible repugnance to sitting for their portrait – which they regard as a vain act, and contrary to "the Christian humility and abnegation" they profess ...'.[43] This clears the way for a positive representation of Browne's decision to flout the conditions laid down for the use of the habit: she had her friend don the holy vestments and pose for the painting (it being, apparently, impossible to position the mannequin satisfactorily).

> This sacrilegious substitution was, of course, kept a profound secret; the 'Sister' to whose use the objects confided to the artist were destined, as well as the Superiors by whose permission they had been at last obtained, remaining in happy ignorance of the fact that they had been desecrated by being placed upon the person of a woman of the world.[44]

Such a breach of contract is seen as perfectly acceptable on three counts: firstly, the preceding comments about the sisters indicate that their regard for the habit is excessive and superstitious and, moreover, that their motives are not entirely to be believed; secondly, the image of the worthy, well-liked and above all respected Browne allows that no dishonour be attached to her most honourable name; and thirdly, that the Church almost deserved it, because the artist was led into such a misdemeanour by her scrupulous painting practice, a loyalty to truth that the Church had impeded at every step.

Charles Kingsley, whose view of the nuns differently stresses their otherness, sees the painting's moral message as proof of Browne's own righteousness. Kingsley, who might be expected to oppose both the subject and style of Browne's paintings (being an Anglican minister noted for his opposition to female orders and a writer and critic known for his disapproval of the Pre-Raphaelites's departure from the Academic ideal),[45] turns out to be one of her greatest supporters. Where the *English Woman's Journal* reveals an Orientalist schema of otherness within the differentiation of European nations and religions, Kingsley directly invokes ideologies of racial difference through the application of degeneracy and evolutionary theories to art. Art, which should aim to represent the ideal in nature to which Man should aspire, has no place to represent disease – something which appears even or 'especially in civilized nations'. But before he proceeds to explain why Browne's depiction of the sickroom is acceptable he delivers a polemic on the function of racial difference in the artistic representation of the ideal. He naturalizes an evolutionary hierarchy of race to endorse the Black man as a pure form within nature whilst simultaneously relegating him to the bottom of the scale.

Imperfect development may be, of course, [a proper subject] provided the imperfection be that of a whole genus, not an individual. High art deals principally with generic forms; nothing individual or personal is allowed in it, it interferes with the generic type; much less anything aberrant or degraded. Thus, a healthy negro may not be so high in the scale of humanity as a deformed white man; but he is, as far as he goes, healthy and what he ought to be by nature, and therefore beautiful; and therefore a proper subject for high art, while the deformed white man, not being what he ought to be, is ugly, and therefore an improper subject.[46]

Kingsley upholds Browne as one whose technique, the result as much of innate good taste as of talent, has found a middle way between the idealists and the realists.

The picture which is the best modern instance of this happy hitting of the golden mean, whereby beauty and homely fact are perfectly combined, is, in my eyes, Henrietta [sic] Browne's picture of the Sick Child and the Sisters of Charity ... I believe that it will surely be ranked hereafter among the very highest works of modern art.

... in all this there is nothing painful. No contortion, no trace of acute suffering ... Neither is there any element of ugliness; ... A child, into whatsoever attitude the limbs may fall, is seldom or never ungraceful ... Ungracefulness, it must be remembered, is always a mere sin in the painter, proceeding either from wilfulness, carelessness, or ignorance of the true anatomy of the human body ... For ungracefulness is the product of deformity ... The average savage of every race, like the wild beast, is always graceful in body, however low in brain.[47]

In an aesthetic in which realism reflects the reality of the world as an evolutionary theatre, race and gender are integral defining terms. The nun is itemized as a separate category of woman, a subgroup with a distinct physiognomy and temperament which, like the healthy savage, is beautiful in itself as an example of type.

It is in the nuns that Madame Browne's power of painting... is shown most perfectly. We have all seen nuns painted; nuns like ghosts, nuns like navigators, nuns like witches, nuns like nothing at all; but here are real nuns; and not mere nuns, but sisters of charity.

[This conception is] so perfect, that it can have been gained only by long personal acquaintance with that good class, and no less by the woman's instinct, enabling her to understand women, and to read many things in countenances, which to the world would seem as impassive and common place as these two sisters' faces seem ... Theirs is the true nun-nature, in which (rightly or wrongly, no matter) passion has been long since driven out as useless and dangerous, and emotion, or indeed any exhibition of personal self-will, has been systematically repressed by a life of discipline. Therefore they have (and in catching that expression Madame Browne has shown her extraordinary genius) that peculiar look which marks the self-inspecting and over-meditative pietist; inward, self-repressed, meditative, hanging on the verge of slyness, and yet not slyness in those whose hearts are pure, though too likely to become such in those whose hearts are not; a look which was common enough in England in Puritan days, but which can only be seen here now in the countenances of some Quaker or Wesleyan women.

It would have been easy for Madame Browne to have excited a little sentiment by making them emaciated, hollow-eyed, and so forth. But she has been too true to fact and nature to do anything of the kind. The two look, at first sight, two fat comfortable ladies ... [whose] softness ... takes off ... the studied, almost stiff attitude, so common in persons under perpetual self-restraint.[48]

To legitimize its claims, the review relies on the essential qualities attributed to the child, the variation of femininity constructed for the nuns (significantly at odds with those who see the nuns as surrogate mothers) and the racial determinism of the 'savage'. These three figures (child, woman, savage) stand as emblems for different stages of evolution and, in the case of the 'negro', as a different genus if not species. In Kingsley's hierarchy the white boy child has every chance of acceding to the sovereignty due to Western rationality; the woman less; the negro none. Browne's ability to draw out the noble essences of these three types is proof of her moral stature as well as her talent. For once, in an assessment of her skill as an artist, gender is relatively immaterial.

[T]o paint such pictures ... the artist must be a good man. Henrietta Browne (or whatever her name in the world may be) is said to possess a heart pure, noble, charitable, and pious. I believed it when I saw that picture; for had she not been what she is reported to be, neither would the picture have been what it is ...[49]

Kingsley's review highlights the Orientalist schemas and racialized discourses that structure, in different ways, the reception of the religious subjects in Britain and France. Regarded in this light, we can see how these seemingly innocuous pictures connect to the network of discursive clusters around race, gender and class that I outlined in Chapter 1.

Whilst we can detect codes of Orientalist otherness in the reception of *The Sisters of Charity*, reviews in both countries are overwhelmingly approving. I think that this is made possible by Browne's treatment of a subject that, whilst its contemporaneity raises the question of female labour and women's social role, does not necessarily disallow the comfortable image of female devotion and steadfast morality that was beloved by both sides of the political divide. It is interesting that although *The Sisters of Charity* was exhibited at both the Salon and Gambart's with another of Browne's pictures of nuns, *The Convent Dispensary*, no critic makes more than passing mention of this second canvas either in 1859, or in 1862 – when British and French critics had the opportunity for a second viewing when it hung with a selection of her work at the French Exposition Universelle. If we look at differences between the two pictures we can begin to understand how *The Sisters of Charity* was able to so successfully bypass the potential pitfalls of its subject.

The figures in *The Convent Dispensary* are, like those in *The Sisters of Charity*, of various ages and indifferent looks, their bodies obscured in heavy habits. But whereas *The Sisters of Charity* is a large painting (167 × 130cm.) offering a close-up portrait of the seated woman and child in the left foreground, *The Convent Dispensary* is described as a cabinet picture (probably of similar dimensions to Browne's other works of this disposition, i.e. c.65 × 80cm.) and depicts a number of women busily engaged in pharmaceutical tasks, only one of whose faces is available to the viewer. Whilst there is nothing overtly shocking about such an image, it does not present the same touching and feminine vision of nurture and charity that was so beloved in *The Sisters of Charity*. Whereas Kingsley, as we have seen, uses the sisters' nonedescript features as a key to their authenticity as a particular type of woman, I would suggest that there is no obvious reference to repression or self-denial in either of these paintings; they could just as easily be interpreted as representing the women and their work with dignity and stature. (Far rarer are Browne's contemplative figures such as *A Nun*, 1859, seen in England 1866.)

Although the size and provenance of *The Sisters of Charity* positioned it as the young artist's masterpiece, its subsequently unshakeable place (in Britain at least) as her *chef d'oeuvre* must also be to do with its choice of subject. It is no coincidence that British art critics in the mid-century prefer the image of a woman nursing a child over one of women working outside of familial references: images of women and children, generally mother and child, were phenomenally popular at this time, and the more sentimental the better. As Lynda Nead has shown, the popularity of such scenes celebrates not only the bourgeois ideal of wifely maternalism but also fends off the spectre of disease and death associated with the previously preferred practice of wet-nursing, recently replaced by the actively child-rearing bourgeois mother.[50] We have already seen how the middle-class Anglican nursing orders were able to sidestep the class problems raised by paid nurses, and how the Frenchness of the Sisters of Charity, or of Mercy, would have similarly separated them. So it becomes possible to see how pictures like Browne's *The Sisters of Charity* could be read as properly feminine displays of maternal or natural solicitude despite the nuns' obvious rejection of family life.

Compare Browne's painting with *The Young Mother* (1846, Plate 10) by Charles Cope, one of the most successful purveyors of scenes of idealized maternity. Whilst Cope depicts the young mother actually breastfeeding her child (the one thing a nun could never do), both paintings produce a Madonna-like dyad focusing on the intense concentration between woman and infant. But in Browne's, the dyadic enclosure, that is so emphasized in Cope, is broken by the presence of the second nun. And whereas Cope's baby suckles, engrossed in the maternal body, Browne's (older) child gazes away from the nun, out of the picture plane; the non-reciprocity of visual contact between nun and child signifying again the absence of the real mother. In contrast though, the Madonna theme is reinforced by the pose of the child, sprawled limply on her lap like a *pietà*. It seems, then, that Browne's choice of the popular woman and child format for a subject that was a potential challenge to the bourgeois family accounts in part for the plaudits heaped upon her work. In 1868 the *Art Journal* is convinced that, '[S]he will never paint a greater; and this singularly fine, touching and womanly work must always rank among the famous pictures of the century'.[51]

But images of nuns also had a seamier side, and another reason for the success of Browne's work was that it managed to avoid the negative associations of sexual deviancy that were regularly invoked by the debate over female religiosity. For the convent, like the harem, was often seen by its opponents as archaic, self-contained, tyrannous and tempting. Above all it was seen as essentially sexual, a subject of prurient fascination and dread. Nineteenth-century fascination with the presumed perversion of the punishments laid down by the convent rule brings to mind the West's never-ending horror at, and interest in, the sadisms attributed to the East, be it cruelty in the slave market and harem, or 'suttee' in India. Pusey's code of spiritual discipline for the Anglican convents included certain modes of obedience, humility, mortification of the flesh, confession and penitence the details of which (including possibly 'having to eat off the floor . . . or making the sign of the cross on the floor with [the] tongue')[52] intrigued and repelled the public.

The idea that women were responsible for the tyrannous rule of the convent adds a further frisson to the lesbian overtones that colour discussion of the unnaturalness of the orders. Although some people saw the convents as a solution to the 'surplus' million women who were demographically unable to find husbands, others disapproved too much of what they saw as the convents' unhealthy unnaturalness in advocating another form of enforced celibacy. The tension between the benefits of a career for women and the potential disadvantages of female seclusion are apparent in the 1855 lecture 'Sisters of Charity: Catholic and Protestant, Abroad and at Home' given by the art critic Anna Jameson, a strong advocate of training for women. Jameson's obvious conviction that the Sisters of Charity provide a good model for female social work is continually disrupted by the need to prove that she is not a Papist supporter, at the same time as she is acutely aware of the real disadvantages of such prejudice to the furtherance of her cause.

> I know that many well-meaning, ignorant people in this country entertain the idea that the existence of communities of women, trained and organized to help in social work from the sentiment of devotion, is especially a Roman Catholic institution, belonging peculiarly to that church, and necessarily implying the existence of nuns and nunneries, veils and vows, forced celibacy and seclusion, and all the other inventions and tradition which, in this Protestant nation, are regarded with terror, disgust, and derision. I conceive that this is altogether a mistake. The truth seems to me to amount to this: that the Roman Catholic Church has had the good sense to turn to account, and assimilate to itself, and inform with its own peculiar doctrines, a deep-seated principle in our human nature, – the law of life, which we Protestants have had the folly to repudiate.[53]

Despite condemning the effects of 'vulgar, stupid prejudices' Jameson is unable to avoid replicating their terms as she distances herself from similar charges of Papism.

> I am no friend to nunneries. I do not like even the idea of Protestant nunneries, which I have heard discussed and warmly advocated. I conceive that any large number of women shut up together in one locality, with no occupation connecting them actively and benevolently with the world of humanity outside, with all their interests centred within their walls, would not mend each other, and that such an atmosphere could not be perfectly healthy, – spiritually, morally, or physically. There would necessarily ensue, in lighter characters, frivolity, idleness, and sick disordered fancies; and in superior minds, ascetic pride, gloom, and impatience. But it is very different with the active charitable Orders, and I should certainly like to see amongst us some institutions which, if not exactly like them, should supply their place.[54]

We see how the differentiations of nation, religion and class constrain the progress of her argument and force her to make a division between the active and contemplative religious orders which locates all perversions within the closed sphere of the contemplative cloister. Such imputations of homosexuality were the unspoken of many representations of the convent, where

differences of age and beauty are used to institute a heterosexual
model of domination and subordination in relations between
women (analogous to the role of race in the construction of similar
hierarchies in images of the harem where accusations of lesbianism
are often more explicit).[55] The way that Jameson resolves the
problem of the routine demonizing of the Roman Catholic other
is to contain the negative side of Catholic devotion in her picture
of contemplative orders. This produces the social-working Sisters
of Charity as exemplary Christian, rather than Roman Catholic,
women – a role model that should, and could, be available to
upright Protestant British ladies. Similarly, Browne's technique
and choice of subject, combined with her authorial persona as a
known to be respectable French lady artist operate within critical
categories of art to secure a safe place in Britain for *The Sisters
of Charity* that allows it to avoid being overwhelmed by the negative associations of nursing orders.

Indeed, Browne's Frenchness and Catholicism may well have
been integral to the acceptability of *The Sisters of Charity*; naturalizing as alien and other a version of the nun that was at that
very moment threatening to transform British religious life and
the role of women in society. (Thus, the confusion over the specifics
of the title can be subsumed under the generic foreignness and
Catholicism associated in Britain with either appellation.) In
Britain, if Browne – a French woman and a Roman Catholic
could be uncontentious about an issue currently occupying the
minds of the British then it is hardly surprising that she managed
to be so in relation to the more marginal subject of Orientalism.
In contrast, the importance of her early paintings in France
emerges retrospectively when they are re-examined as forerunners
to the Orientalist subjects which were to excite the French art
public in the 1860s and 1870s.[56]

ORIENTALISM IN THE VISUAL ARTS

If Browne's representations of nuns were particularly well
received in Britain, her first Orientalist subjects fairly exploded
onto the French art scene. In 1861 she exhibited two paintings
at the Paris Salon entitled *Une visite (intérieur de harem;
Constantinople, 1860)* (Plate 13) and *Une joueuse de flûte (intérieur
de harem, Constantinople, 1860)* (Plate 12). Referred to generally
as the *Interiors*, these paintings of the Oriental harem – a site

forbidden to Western men – received a large amount of (conflict-ing) critical coverage. In France they prompted Théophile Gautier, who had already published an account of his visit to Turkey,[57] to exclaim that '[o]nly women should go to Turkey'. In Britain they were largely ignored, although at least one (and it is impossible to ascertain which) of the *Interiors* was on show at Gambart's French Gallery in 1862, when it did get some coverage in the British art press. This was the first and last time that Browne explicitly turned to this presumably lucrative and certainly high-profile subject; she continued to produce Orientalist subjects but tended to restrict herself to pictures of children, schools and scholars and individual ethnographic types.

In both Britain and France Orientalism was a popular area of representation. Its critical status was higher in France, where several of the Salon's most prestigious painters regularly selected Orientalist subjects. The popularity of Oriental themes was due to both the conscious deployment of the Fine Arts in the imperial project and the opportunities in technique and content offered by the new sights and colours associated with the East. The French interest in Orientalism began with the first generation of painter-explorers who brought back images of deserts, souks and odalisques that were to become the key tropes of Orientalist painting. Decamps, though obscure today, was the most esteemed Orientalist of his day (1813–60). His impasto and chiascuro tech-nique is often characterized as a glamorous and dramatic vision of the East. But significantly for our analysis, he also painted numerous vignettes of Oriental children that whilst connoting Oriental otherness bear more relation to the mischievous urchins of Southern Europe than to the brutality and sexuality of his adult Orient (see Plate 14). By the 1860s the French tradition had devel-oped into the glossy eroticism typified by Gérôme, whose luscious canvases were invariably greeted with praise for his technique and horror at the immorality of his subject choice.

The British tradition of Orientalism was far less obviously sala-cious. It is typified by the archaeological landscapes of David Roberts, the illustrated travelogues of Edward William Lane and Edward Lear, the detailed and allegedly well-researched pictures of John Frederick Lewis and the typological biblical canvases of William Holman Hunt. Specifically in relation to Turkey, much visual information in the eighteenth and early nineteenth century derives from Luigi Mayer's *Views in the Ottoman Dominions*

(1810), compiled under the aegis of the British ambassador to Constantinople, and Thomas Allom's topographical painting from his visit in the late 1830s. In the nineteenth century British Orientalist painting was an altogether smaller field than in France. Its concern with ethnography and topography was of course informed by the vision of the Orient as different, exotic and archaic, but it tended to avoid the overtly sexual subjects popularized by leading French artists. Instead of explicit sexual fantasies, British Orientalism concerned itself with the anthropological chronicling of lives and customs with an emphasis on exotica and difference.

Typical of this tendency is J.F. Lewis, whose detailed paintings were widely accepted as authentic, since he had lived in Cairo from 1842 to 1851 – although most of his paintings were made in the studio from sketches on his return to Britain. Like Browne his paintings were praised for their accuracy and detail, enhanced by his almost photo-realist watercolour technique (much admired by Gautier and Ruskin). He often painted clothed Oriental women going about their lives which, like *The Arab Scribe, Cairo* (1852, Plate 15) and *The Reception* (1873, Plate 16) are not unlike Browne's in subject. But in Lewis' paintings, although the figures are dressed, we find more emphasis on the luxury and exotica associated with the Orientalist fantasy (the gazelle, the pool, the young Black male servant and intricately inlaid windows and floors). Lewis provides a beautiful and less morally troubling Orient than Gérôme, relying on spectacle, authenticity and humour for effect. Although he represents women as active social beings, rather than just as passive objects, he still maintains the erotic charge of the harem: typical of his work is the considerable bosom revealed by the reclining déshabille of the sleeping figure in *The Siesta* (1876, Plate 17).

Although European Orientalism was a heterogeneous phenomenon, it can be argued that the cult of the harem was central to the fantasies that structure Orientalist discourse. The mystique of the forbidden harem stemmed from the vision of it as a segregated space, a polygamous realm, from which all men except the husband (generally conceptualized as the Sultan) and his eunuchs were barred. Although some artists include the Sultan, eunuchs or male guards at the harem entrance, the presence of men is most often signified by their absence. The erotic charge of the harem has two main trajectories: the fulfilment of seeing the forbidden faces and bodies of Muslim women; and the fantasy of one man's sexual ownership of many women. In addition to this is the persistent but less obviously articulated frisson of the women's sexual (lesbian) activities in the master's absence. As in Orientalist discourse, where the harem women's existence centres around the absent and controlling man, Orientalist paintings are organized by the needs of the absent and controlling Western viewer; women bathe and prepare themselves for the Sultan/ husband and by proxy for the artist and viewer. Harem pictures are generally scenes of minimal activity where the location simply provides a new setting for a single or group nude with the added pleasure of seeing the forbidden. The represented women rarely interact with each other as they do in Browne's *Interiors*. Typical of the representation of the harem as a frozen tableau of erotic ennui are Jean-Auguste-Dominique Ingres' *Bain turq* (1862, Plate 18) and Jean-Jules-Antoine Lecomte du Nouy's *White Slave Girl* (1888, Plate 19), where the dark skinned woman's gaze fails to connect with the foreground figure who stares into space as we (and the Black woman?) admire her.[58] Although Browne is unusual, she is not alone in picturing Oriental women in a more flexible relationship to social and private spaces than the stereotypically enclosed walls of the fantasy seraglio. There always was a body of work that represented women's access to other sites (balconies, gardens, journeys) although the manner of representation may have retained the myth of sexuality and indolence.[59] Gautier's characteristically prosaic acceptance of Turkish customs gives way to a fantasy rhetoric of longing and excess when he discusses the hidden women of the harem.

> I could not forbear to think of all the wealth of loveliness thus lost to human sight; the marvellous types of Grecian, Circassian, Georgian, and Indian beauty, which fade there, without having been reproduced or perpetuated, by the pencil or the chisel ... Violantés, without a Titian; and Fornarinas, to whom no Raphael will ever be known ...

> Speak to me of the Padischa! – the Sultan! ... whose eye rests only upon forms the most perfect, never sullied by mortal gaze; – forms which pass from the cradle to the tomb, guarded by sexless monsters, in those magnificent solitudes which the boldest dare not seek to penetrate; and surrounded by a mystery and seclusion which offers no scope to even the most vague desire.[60]

This eruption of lyricism anticipates his level of excitement eight years later when Browne's *Interiors* promised to decode the mysteries of the 'hermetically sealed' harem (a zone that is also, he notes, forbidden to Muslim men other than brothers and fathers). Gautier's stress on the hidden pleasures of the harem is symptomatic of Orientalist discourse, where the secret of conquering the East is conceptualized as the breaching of the harem's walls. Not for nothing did the subject predominate in art and literature of the period.[61] But Gautier also reveals the vulnerability of the desirous Western man whose wants make him gullible to ruses pretending to offer access.

Although Orientalism was a popular genre, many critics in France and Britain had trouble approving its morally dubious subjects, regardless of the artist's gender. It was not simply that some subjects were morally disturbing and others were not (although some undeniably caused more problems than others) but that subjects became disturbing when treated in morally dubious ways. This inevitably brought into question the morals of the artist which, as we have seen, was often articulated most clearly in the mixed reception of Gérôme's work.

Linda Nochlin has analysed how Gérôme's use of detail authenticates the Oriental setting of his salacious scenes and presents the pictures as a slice of life, thus obscuring the presence of the artist and facilitating a voyeuristic viewing position for the Western audience without implicating them in the (often) tawdry, un-Christian, but nonetheless titillating scenes on display.[62] One of the most obvious differences between Browne's *Interiors* and Nochlin's example of Gérôme's *Slave Market* (Plate 11) and *Snake Charmer* is Browne's lack of luscious surface and opulent detail. The critics who, as we will see, berate Browne for abandoning and therefore throwing into question Decamps' tradition of Orientalism (of which Gérôme is heir) are not just defending a favourite artist. The detailed luxury of that strand of Orientalism is an important part of the discursive construction of the Orient as other and inferior to the West. As Nochlin points out, luscious detail allows the eye to feast on the beauty of the painting as a whole and reduces the Oriental figures to just one more interesting, exotic and potentially dehumanized detail, effectively distancing us from them, their context and the power relations of the picture. In Britain and France critics struggled to contain their admiration for Gérôme's skill

with their repugnance at his immoral subjects. In 1868, reviewing Gérôme's thirteen paintings on display at the 1867 Paris
Exposition Universelle, the *Art Journal* is again highly critical:
'Heartlessness, cruelty, lust, Gérôme has glorified, while that
which is noblest in humanity his pictures ignore or outrage'.[63]
The writer then goes on to praise Browne (who exhibited eight
paintings) for producing virtuous scenes which appear to have no
links with the errors of her compatriot and arch Orientalist. The
same issue comments on the authenticity and charm of *Rhodian
Girl* and *Israelite School at Tangiers* in its review of Gambart's
London exhibition, illustrating how Browne's work managed to
run along parallel tracks, activating the interest in the Orient
but avoiding charges of immorality. Nation-specific criticisms of
her work tend to avoid the outrage levelled at Gérôme. Gérôme,
despite his fame, was persistently criticized in Britain as embodying the worst of all that was French: '[his style] is, for
the most part, a finished effeminacy, [his subject], but too often,
a culpable lasciviousness ... The evil vein which so notoriously
and lamentably permeates French novel literature, is here
fully and execrably exemplified and emulated'.[64] Generally it
is Gérôme's technical skill that saves him from total condemnation, but in this review it is his technique itself that
denotes sexual deviance (his effeminacy). Combined with an
analysis of his content as morally culpable the hero of beautifully
constructed patriarchal fantasies is demoted to the level of eunuch
or demasculinized/emasculated man.

The French press obviously does not blame Gérôme's faults on
his nationality. Vignon in *Journal des desmoiselles* deplores his
choice of subjects in 1861 and advised her young readers against
joining the crowds around his paintings. But, writing the same
year in *Le Correspondent*, she does not berate Gérôme in the
same way, leading me to assume that readers of *Le Correspondent*
are considered more able to withstand the shock of Gérôme's
canvases than the dear desmoiselles. The 1867 *Revue du monde
catholique*'s Salon review of Gérôme's *Slave Market* is torn
between admiring his skill, condemning his taste and condemning
the iniquities of the slavers.

> ... the foul Jew puts his fingers into her mouth and forces her
> to open it wide to show that the teeth are intact ... Shame,
> shame, to represent such scenes in which the brutal indecency

adds nothing to our horror of the abominable moors. It is not difficult however to recognize that there is always talent there, great talent . . .[65]

Bourniol puts his finger on the problem; the paintings rely on the assumption that the civilized and superior Western viewer will deplore slavery and hence read the painting 'properly'. But nothing in the construction of the picture flouts the traditions of voyeurism and the nude to disallow the viewer's pleasure in the scene. The review struggles to condemn the content (slavery – here displaced onto bad Arabs and Jews) and save the artist (the esteemed Frenchman who chooses to paint such deplorable scenes). We will see later how this journal is one of the few to level similar accusations of insufficiently clear moral values at Browne's paintings.

Given that women's accession to both colonial subjectivity and cultural production was filtered through discourses of femininity as well as nation, the search for imperial culture made by women must relate to the different, gendered, axis of women's experience of empire. This means extending the boundaries of Orientalism to include the productions of amateur as well as professional artists. (Whether in Surrey or Syria the women of the ruling classes engaged in the accomplishment arts and social niceties that anchored their classed and gendered sensibilities). The existence of Orientalist images made by amateur women artists, which had a predominantly or even exclusively family audience, illustrates the pervasiveness of imperialism and ideologies of racial difference in the formation of specifically female social and subjective matrixes.

Briony Llewelyn is inclined not to categorize women's amateur art as Orientalism since she thinks it displays not so much a (learned) interest in Oriental culture as a tourist's desire to sketch picturesque views and people.[66] Most of the visual Orientalism produced by women was topography in the form of sketches and watercolours made during trips abroad. Because the images often served as mementos of journeys and holidays, women were more likely to paint out of the way places that appealed to them, or had pleasurable memories, as well as the sites of famous ruins as immortalized by Roberts. The Searight Collection at the Victoria and Albert Museum in London contains examples of this type of amateur production: landscapes by Maria Harriet Matthias (active

1856–7, see Plate 20) and an album of sketches by Charlotte Inglefield and her family (d. 1901) that concentrates on landscape and street sights curious to Western eyes.

But I would claim that much of this work can indeed be included under the remit of Orientalism because the inscribed mode of viewing is based on an Orientalist paradigm of difference and superiority. Further, we may learn just as much about contemporary attitudes from the tourist's unselfconscious selection of significant sights as from the more overtly mediated subject choice of the professional artist. But the inclusion of Oriental subjects in amateur art is not a neutral event – although rich women may have sketched regularly whatever the location, they always made choices about which subjects were suitable based on prevailing aesthetic and social value systems. The very acceptability of Oriental lands and peoples as subjects for amateur art attests to the hegemonic status of imperial and Orientalist ideologies. In addition, as Melman's research indicates, it was often an Orientalist or imperialist motivation that took women to the East in the first place: in her sample of evangelical women missionaries it is clear that painting and sketching served a crucial function in their spiritual appreciation of the Biblical landscape.[67]

Opportunities for women and men to travel were increasing. The extension of industry and empire had combined new technology and terrain to open up the globe for more comfortable and accessible travel than ever before. Men who worked abroad in business or colonial administration were often, and in our period increasingly, accompanied by sisters, wives and daughters. The tourist industry had begun and the rich could now visit, with relative ease, parts of the world that hitherto had been the goal of only the hardiest explorers.[68] For rich women, travel to the East or Africa became less foreboding as social networking extended beyond Europe into the colonies and areas of Western influence. The chance of independence and freedom from the restraints of polite society that inspired the generations of women travellers and explorers, as well as the dangers and hardships that marked their journeys, were mostly eradicated from the newly colonized and 'civilized' areas of North Africa and the East that were now appearing in the press as favoured destinations for holiday tours.[69] Unless one travelled into the interior away from the main centres of European influence it would have been difficult to avoid contact with expatriate and travelling communities. Indeed,

Melman suggests that the model of the travelling spinster lady was atypical and that most women travelling or working in the Orient were there as the companion to a male relative. In this Browne was typical.

In relation to art, the greater experience of travel outside Western Europe blurred the differences between conventions of the picturesque and Orientalism, leading to an overlap between the two areas of representation. Orientalism, as a mode of viewing based on difference and Western superiority becomes both more overtly available to women (who have more first-hand experience) and more pervasively implicit in the experience and representation of non-Western Europe (perceived as similarly 'primitive'). It is against this backdrop of Europeanization that Browne's trips to the East need to be placed. These journeys cannot be separated from French imperial interests even where they were not specifically initiated by de Saux's diplomatic obligations. They would have brought them into contact with new and known members of the French diplomatic and European ruling-class communities abroad. However, none of the contemporary accounts of Browne's travels treat them as anything other than a productive excursion on the part of a member of the fashionable sophisticated rich. T. Chasrel, in an 1877 retrospective of Browne in the French periodical *L'Art*, highlights the stresses of painting in a hot climate, but does not suggest that such activities are unsuitable for a woman.[70] But his comment that '[i]n addition to enlarging the framework of her talent they [her travels] also assured her the liberty to paint' is highly unlikely: as the wife of a diplomat, Browne's household and social duties would simply have been transposed from Paris to Constantinople. Accounts of colonial expatriate society paint a world where social interaction mattered more not less, and if anything, was more rather than less time-consuming than at home. Chasrel's commentary, for all its apparent sympathy, misrecognizes the boundaries and function of women's apparent leisure.

As we have seen, the relationship between amateur and professional women artists was fraught with difficulties. Although many European women chose a life of travel as an escape from the constraints of life at home, the heightened stress on conformity and manners that characterized expatriate society meant that women artists in the Orient may well have had even less chance of breaking out of the clearly gendered spaces of proper society.

All Western women would have found themselves caught up in a similarly gendered interaction with the Orient – professional women not only occupied similar social spaces to non-professionals, but also shared a gendered access to representation, in terms of subject, technique, and often reception.

The number of professional women artists who painted Orientalist subjects grew as the century wore on (due in part to the increased ease and safety of travel). As might be expected, the majority stuck to safely feminine areas of representation such as topography, portraiture, children and ethnographic types (among which can be included some of Browne's work). Others, however, ventured into what we might consider to be the more dangerously immoral area of the Orientalist pseudo-classical nude. Whilst there were some artists whose work clearly fell into one camp rather than another, many women painted both 'feminine' cameos of Oriental daily life and nudes and odalisques. The range of subjects and styles adopted by women artists in relation to the Orient suggests that the boundaries of the field were more fluid than had previously been supposed and also indicates the changing nature of women's relationship to art. Certainly, by the 1880s when the British artist Margaret Murray Cookesley (d. 1927) was exhibiting, her pseudo-classical Oriental nudes appear to have been quietly received; her *Nubian Girl* of 1886 (Plate 21) leans against an urn, proudly bare-chested, clad only in an 'Oriental' drape and was shown to no great notoriety.

Cookesley's work is very similar to mainstream British Orientalism of the 1880s and does not appear to have been discussed as a particularly authentic view of the harem. Although she did travel to the Middle East, I think her work largely reproduces the generic codes of Orientalism that were challenged by the work of other women artists like Browne. Cookesley's scenes of the harem (like *Entertaining in the Harem*, 1894 and *Smoking the Pipe*, 1893, Plates 22 and 23) are obviously cobbled together Oriental-ish tableaux (the women in both paintings wear the same pseudo-classical drapery). Rather than indicating anything about the specificity of the female gaze, these paintings demonstrate that Orientalism was, by the turn of the century, so large and popular a field that anyone could venture in without necessarily being understood to be making a major intervention. In addition, the increased availability of art education and the life class for women means that we should expect to see larger numbers of women participating in all areas of cultural production.

More difficult to explain or categorize is the mixed oeuvre of the Polish/Danish artist Elisabeth Jerichau-Baumann (1819–1881) – noted by the *Art Journal* as having 'sometimes been under obligation' to Browne[71] – who enjoyed popularity as a portraitist in royal courts of Europe and the Orient in the 1860s and 1870s.[72] Apart from portraits, Jerichau-Baumann's work consisted of cameos of daily life (see, for example, *A Turkish Beauty with her Nurse and Child*, 1880, Plate 24) including several pictures of Fellaheen women and their children as well as some which, like *Vandbaersker* (1875, Plate 25) and *An Odalisque* (n.d., Plate 26), contain a level of nudity that seems surprising for a woman artist of this period. Jerichau-Baumann exhibited in Britain and France from the 1860s, building a thriving portrait practice in Europe and, upon travelling to North Africa and the Middle East armed with introductions from European royalty, gained entry into Oriental high society where she received several portrait commissions from the royal families of Turkey and Egypt.[73] It seems that one way in which these potentially transgressive pictures were legitimized was in terms of prevailing discourses of ethnography; The *Art Journal* praises Jerichau-Baumann's semi-naked women in terms of her 'pronouncedly ethnographical' style and accurate depiction of 'nationality'.[74] Thus, a space is opened up for women to paint the nude if such images could be favourably received because, like Jerichau-Baumann's use of Oriental settings and accoutrements, they could be coded as authentic (pseudo) scientific enquiry.[75] How else can the British bourgeoisie invite Jerichau-Baumann into their respectable homes to paint their daughters?[76]

There are a number of British women artists whose Orientalist subjects were generally less contentious. Eliza Fox Bridell, who originally exhibited genre and portraiture, later built a reputation for Oriental landscapes after a sojourn in Algeria in 1863.[77] Mrs. Clayton noted that Bridell, like other women travellers and artists, benefited from contacts with high-ranking officials in the East; again emphasizing the variety of ways in which women travellers were dependent on expatriate society. Emily Mary Osborne (b. 1834), a successful artist best known for her scenes of social commentary, also travelled and painted landscapes in Algeria.[78] Likewise, Sophie Anderson (1823–1903), who is best known for

Italianate genre scenes and fancy images of children, also painted Orientalist subjects, including *In the Harem, Tunis* (n.d., Plate 27) and the *Portrait of Toklihili, The Indian Princess*, (n.d., Plate 28). Other artists include the feminist campaigner Barbara Leigh Smith Bodichon (1827–91), who travelled to and painted landscapes of North Africa,[79] Edith Martineau (1842–1909), who exhibited ethnographic portrait types (such as *Head of a Balkan*, 1867) and Frances E. Nesbitt (1864–1934), who painted watercolours of local life in North Africa and Palestine. In France, the Princess Mathilde Bonaparte (1820–1904), Jaqueline Commère Paton (b. 1859) and Laure Houssaye de Léoménil (1806–66) sent Orientalist subjects to the Salon.[80] Like Browne, most of these women produced a mixed oeuvre, different elements of which achieved prominence at various stages of their careers. (We shall be returning to some of these artists later.)

Despite women's evident involvement in Orientalism, they were still treated as a special case by critics as well as facing the usual discriminatory treatment given to women's art. Some of the problems posed by women artists using Orientalist subjects can be clarified by looking at their work in relation to gender and genre. In relation to gender we have seen how the biographical knowledge of the gendered artist was an important part of interpretation: in Browne's case, her venture into what was seen as the possibly immoral sphere of Orientalism was safeguarded from moral danger by artist-centred commentaries that produced the paintings as worthy offerings from a morally respectable brush. In relation to genre, the tendency to read them as womanly representations of a womanly space, situates them within the strong moral narratives associated with domestic genre painting, a transposition of the paradigm of domestic genre painting for which she was already famous. This is assisted by Browne's choice of some subjects (portraits, family, the education and care of children and devotional scenes) and avoidance of others (slave markets, prostitutes, executions and low-life street scenes) which again minimized the deviation of a female Orientalist. Although all Orientalist subjects could be imbued with sexuality by the West, Browne rarely enters such dangerous waters. One exception (apart from the obvious case of the harem) is her 1869 painting *Dancers in Nubia, Assouan* (Plate 29), a subject with the potential for overt immorality that she usually avoided.

But her first Orientalist subjects were hard to ignore. They were not innocuous landscapes or genre pieces transplanted to the Orient. They marked a deliberate and, I would argue, necessarily self-conscious foray into the key myth of Orientalism: the forbidden harem. As such they posed a conundrum within the logic of Orientalism: although only a woman could report accurately on this enticing subject, the resulting information threatened to challenge long-cherished fantasies and invalidate the vision of established male Orientalist artists. Griselda Pollock in an extension of the point that I discussed in Chapter 1 – that the act of painting is itself constitutive of sexual difference – argues that the social spaces open to and occupied by women artists are linked not only to the spaces they represent but also to the viewing position inscribed in the paintings.

The space of the look [of the producer] at the point of production will to some extent determine the viewing position of the spectator at the point of consumption.[81]

If we take from this the argument that the social spaces occupied by Browne the painter will have a determining effect on the subjects she can paint and the viewing position they foreground, we begin to conjecture how her take on the Orient will be different, and differently received, to that of men. This is not because her gender makes for an innate empathy with Oriental women, but because the (gendered) enunciative position from which she represents will affect the choice of both subject and technique. Thus, the social, historical, racialized and gendered specificities of Browne's Orientalism cannot but deconstruct a homogeneous notion of Orientalism, indicating instead a discursive field of multiple voices and visions.

NOTES

1 The *Athenaeum*, August 1859, p. 213.
2 Larrouse also suggests that her anglicized surname might have contributed to her success in Britain. Pierre Larrouse, *Grand dictionnaire universel de XIXe siècle*, Paris, 1864–76, p. 1325.
3 The *Athenaeum*, August 1859, p. 213.
4 I am grateful to Anne Summers for her comments on this issue. See also, Anne Summers, *Angels and Citizens: British Women as Military Nurses 1854–1914*, London, Routledge, 1988.
5 The *Art Journal*, September 1859, p. 291.

6 See Geoffrey Rowell, *The Vision Glorious: Themes and Person-alities of the Catholic Revival in Anglicanism*, Oxford, Oxford University Press, 1983; Peter F. Anson, *The Call of the Cloister: Religious Communities and Kindred Bodies in the Anglican Communion*, London, S.P.C.K., 1964, pp. 25–8; Summers, *Angels and Citizens*.

7 This was not without tensions: working-class nurses being represented by Nightingale *et al.* as unhygienic. Anne Summers, 'Pride and Prejudice: Ladies and Nurses in the Crimean War', in *History Workshop Journal*, no. 16, Autumn, 1983.
     The definition of 'decent' nurses excluded racialized as well as classed others. See Ziggi Alexander and Audrey Dewjee (eds), *Wonderful Adventures of Mrs Seacole in Many Lands*, (1857), second edition, Bristol, Falling Wall Press, 1984.

8 However, the sisters' status as brides of Christ was an acrimonious issue in the Anglican Church. See Susan Casteras, 'Virgin Vows: The Early Victorian Artists' Portrayal of Nuns and Novices', in *Victorian Studies*, no. 2, vol. 24, Winter 1981.

9 A heated debate about the cloistered life was carried out in fiction where a series of tractarian novels celebrating the spiritual fervour of the convent was rigorously countered by a campaign of anti-Revivalist stories produced by adherents of the evangelical Churches and scorn from the mainstream. As with any type of literary produc-tion in this period, we find many women listed among the authors on both sides. See A. L. Drummond, *The Churches in English Fiction*, Leicester, Backus, 1950.

10 *Punch* 19, 19 October 1850 p. 163, in Casteras, 'Virgin Vows'.

11 Charles Kingsley, *Yeast, a Problem*, London, 1860.

12 She finds that although images of nuns in the first three decades of the nineteenth century were not unknown, they were quite rare, whereas from 1839 to the end of the century at least one such subject was on display at the Royal Academy or British Institution every year. Casteras, 'Virgin Vows'.

13 See, Lindsay Errington, *Social and Religious Themes in English Art 1848–1860*, New York, Garland, 1984; Jan Marsh, *Pre-Raphaelite Women: Images of Femininity in Pre-Raphaelite Art*, London, Weidenfeld and Nicolson, 1987; Susan Casteras, *Images of Victorian Womanhood in English Art*, London, Associated University Press, 1987.

14 It was only after being personally assured by Collins that he had ended his association with Anglo-Catholicism that Ruskin revised his opinion and accorded the picture moderate praise. John Ruskin, in *The Times*, 13 May 1851 and 31 May 1851, quoted in Casteras, 'Virgin Vows', p. 173.

15 Although the *Athenaeum* comments on the 'awkwardness and weak-ness of the woman using the unaccustomed spade' and the nuns' 'hard and painful faces', I take this to be an approving interpretation of these details as criticism of the hardships of convent life. The *Athenaeum*, 1859, p. 586.

16 Casteras, *Images*, p. 178.
17 See Casteras, 'Virgin Vows', pp. 174–5.
18 Casteras, 'Virgin Vows', pp. 180–2.
19 See Linda Nochlin, *Realism*, Harmondsworth, Penguin, 1978, pp. 82–8; Theodore Zeldin, *France 1848–1945, Vol. 2: Intellect, Taste and Anxiety*, Oxford, The Clarendon Press, 1977, section 20, part III.
20 See Fred Orton and Griselda Pollock, 'Les Données Bretonnantes: La Prairie de Représentation' in *Art History*, vol. 3, no. 3, September 1980; Griselda Pollock, 'Van Gogh and the Poor Slaves: Images of Rural Labour as Modern Art', in *Art History*, vol. 11, no. 3, September 1988; Michael Orwicz, 'Criticism and Representations of Brittany in the Early Third Republic', in *Art Journal*, vol. 46, no. 4, Winter, 1987; Nicholas Green, *The Spectacle of Nature: Landscape and Bourgeois Culture in Nineteenth-Century France*, Manchester, Manchester University Press, 1990.
21 The *Art Journal*, May 1868, p. 53. See also the *Art Journal* 1862, p. 166 and 1868, p. 12.
22 See J.P.T. Bury, *France 1814–1940*, (1949) fifth edition, London, Methuen, 1985, pp 79–97
23 The Christian press regularly reviewed the Salon, and although not all titles covered it each year, the recurrence of the same writers in different publications suggests that there was an elite of Christian writers specializing in art criticism.
24 A. de Belloy, 'Salon de 1859', in *L'Artiste*, vol. 6, 24 April 1859, pp. 257–9.
25 Théophile Gautier, 'Exposition de 1859', in *Le Moniteur universel*, September 1859, p. 831.
26 Although Gautier moved in elevated court and artistic circles and was noted for the inclusiveness of his reviews, rarely leaving anyone out, he cannot be dismissed as a sycophant; his reviews were accessible, widely read and profoundly influential. See Joseph C. Sloane, *French Painting Between the Past and the Present: Artists, Critics and Traditions from 1848–1870*, Princeton, Princeton University Press, 1951, chs. 2 and 7.
27 Claude Vignon, 'Causerie artistique: Salon de 1859', in *Journal des desmoiselles*, June and July 1859, p. 193.
28 Every issue has fashion plates reproduced in colour; paper patterns for dressmaking, embroidery and lace-making; musical scores; and articles of an edifying and respectable tone. Whilst the colour reproductions mark the magazine as an expensive, luxury commodity affordable only to the very wealthy, the presence of paper patterns suggests a middle-bourgeois reader who either makes her own clothes or takes patterns to a dressmaker (rather than patronizing a couturier). I am indebted to Kate Stockwell for this last point.
    Whilst Bellanger includes *Journal des desmoiselles* in his list of 'la presse enfantine', I think we can safely assume its readership to have been young and adolescent women, rather than actual children. The dress designs are for adults and Vignon's comments about marriage in a later issue indicate the assumed proximity

of such an event in her readers' lives. Claude Bellanger, *Histoire générale de la presse française*, Paris, Universitaires de France, 1969.

29 See Charlotte Yeldham, *Women Artists in Nineteenth-Century France and England. Their Art Education, Exhibition Opportunities and Membership of Exhibiting Societies and Academies, with an Assessment of the Subject Matter of their Work and Summary Biographies*, New York, Garland, 1986, p. 345.

30 Founded in 1858, the *Journal* joined the *Alexandria Magazine* to become, in 1866, the *Englishwoman's Review* which ran until 1910. Although the later *Review* adopted a current affairs, short report format, the *Journal* was more in the tradition of the review periodical with long features and greater arts coverage. Doughan and Sanchez cite a circulation of five hundred for the *Journal* but estimate that the actual readership was much greater. See David Doughan and Denise Sanchez, *Feminist Periodicals 1855–1984*, Brighton, Harvester Wheatsheaf, 1987, item 4.

31 A.B., 'Madame Henriette Browne', the *English Woman's Journal*, April 1 1860, pp. 85–92.

32 A.B., 'Madame Henriette Browne', pp. 86–7.

33 A.B., 'Madame Henriette Browne', p. 85.

34 A.B., 'Madame Henriette Browne', p. 89.

35 A.B., 'Madame Henriette Browne', p. 89.

36 Gloves were a key signifier of female respectability for women of all classes. See, Liz Stanley (ed.), *The Diaries of Hannah Cullwick. Victorian Maidservant*, London, Virago, 1984, p. 266, Davidoff, 'Class and Gender'; Heather Dawkins, 'The Diaries and Photographs of Hannah Cullwick', in *Art History*, vol. 10, no. 2, June 1987.

37 It is clear that many women in public life gave serious thought to the matter of personal style, using it to create a preferred image, be it arty, respectable or serious. As Cherry points out, whilst dress and demeanour would of course have signified to men, it was other women who were the most informed and acute observers of each others' style, as is suggested by the detailed tone of the *English Woman's Journal*. Deborah Cherry, *Painting Women: Victorian Women Artists*, London, Routledge, 1993, pp. 83–9.

38 We know this relationship was often remarked on, for Gambart, who was apparently protective of the Bonheur/Micas relationship, went to some trouble to quash rumours. It is impossible to know if this was a knowing defence of a lesbian relationship or a chivalrous protection of what he saw as an irreproachable friendship. See Alfred Boime, 'The Case of Rosa Bonheur: Why Should a Woman Want to be More Like a Man?', in *Art History*, vol. 4, no. 4, December 1981; Maas, pp. 75–80.

39 A.B., 'Rosa Bonheur: An Authorised Memoir', in the *English Woman's Journal*, vol. 1, no. 4, June 1858, p. 229.

40 A.B., 'Rosa Bonheur', p. 242.

41 A.B., 'Madame Henriette Browne', p. 89 (original emphasis).

42 A.B., 'Madame Henriette Browne', pp. 90–1.

43 A.B., 'Madame Henriette Browne', p. 90.

44 A.B., 'Madame Henriette Browne', p. 91.
45 See Errington, *Social and Religious*.
46 (Reverend) Charles Kingsley, 'Henrietta Browne's Picture of The Sisters of Charity', in *Fine Arts Quarterly Review*, no. 1, vol. 1, May 1863, pp. 299–300.
47 Kingsley, 'Browne', p. 303.
48 Kingsley, 'Browne', pp. 304–6.
49 Kingsley, 'Browne', p. 306.
50 See Lynda Nead, *Myths of Sexuality: Representations of Women in Victorian Britain*, Oxford, Blackwell, 1988, pp. 26–8.
51 The *Art Journal*, May 1868, p. 53.
52 Casteras, 'Virgin Vows', pp. 166–7.
53 Anna Jameson, *Sisters of Charity and the Communion of Labour: Two Lectures on the Employment of Women*, (1855) London, Longman, Brown, Green, Longmans and Roberts, 1859, p. 18.
54 Jameson, *Sisters of Charity*, p. 34.
55 And not only in the nineteenth century; Casteras also ignores the spectre of lesbianism implied by Jameson and reads her words as a criticism of enclosure and the Church's supplanting of parental or patriarchal authority. Despite the frequent use of loaded terms like 'unhealthy' and 'unnatural', Casteras fails to interrogate what such accusations might mean, leaving lesbianism as the unspoken of her text as well.
56 Olivier Merson introduces his review of Browne's harem subjects with reference to the English admiration for *The Sisters of Charity* and Larrouse also references her popularity across the Channel. Olivier Merson, *Exposition de 1861: La peinture en France*, Paris, Libraire de la Société des Gens de lettres, 1861, pp. 274–5.
57 Théophile Gautier, *Constantinople of Today*, (1853) trans. Robert Howe Gould, London, David Bogne, 1854.
58 For an exploration of the gendered gaze in relation to Ingres see Wendy Leeks, 'Ingres Other-Wise', in *Oxford Art Journal*, vol. 9, no. 1, 1986.
59 For examples see Lynn Thornton, *Women as Portrayed in Orientalist Painting*, Paris, Edition ACR, 1985.
60 Gautier, *Constantinople*, pp. 187–8.
61 Jacques Bosquet, in his review of dream narratives in Romantic literature, notes the predominance of fantasies of sexual access to the multitude of women in the harem. Jacques Bosquet, *Les themes du rêve dans la littérature Romantique*, Paris, 1964, in Rani Kabbani, *Europe's Myths of Orient*, London, Macmillan, 1986.
62 Nochlin, 'The Imaginary Orient', in *Art in America*, May 1993.
63 The *Art Journal*, May, 1868, p. 12.
64 The *Art Journal*, 1861, p. 183.
65 Bathild Bourniol, 'L'amateur au Salon', in *Revue du monde catholique*, no. 141, June 10, 1867, pp. 468–508.
66 Briony Llewelyn in personal conversation. See also Briony Llewelyn, *The Orient Observed: Images of the Middle East From the Searight Collection*, London, Victoria and Albert Museum, 1989.

67 See particularly the sections on Matilda M. Cubley's, *The Plains of Palestine*, 1860, in Billie Melman, *Women's Orients. English Women and the Middle East, 1718–1918*, Basingstoke, Macmillan, 1992, ch. 9.

68 See E.J. Hobsbawm, *The Age of Capital 1848–1875*, London, Weidenfeld and Nicolson, 1975, ch. 11 and *The Age of Empire 1874–1914*, London, Penguin, 1987; John Pudney, *The Thomas Cook Story*, London, The Non-Fiction Book Co., 1954.

69 See Dea Birkett, *Spinsters Abroad: Victorian Lady Explorers*, Oxford, Blackwell, 1989; Sara Mills, *Discourses of Difference: An Analysis of Women's Travel Writing and Colonialism*, London, Routledge, 1991.

70 T. Chasrel, 'Henriette Browne' in *L'Art revue hebdomadaire illustré*, vol. 2, 1877, pp. 97–103.

71 The *Art Journal*, June 1866, p. 194.

72 Clement, pp. 98–107; the *Art Journal*, 1869, p. 382, both in Yeldham, *Women Artists*, p. 348.

73 She wrote two books about her career and travels, including visits to harems in Constantinople, Smyna and Cairo. Elisabeth Jerichau-Baumann, *Brogede Rejsebilleder*, Copenhagen, Thieles Bogtrykkeri, 1881. See also Nicholaj Bøgh, *Elisabeth Jerichau-Baumann; En Karakteristik*, Copenhagen, Trykt hos J. Jørgenson and Co., 1886.

74 The *Art Journal*, 1871, p. 165.

75 For a more detailed analysis of the work of Jerichau-Baumann and Sophie Anderson see Reina Lewis, 'Women Orientalist Artists: Diversity, Ethnography, Interpretation', in *Women: A Cultural Review*, vol. 6, no. 1, 1995.

76 For example, the Royal Academy Index lists three portraits of English families in 1866 and 1867.

77 See Yeldham, *Women Artists*, p. 295.

78 See Nunn, *Victorian Women Artists*, London, The Women's Press, 1987, pp. 22–4.

79 See review of the Society of Female artists in the *Art Journal* 1868, p. 46.

80 See Chris Petteys, *Dictionary of Women Artists Born Before 1900*, Boston, G.K. Hall, 1985; and Thornton, *Women*.

81 Griselda Pollock, 'Modernity and the Spaces of Femininity,' in Pollock, 1987, p. 66.

Plate 1 Henriette Browne, *Les soeurs de charité, The Sisters of Charity*, 1859. Oil on canvas, 101.6 × 78.7cm. © 1992 Sotheby's, Inc. Courtesy of Sotheby's Inc., New York.

Plate 2 Henriette Browne, *La pharmacie, intérieur, The Convent Dispensary*, 1859. Materials and dimensions unknown. Photograph: the Witt Library, Courtauld Institute of Art.

Plate 3 Rosa Bonheur, *The Horse Fair*, 1855. Oil on canvas, 120 × 254cm. The Metropolitan Museum of Art, gift of Cornelius Vanderbilt, 1887 (87.25).

Plate 4 Elizabeth Butler, Lady Thompson, *Calling the Roll After an Engagement (The Roll Call)*, 1874. Oil on canvas, 91 × 182.9cm. The Royal Collection © Her Majesty Queen Elizabeth II.

Plate 5 Jean-Léon Gérôme, *Phryne Before the Areopagus*, 1861. Oil on canvas, 80 × 128cm. Hamburger Kunsthalle.

Plate 6 Charles Collins, *Convent Thoughts*, 1851. Oil on canvas, 82.6 × 57.8cm. Ashmolean Museum, Oxford.

Plate 7 John Everett Millais, *The Vale of Rest*, 1859. Oil on canvas, 102.9 × 172.7cm. Tate Gallery, London.

Plate 8 Alfred Elmore, *The Novice*, 1852. Oil on canvas, 73.7 × 90.2cm. Engraving after the painting in the *Art Journal*, no. 27, 1865. Courtesy of the Board of Trustees of Victoria and Albert Museum.

Plate 9 Henriette Browne, *Le catéchisme, The Catechism*, 1857. Oil on canvas, 54 × 46cm. Photograph courtesy of Sotheby's, London.

Plate 10 Charles Cope, *The Young Mother*, 1846. Oil on panel, 31.2 × 26cm. Courtesy of the Board of Trustees of Victoria and Albert Museum.

Plate 11 Jean-Léon Gérôme, *Slave Market*, n.d. Oil on canvas, 84.3 × 63cm. Stirling and Francine Clarke Art Institute, Williamstown, Massachusetts.

Plate 12 Henriette Browne, *Une joueuse de flûte (intérieur de harem, Constantinople, 1860), A Flute Player (Harem Interior; Constantinople, 1860)*, 1861. Oil on canvas, dimensions unknown. Photograph courtesy of the département des livres imprimés, Bibliothèque Nationale, Paris.

Plate 13 Henriette Browne, *Une visite (intérieur de harem, Constantinople, 1860), A Visit (Harem Interior; Constantinople, 1860)*, 1861. Oil on canvas, 86 × 114cm. Photograph courtesy of Sotheby's, London.

Plate 14 Alexandre Gabriel Decamps, *The Turkish School*, 1843. Materials and dimensions unknown. Amsterdams Historisch Museum – Fodor Collection.

Plate 15 John Frederick Lewis, *The Arab Scribe, Cairo*, 1852. Watercolour heightened with white, 46.3 × 60.9cm. Bridgeman Art Library.

Plate 16 John Frederick Lewis, *The Reception*, 1873. Oil on canvas, 63.5 × 72.6cm. Yale Centre for British Art, Paul Mellon Collection.

Plate 17 John Frederick Lewis, *The Siesta*, 1876. Oil on canvas, 87.5 × 109.4cm. The Tate Gallery, London.

Plate 18 Jean-Auguste-Dominique Ingres, *Bain Turq, The Turkish Bath*, 1862. Oil on canvas, 108cm diameter. Clichés des Musées Nationaux – Paris. © Photo R.M.N.

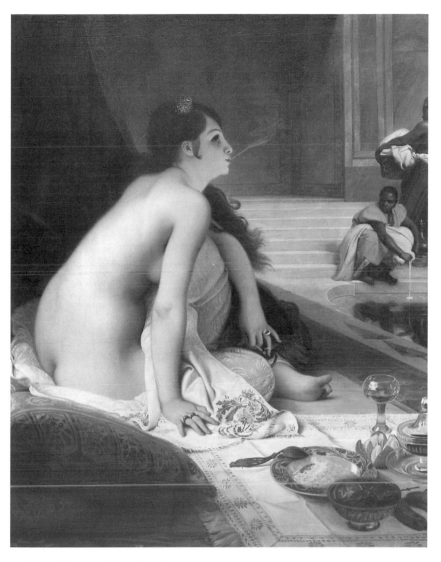

Plate 19 Jean-Jules-Antoine Lecomte de Nouy, *L'esclave blanche*, *The White Slave*, 1888. Oil on canvas, 146 × 118cm. Cliché Ville de Nantes – P. Jean.

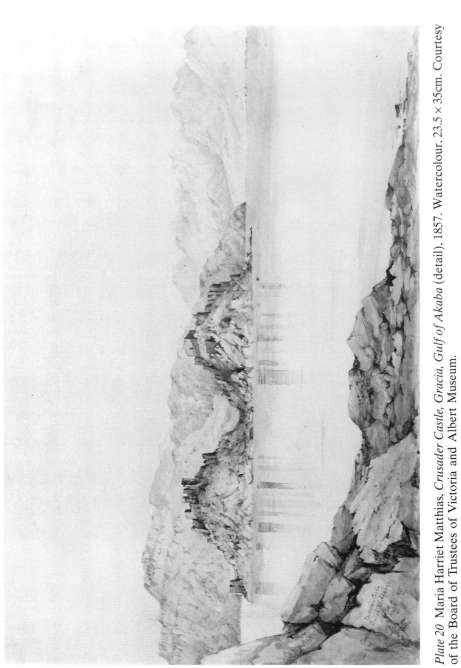

Plate 20 Maria Harriet Matthias, *Crusader Castle, Gracia, Gulf of Akaba* (detail), 1857. Watercolour, 23.5 × 35cm. Courtesy of the Board of Trustees of Victoria and Albert Museum.

Plate 21 Margaret Murray Cookesley, *Nubian Girl*, 1886. Materials and dimensions unknown. Courtesy Mathaf Gallery, London.

Plate 22 Margaret Murray Cookesley, *Entertaining in the Harem*, 1894. Oil on canvas, 29 × 39cm. Photograph courtesy of Sotheby's, London.

Plate 23 Margaret Murray Cookesley, *Smoking the Pipe*, 1893. Oil on panel, 30 × 46cm. Courtesy Mathaf Gallery, London.

Plate 24 Elisabeth Jerichau-Baumann, *A Turkish Beauty with Her Nurse and Child*, 1880. Oil on canvas, 60 × 80.5cm. Photograph courtesy of Sotheby's, London.

Plate 25 Elisabeth Jerichau-Baumann, *Vandbaersker*, 1875. Engraving, illustrated in Jerichau-Baumann, 1881. By permission of The British Library.

Plate 26 Elisabeth Jerichau-Baumann, *An Odalisque*, n.d. Oil on canvas, 99 × 74.2cm. Photograph courtesy of Christies, London.

Plate 27 Sophie Anderson, *In the Harem, Tunis*, n.d. Oil on canvas, 75.5 × 63cm. Photograph: the Witt Library, Courtauld Institute of Art.

Plate 28 Sophie Anderson, *Portrait of Toklihili, the Indian Princess*, n.d. Oil on canvas, 103 × 66cm. Photograph courtesy of Sotheby's, London.

Plate 29 Henriette Browne, *Danseuses en Nubie; Assouan, Dancers in Nubia, Assouan*, 1869. Engraving after the painting, illustrated in Chasrel, 1877. By permission of The British Library.

Plate 30 Henriette Browne, *La perruche, The Budgerigar*, 1875. Oil on canvas, 147.4 × 91.5cm. Russell-Cotes Art Gallery and Museum, Bournemouth.

Plate 31 Henriette Browne, *Jeune fille de Rhodes, Rhodian Girl*, 1867. Oil on canvas, 147.3 × 114.3cm. Photograph courtesy of the département des livres imprimés, Bibliothèque Nationale, Paris.

Plate 32 Henriette Browne, *Une école israélite à Tanger, Jewish School in Tangiers*, 1867. Engraving after the painting, illustrated in Chasrel, 1877. By permission of The British Library.

Plate 33 Frederick Goodall, *A New Light in the Harem*, 1884. Oil on canvas, 122.7 × 215.3cm. Board of trustees of the National Museums and Galleries on Merseyside (Walker Art Gallery, Liverpool).

Plate 34 Jean-Léon Gérôme, *Dance of the Almeh*, 1863. Oil on canvas, 50.2 × 81.3cm. The Dayton Art Institute, gift of Mr. Robert Badenhop.

Plate 35 Edward Lane, 'Dancing Girls', 1836. Engraving from a drawing by Lane in *Manners and Customs of the Modern Egyptians*. By permission of The British Library.

Plate 36 Henriette Browne, *L'étude du Coran*, *Egyptian Boys Chanting From the Qur'an*, 1869. Materials and dimensions unknown. Photograph courtesy of département des livres imprimés, Bibliothèque Nationale, Paris.

Plate 37 Henriette Browne, *A Turkish Scene*, 1864. Materials and dimensions unknown. Photograph: the Witt Library, Courtauld Institute of Art.

Plate 38 Henriette Browne, *Un bibliophile*, *A Scribe*, 1876. Oil on canvas, 62 × 50cm. Courtesy of Mathaf Gallery, London.

Plate 39 Henriette Browne, *Un poète; Les Coptes dans la Haute Égypt, A Poet: Copts in Upper Egypt*, 1874. Engraving after the painting, illustrated in *L'Art*. Photograph: Witt Library, Courtauld Institute of Art.

Plate 40 Sophie Anderson, *Guess Again*, 1878. Oil on canvas, 98.4 × 74.3cm. The FORBES Magazine Collection, New York.

Chapter 4

'Only women should go to Turkey'
Henriette Browne and the female Orientalist gaze

How did contemporary viewers respond when a properly respectable lady artist like Henriette Browne started to paint subjects drawn from the popular but morally contentious field of Orientalism? This chapter analyses responses to Browne's Orientalist paintings in relation to the field of men and women's visual Orientalism (as laid out in Chapter 3) and to written accounts of life in the harem by Occidental and Oriental women.

It is my contention that Browne's Orientalist work offers a feminized vision of the Orient; a choice and treatment of subjects that functions as an extension of the domestic narrative painting for which she was already famous. Her gaze on the Orient is both as woman and as Westerner: the enunciative position from which she paints foregrounds a relation to the Orient that, whilst it retains a sense of difference, challenges Western assumptions about the inimical otherness of the Orient. This is achieved by portraying points of similarity between the two – the Oriental domestic as analogy for the Occidental domestic. This marks a threat to the conventional assumption of absolute difference that is also a challenge to the West's assumption of absolute superiority. In offering this analysis, I am partially in accord with Billie Melman's work on nineteenth-century British women's written Orientalism. She argues that European women desexualized the harem, domesticating it to reproduce the *haremlik* (the segregated quarters of women and children) as an 'image of the middle-class "home": domestic, feminine and autonomous'.[1] I shall be analysing the transposition of Western concepts of femininity and domesticity in women's Orientalism in the rest of this chapter in order to see the ways in which Browne's work related to what we are now discovering to be the substantial and varied involvement of European women in the cultural codes of Orientalism. Also (and this is where I depart from Melman), I explore what those cultural interventions can tell us about the formation of imperial female subjectivities.[2] It will be argued that like other women travellers Browne retains a sense of difference from the Orient, despite the experience of points of similarity, that is not necessarily registered as pejorative in the totalizing sense characteristic of hegemonic Orientalist discourse. Instead, it is contingent on a gendered set of differentiations whose possibility of a total superiority is compromised by the parallels between Western and Eastern gender relations and by the gender-specific restrictions on women's activities in work, creativity and politics.

As in other chapters, I am drawing on contemporary art criticism to explore the meanings associated with Browne's paintings. The criticism's dispersion of Orientalist 'truths' about the harem will be counterposed by an alternative set of knowledges constructed through Western and Oriental women's reports of harem life. Therefore, I shall in fact be reading readings of Browne's images. In so doing I am not making assumptions about their accuracy but analysing the different discursive strategies that claimed for her the gendered authority associated with women's Orientalism. Thus, I shall be addressing both the critical tendency to read women's work as straightforwardly truthful and the autobiographical claim to an unprejudiced natural vision inherent in women's written accounts of the harem. These both will be regarded as (often conflicting) attempts to establish differently gendered knowledges about the East and West. As such, they will be used to provide an index to the issues at stake in the (female) representation of the harem rather than regarded as a truth of it. Note that whilst I refer to the harem in the singular, I am not suggesting that there is only one real harem or type of harem or, indeed, assessing how representations relate to the real thing. Rather, I treat the term 'harem' as a concept, a set of ideas that had an iconic status in the West at the same time as the word harem also designates the actual (and varied) living arrangements of women in Islamic households.[3] Looking at Browne's Orientalism in this context will allow us to explore how far a white Western woman could accede to the enunciative position of Orientalist discourse; or rather, to unpick the singularity of that positionality and reframe it in relation to the evident, if necessarily partial, access available to a gendered subject like Browne.

CRITICAL RESPONSES TO BROWNE'S *HAREM INTERIORS*, 1861

Browne's first Orientalist paintings, the two *Harem Interiors* (*A Visit: Harem Interior, Constantinople 1861*, Plate 11 and *A Flute Player, Harem Interior, Constantinople, 1861*, Plate 12) were shown at the Paris Salon in 1861 and caused a stir. Interest stemmed less from their artistic merit than from their being known to have been produced by a woman who claimed to have seen inside the harem. The reviews dealt in various ways with the contradictory dynamic in which, on one hand, women travellers' different access (real or imagined) to the forbidden territories of the harem appeared to offer a source of reliable information and, on the other, brought back 'evidence' that often conflicted with the West's cherished visions of the Orient.[4] This was true of the Orient in general: travellers wrote of the disappointment of coming face to face with landmarks, buildings and people that bore no relation to the splendour ascribed to them in Western legends.[5] Travel writers like Chateaubriand grappled with the desire to adulterate the truth in order to retain the vision that flourished in Europe. In painting, Ingres used Lady Mary Wortley Montagu's account of her visit to a Turkish bath as a source for his bath scenes, but ignored her insistence that the women's behaviour was perfectly proper when he wanted to produce a picture of sex and excess in keeping with Europe's treasured myths. Subsequently, an account like that offered by Browne was likely to be both welcome and contentious since its 'authentic' information was a potential challenge to Orientalist conventions. What is not explained by Melman's valuable account of the growing market for women's Orientalism (which was certainly well established by the mid-nineteenth century), is the persistence and longevity of hegemonic Orientalist tropes, even though it seems they were regularly disproved by readily available women's accounts. In what follows, I am concerned to see how the authenticity attributed to Browne's work – and here I agree with Melman that women's work was read as authentic on account of their presumed feminine empathy with their Oriental subjects[6] – was perceived as both a challenge to and potential support for elements of the Orientalist harem fantasy. The different critical strategies adopted in response to her paintings illustrate both the flexibility and the limits of the power/knowledge dialectic of Orientalist discourse.

The interpretations of the painting rely on the artist's presumed presence at the scene. This immediately disrupts the traditions of Western voyeurism outlined by Nochlin.[7] Rather than hide the presence of the Westerner at the scene, the construction of the paintings as testimony foregrounds the presence of the artist: the image would not have been possible if Browne had not been there, even though the figure of the artist is not actually depicted in the painting. Her presence is projected into the scene by a combination of the viewer's allegiance to Orientalist knowledges about the harem (in which a woman's view has a privileged access to a forbidden sight) and the pictures' traditional composition (where the viewing position accords with that of the artist) which lends itself to such a reading. Add to this Browne's existing reputation as a naturalistic painter who prioritized study from life to get her details right (remember the lengths she went to in order to get her hands on a real habit for *The Sisters of Charity*) and we have a painting whose meaning is inextricably linked to its point of production.

Browne's paintings are differently detailed from those of Gérôme. Where his display polished surfaces, opulent sets and lavish detail, hers are restrained in tone and understated in detail. Her different vision connotes an insider's knowledge rather than obscuring evidence of the artist's presence. This tautologically reinscribes the woman artist as the owner of the gaze that reveals the mysteries of the Orient. Browne does not use an armoury of detail and her finish is not that of the seamless, invisible brushwork practised by Gérôme. Some writers criticize her work as being too sketchy but this is a standard accusation levelled at women artists, and working from black and white photographs I cannot tell if this is an accurate description or unjustified criticism. The actual paintings of Browne's I have seen appear to be quite highly finished and no looser in brushwork than was usual in this period. Her relatively sparse compositions are seen by some as a fault in her technique and by others as proof of the reality of her version of the harem. For her supporters, the scarcity of detail is simultaneously a sign of the painting's veracity (Browne tells it is how it is) and a claim to fame for the artist who moves on from outmoded Orientalist conventions. Melman argues that women's Orientalism was seen to bear the mark of a particularly feminine eye for detail – men being inclined to ignore detail in their lofty contemplation of the whole – which was in turn tied back into women's presumed empathetic and experiential knowledge of the Orient. Thus, Browne's detail (though it is not lush it accords with other women's accounts of the *haremlik*) functions as both proof of her having been there and as substantiating her femininity.

Again, we find that the response to Browne's work is split across the French/English divide, but this time in reverse: where the religious and domestic narrative pictures had been hugely successful in Britain but marginal in France, the *Interiors* mark the start of her rising French reputation as an Orientalist but were practically ignored in Britain.

The British art press reviews of the 1861 Salon mention Browne but pay no attention to the Orientalist paintings that were so remarked upon in France. The exhibition of one of them at Gambart's also received scant critical attention. The *Art Journal* noted that the French Gallery's exhibition had popularized French artists and identifies Browne as a 'distinguished lady artist [like Rosa Bonheur]' but of the picture it merely mentions that it is 'widely differing from the "Soeurs de Charité" she has recently painted'.[8] The *Athenaeum* only records that Browne has sent in 'the fruit of a recent tour in her "Scene in the Seraglio" '.[9]

Does this silence mean that the British reviewers did not like her new work or that they did not see it as anything very different from the genre scenes that they expected from her easel? It is not that Browne is out of favour – in 1862 the *Art Journal* welcomes the publication of an engraving of *The Sisters of Charity* (a sure sign of popular status) – but the new work certainly does not arouse the same excitement as the religious scenes. That fewer British than French critics situate her work in relation to mainstream Orientalism may be accounted for by Orientalism's greater standing in the French art world. Also, Browne's work has a greater affinity with that of Lewis, Britain's leading exponent of Orientalism. In terms of British Orientalism, therefore, her work marks less of a departure than it did in France and was, perhaps, considered less remarkable. (Although, it must be noted, that there was sufficient interest in Britain in women's representation of the harem to sustain the publication of a quantity of women's written accounts: all the written sources I have used were available in English.)

As we shall see in relation to her later Orientalist subjects, the British reception of Browne's work tends to mobilize discourses of ethnography. It is possible that the presentation of the pictures with titles classifying subject and location in much the same way as an ethnographic case study mitigates her potentially illicit venture into the masculine and sexualized field of Orientalism: titles like this include, *A Turkish Scene* (1864, Plate 37), *Jeune fille de Rhodes* (Plate 31) and *Une école israélite à Tanger* (Salon and Exposition Universelle 1867, Gambart's 1868, Plate 32), *Danseuses en Nubie; Assouan* (Salon 1869, Plate 29) and *Les oranges; Haute Égypte* (Salon 1870, not illustrated).[10]

In France Théophile Gautier gives an enthusiastic reception to Browne's harem scenes. He valorizes the *Interiors* on the grounds that they are the realistic depiction of the eye-witness account only a woman could produce. His rhetoric expands this into a hyperbole asserting that there is no point in men visiting the Orient at all, since so much is hidden from them.

In Constantinople, when our curiosity is allowed to run the streets, enter the houses it irritates us to be unable to go past the selamlik with our cups of coffee and chibouks, we often say to ourselves 'Only women should go to Turkey – what can a man see in this jealous country? White minarets, guilloche[11] fountains, red houses, black cypresses, mangy dogs, hammals with loaded camels ... or photographs and optical views.' Nothing more. For a woman, on the contrary, the odalisque opens itself, the harem has no more mysteries; those faces, doubtless charming, for which the bearded tourist searches in vain ... she contemplates stripped of their veil, in all the brilliance of their beauty; the feredge [cloak], a domino from Islam's permanent carnival, could not conceal more gracious bodies and splendid costumes.[12]

The dream which we have Mme Browne has truly brought into realization; she has reported a new Orient fresher than those of the *Thousand and One Nights*, to which we must make a comparison.

A Visit shows us at last the interior of a harem by one who has seen it, a thing rare and perhaps unique, because however well male painters often do make odalisques, not one is able to boast of having worked from nature. – for architecture, don't go imagining an Alhambra or a fairy palace, but [instead] a very simple room, with some colonettes and white walls decorated with divans – The visitors arrive, the cadine receives them at the top of the stairs, they haven't yet taken off the yashmak and feredje, one is in red the other in blue, and the transparent muslin of their chinstrap allows one to see that both of them are pretty; they have brought with them a little girl. The harem women, sitting or rather squatting, on the divan, have the air of trying an activity which breaks into their nonchalance in order to celebrate the new arrivals. Their occupations were never very important, one was smelling a flower, and the other, leant against the partition of the wall, smoking a papipos – the cigarette of the Orient – when, as well they know, the narghile is beginning to go out of fashion there.

Nothing is as elegant as these long robes of such delicate colours, which trace the figure and give the body so much grace and svelteness. It makes us hold crinolines in horror! Above these long robes, like flowers on their stems, are poised fresh faces that cannot be imagined by one accustomed to European complexions, because they have never been exposed to the open air.[13]

Gautier's typically detailed descriptions of the paintings emphasize their ethnographic details.

A Flute Player initiates us into the diversions of the harem. Draped in white muslin, a young musician plays on a derviche's flute one of those melodies of strange charm which seizes you as if invisibly, and you recall the memories of airs heard in a previous existence; three women cadines or odalisques are listening leant against the wall in an attitude of ecstatic dreaming. One of the flute player's companions, recognizable by her guzla, teases a tortoise to crawl along on a stool. A third musician watches her do it.[14]

For him, Browne's entry into the female quarters marks out her paintings as real representations of the East as opposed to fantasies.

These two scenes have a character of oriental intimacy which distinguishes them from all the fantasies of *'le turquerie'*. This is really the truth about Turkish women. M Browne found, after Decamps, a new way to paint white walls, instead of thickening them, or scratching them, or trowelling, she stuccoes them, so to speak, leaving all the pattern to the figures; the resultant effect is very happy.[15]

Gautier's pointed intervention highlights the importance of the battle over technique between the followers of Decamps and

Browne. Considering that the paintings are clearly Orientalist, it is surprising that technical differences aroused such condemnation – the conventions of harem walls à la Decamps must have more riding on them than a dispute over how to depict plaster. They signify the very structures of Orientalist discourse. Thus Browne's walls disrupt the codes of viewing critics expect from Orientalist painting. Gautier relates the different way that Browne paints walls to the claims of veracity afforded by her visits to the harem. The plainness of the rooms she depicts may surprise some – 'don't go imagining an Alhambra . . .' – and may dismantle treasured dreams about the harem but Gautier welcomes them as a sign of reality.

He contrasts Browne's intimacy with the Orient to other artists' fantasies, making her paintings function as visual reports. Some may feel that these scenes are too tame and domestic, but Gautier utilizes their claim to reality to give them novelty value and thus promote the paintings. His detailed reading of the content relies on an acknowledgement of the class-, gender- and nation-specific spaces from which Browne paints. He uses the particularities of her relationship to the harem to construct a critical space in which he can discuss the paintings as mainstream Orientalism (not just as ethnographic portraiture or topography as is the case with other women's amateur and professional Orientalism)[16] without having to contend with the unfeminine immorality associated with the genre. He thus manages to meet the challenge of Browne's de-sexualized harem and incorporate it within dominant Orientalism by offering a modified fantasy of the harem – if some viewers dislike the paintings it is because they lack the taste to appreciate the real thing. Gautier establishes a relationship between the woman artist and the represented space in keeping with the European linkage of women and the domestic. Thus gender determines Browne's access to the harem (on which rests the paintings' claim to truth) and foregrounds a special relationship to the domestic (on which rests his readings of the paintings as truthful and as womanly). Because of the projection of the idea of women's innate empathy with the domestic, the exotic erotic fantasy harem of Ingres and Gérôme becomes a knowable domestic location. The details of exotic costume and customs become ethnography, albeit picturesque, rather than titillating, lascivious vignettes. The fascination with the harem is amended from one that is overtly sexual to one that is overtly ethnographic, where the harem's sexual significance is implicit rather than explicit (caught up, for example, in the emphasis on the women's beauty). But for all their affinities, it is important that the Occident not be confused with the Orient. Gautier may praise the feredge over the crinoline, but he maintains enough strategic distance to portray the Orient as inferior to European civilization. (Islam as a 'carnival' is spectacular but spiritually worthless, the animals are mangy, the women lazy, etc.)

The review favours the humble details of domestic life available to a woman over the myths of Orientalism available to a man; the key tropes of the Orientalist fantasy (cypresses, minarets, camels, odalisques) and industry (photographs and panoramas) no longer thrill. Instead, the reviewer revels in a new vision of the Orient. Browne's claim to reality is endorsed by the contemporaneity of her details, such as the new fashion for papipos over narghile pipes, which Gautier, with his travel experience, is able to decode. The introduction of fashion, a phenomenon that requires both a concept of time and channels of communication, potentially undermines the image of the harem as an anachronistic prison and emphasizes the temporality of the Orient, in distinction to its traditional representation as timeless and archaic.[17] But the painting displays sufficient traditional tropes to enable the (re)viewer to contain it within the Orientalist myth: Gautier is able to extrapolate the flute melody as a reminder of previous lives in practically the same breath as he remarks on the modernity of the pipes. This contradiction is typical of Gautier's critical approach which is based on connoisseurship and a Romantic immersion in the art object. As such, to be transported (into an evocation of previous lives) was a sign of a painting's success. Gautier's Romantic belief in reincarnation and 'intellectual homelands' (his was ancient Egyptian, Delacroix's Anglo-Hindu ...) worked particularly well in the case of his Orientalist friends because it mapped onto the traditional view of the Orient as the cradle of Western civilization.[18]

Claude Vignon is less than impressed with Browne's harems. Unlike Gautier, she sees no advantage deriving from the artist's gender. In fact Browne, who she previously liked to praise as a masculine and virile artist, is found to have succumbed to the weaknesses of her sex and is demoted to the status of female.

Madame Browne, whose talent we recognized from the first
. . . counts among the three or four best portraitists . . . The two
Harem Interiors do not at all indicate a progress of the artist
[who showed] . . . for a short while, a totally virile talent. It is
feminine painting, a little shallow, a little cold, such at last that,
if the *Interiors* were not placed next to the portrait of Baron
de S and signed with the same signature, they would not arouse
a second glance. Mme. Browne owes us more, it is said that
she has captured nature in the *Interiors*, [but I think] she was,
despite herself, influenced by the harem's enervating atmos-
phere.[19]

Where Gautier thinks Browne has made a coup by depicting the
truth of the harem, as far as Vignon is concerned the artist was
betrayed by her own nature. It seems femininity, like blood, will
out. Although Vignon criticizes the harem's effects on women,
note that her condemnation of Browne is not couched in the terms
of moral repugnance that we earlier saw her direct at Gérôme in
that year's *Journal des desmoiselles*.[20] Meanwhile, she continues
to praise Browne in the *Journal des desmoiselles*. She does not
refer to the disappointing *Interiors* at all, leading me to deduce
that the importance of Browne as a role model for the young
women readers overrides her dislike of the recent work. Gender,
which in *Le Correspondent* accounts for Browne's failure, in
Journal des desmoiselles is the grounds of her success. This
example shows how the review's presumed readership impacts on
the operation of discourses of gender and art.

Hector de Callias in *L'Artist* cannot rest easy with Browne's
rejection of Decampian conventions. He is impressed with her
paintings and accepts their documentary status but wants to
retain some of the favourite elements of the Orientalist fantasy.
His tone suggests that realism is all very well, but since the
fantasy is so well-established it is perverse to go against it in
case the resultant image is less credible to Western eyes. If
Browne equals documentary then what de Callias wants is docu-
drama!

She has journeyed in the Orient. Like Lady Montagu, she
penetrated into the harems, there she filled her palette with
the richest colours and brings back to us interiors peopled with
indolent beauties. . . . The harems' white walls are uniform and
stucco. We reproach the artist who opposes herself to Decamps'

cncrusted and engraved walls. One does not dream that such walls would bc cntircly out of harmony with the general contents of the paintings . . .[21]

De Callias' fervent championing of Decamps reveals the level of resistance to other versions of the Orient, although his reference to Lady Montagu substantiates the importance of the female eyewitness account.

Olivier Merson is disappointed with Browne's account of the harem. Rather than dispute whether she actually saw what she painted, he minimizes the centrality of the *Interiors* by presenting them as just one version among many. This defuses their challenge to the Orientalist 'dream' which, it is implied, continues in reality elsewhere (in the harems of the very rich). Whilst on one hand this seems perfectly reasonable (why should there not be different types and classes of harems, just as there are different types of houscs in Europc?), on the other it dilutes the significance of the *Interiors* by refusing their claim to rclate to harems as a whole.

Having been able to clear the threshold of the harems, she [Browne] painted from nature those strange and jealous interiors, . . . This then is thc harem. Instead of diamond palaces and rejuvenated Alhambras, marble basins and gushing fountains, sumptuous rugs and naked odalisques rolling about in their pearled costumes, on piles of cushions or mosaics, we see a room that is austere and serious, without ornamentation, with colonnettes and white-washed walls, a mat unwinding on the flags, a divan dominating all around, and populated with silent women, bored, somnolently graceful, chaste in the muslin of their long robes which outline their fragile and languid bodies. I confess that these pictures disturb our Oriental dreams a little. It is true, if the artist had painted the seraglio of a Grand-Seigneur, perhaps we would have been less disappointed, perhaps we would rediscover the voluptuous setting, that sensual and breathtaking luxury that permeates the stories of *A Thousand and One Nights*.[22]

Merson offers the most telling criticism of Browne's technique. He tells us quite clearly that she has broken the rules of verisimilitude required in the representation of foreign subjects, and so fails to convince.

Now, the painter permits us a technical observation. The inside of the rooms are whitewashed. To give this effect, Mme Browne has covered the background with a paste sufficiently resistant, and this is for the best. Then, the shaded parts of the figures that must project from this solid background, she has only covered with a wash of colour as light as the weave played across toile. This time she is mistaken. In order to free oneself for a foreign plan, it is not enough to give it a more definite location; it is important also that the manner in which it is put is close to natural in the eye of the spectator. This is not a cunning trick of the trade, it is a positive rule whose application we see in all the pictures of the master colourists. On the contrary, in *The Visit* and *The Flute Player* if I see the shaded tones of people sinking deeper instead of moving away, it is less because of their quality of colour than because they were placed there for opposite reasons to the effect they were called upon to express.

It seems that Gérôme had it right all along. Browne's deviation from Orientalist conventions (and the review starts with a passage on the particular colour opportunities offered by the light of the Orient) is not a matter of interpretation, it is a mistake.

The ease with which Merson and the other critics sum up the characteristics of the Oriental dream shows how familiar, and how cherished, it was. Women who reported back on the harem were faced with an audience curious for knowledge but resistant to changes in the accepted knowledges about the East. Of course not all women agreed on what the harem was like. Léon Lagrange in the *Gazette des beaux-arts* plays women off against each other, using the Italian Princess Belgiojoso's travel writings to dispute the authenticity of Browne's image of the harem.[23]

> *The Visit* and *The Flute Player*, which present themselves as revelations of the mysterious life of the harem, do not exceed in value and interest, a woman's travelogue; again the indiscretions of the princess Belgiojoso have a completely different version of the truth. It is possible that in 1860 the young Paris milliners taken to Constantinople by the Crimean War, amused themselves by playing out innocent and insipid entertainments [*berquinades*] in front of Madame Browne which she fixed quickly in her notebook.[24]

Both women's products are trivialized by reducing them to the level of childish amusements like those indulged in by bored milliners. The combination of Parisian milliners, who featured regularly in the list of working-class women suspected of clandestine prostitution, and the term 'innocent' lends an air of sexual duplicity that reinforces Belgiojoso's 'indiscretions' as a more accurate view of the harem.[25] In this case it is implied that Browne was the innocent dupe of the sexually knowing, which undermines her alleged access to the truth. Having thus demolished her claim to serious critical attention he delivers the *coup de grâce* by claiming that only the Parisian obsession with Orientalism protects the canvas from serious critical discussion.

> Madame Belgiojoso peoples harems with massive beauties, that strictly conform to the Mohammedan ideal of the houri type figure, and dressed with the bad taste which character izes this exquisite flower. For us it is impossible to recognize [this] in the luminous pastels that light up the *Interiors* of M. Browne. . . . The walls too appear naked to us. What! No flashy mirror, no covering from Paris or London, and, similarly with the furniture, no piano, no porcelain clock, likewise no music box. Verisimilitude does not bow in favour of M. Browne: only the totally Parisian fondness for Turkish subjects protects them from the most serious reproaches that criticism would be within its rights to make of them in the name of art.[26]

Browne's work is characterized as silly and dilletante, a fad of fashion, and thus of no lasting consequence. It is unclear whether the sarcastic reference to the absence of Western goods points to the increased two-way trade between East and West in this period, and is thus an accusation of inauthenticity, or is a sneer at the genre in general for its fondness for interiors crammed with goods. As Kabbani points out, this 'catalogue of goods' available to the Western viewer is one of the main pleasures of the Oriental text – a fantasy of ownership that extends to the women pictured in the Oriental interior.[27] The absence of luscious accoutrements in Browne's paintings therefore threatens to disrupt the expected mode of viewing and satisfactions of the Western audience. Although Orientalism is characterized by the European acquisition of Eastern goods, Western products were also sought after in the East. This was particularly the case with clothing. After the dress reforms of the 1830s many rich Turks wore Western dress, but this 'inauthentic' clothing was generally edited out by Western artists – even though the display of Western artefacts in rich Ottoman households was often seen by their owners as a sign of progressiveness[28]. Gautier, who approves of the Sultan employing Donizetti's brother as leader of his musical staff, is still somewhat staggered by the Turks' taste for vulgar French clocks or reproduction pictures, all of which are held in high esteem because of their European origin.[29]

Although in many ways the *Interiors* conform to the image of Ottoman houses in Orientalist art (the *mouchearabia*/lattice screened windows, yashmaks and *feredjes*, the coffee pot, the tiled floor, low level seating, arches and columns) they also differ in that the furnishing is sparse and the room, as Lagrange points out, is bare and simple.[30] This is quite in keeping with Ottoman interiors where space and coolness were maximized by storing furnishings and linens in cupboards when not in use. The dark-skinned woman at the right of the picture is carrying a cushion, such as would be brought out of store for use when guests arrived. This practice contradicts the Western vision of the multitudinous splendours of the Orient that was transposed from their own domestic predilection for interiors crowded with ornament and display. No doubt some visitors to the public areas of Oriental houses were met with an impressive array of luxurious furnishings, but the vision of rooms crammed like an Aladdin's cave full of treasures would disappear when belongings were packed away once the room was vacated.

Several of the architectural and social details of the paintings seem reliable. Charles Newton, curator of the Victoria and Albert Museum's Searight Collection, considers *A Visit* to be a fairly authentic representation of the interior of a wealthy Ottoman household. The stone structure indicates an expensive, large and probably old house. (Modern houses in nineteenth-century Constantinople were generally built of wood since few people could afford to build in scarce and expensive stone.[31]) The dimensions of the room in *A Visit* suggest that it is the main reception hall of the *haremlik* in a moderately wealthy household. Another possible illustration of the family's wealth is the carpet in *A Flute Player* which, judging by the pattern, may be a Western import. (Although it is impossible to tell clearly from a black and white photograph.)

These images of domestic detail and social interaction relate more to the English school of Orientalism exemplified by Lewis than to French high Orientalist fantasy. Orientalist paintings are caught up in a complex of intertextual relations wherein they invoke each other in a general sense (Europe's knowledge of the Orient is derived from the repetition and authentification of its signs about it) and reference each other specifically. In Merson's review, for example, there is a sense in which he acknowledges that the dream of the Orient challenged by Browne's *Interiors* is a fantasized reality based on representations. As such, an anti-dote to the disappointment of the *Interiors* can be provided by re-activating the pleasures of *A Thousand and One Nights*. Although Browne deviates from some strands of Orientalism (for example, she does not quote reclining nude odalisques) her realist style quotes enough conventional details of the field to counter-balance such omissions and authenticate the particular image of the harem on offer. The presence of well-rehearsed signs of the Orient, such as the women's yashmaks and curved 'Turkish' slip-pers, gives the paintings a sense of ethnographic verisimilitude. Some critics were able to read this as the detailed representation of an everyday event available only to a female witness. Although some criticize her content and style, for her champions Gautier and Chasrel it is this combination of new and 'known' informa-tion about the harem that proves their worth.

Chasrel's 1877 retrospective depicts Browne as an important Orientalist and traveller-artist. Entering into recent art world debates about the usefulness of travel for artists, he cites Browne, alongside Gérôme and Fromentine, as one who truly benefits from tours abroad (similar to the inspiration Millet finds at home). This is contrasted to the multitude of talentless artists whose search for ideas on any continent is futile. Browne's presence among such hallowed company is couched in the sugary terms of femininity:

Without attempting a comparison which would pose as flattery we do not regret the advantages of circumstances which made space for the elegant talent and sensibility [*sympathique*] of [Browne] . . . who has added a new note to the rich and varied scale of Orientalist painting. A feminine note with all the deli-cacy, all the drama and all the distinction which gives the impression of a woman adding to the essence of art. The addi-tion is but a semi-tone, or even, if you like, a quarter-tone to

[our] Oriental gifts, but this quarter-tone belongs to the artist who has had the good fortune to penetrate some of the mysteries of the intimate life of the Orient, and the talent to turn to painting's profit the womanly privileges of discovery she gained. We are reminded of the instant success of *A Visit to the Harem* in the salon of 1861. If not a revelation, it was at least an amendment which had the mark of direct and personal observation. It was what others had caught fleeting glimpses of, guessed at or simply imagined, Mme. Henriette Browne saw it herself, it was part of a privilege; and that she succeeded in communicating to the lay public all the freshness and all the vivacity of this initial impression, is part of her talent.[32]

Browne's talent is relentlessly traced to her gender at the level of both form and of content: Chasrel follows the trend of earlier British reviewers and relates Browne to Millet and the painters of peasants, but he does not base his belief in the authenticity of her representations to the naturalistic style she shares with them. The paintings' credibility rests on the innate femininity of the woman herself:

That which we find pleasing about this talent is . . . the natural distinction and the modesty of the woman . . . [an artist] recognized by her peers and her masters, without her work betraying the infatuation of newly arrived dilettantism.

The touch, without overly precious scrupulousness, [tends] to the delicacy and quality of fine needlework. The accent is precise without any trace of the search for virile energy which too often spoils the most charming qualities. The sentiment is discreet without losing its intensity . . . [her] painting holds itself equidistant from grandeur and from affected winsomeness, from power and from affectation, and finds in the right milieu of its nature the sign of good taste and charm of which any upstart in Art would be incapable.[33]

Although all the critical material on Browne assumes gender to be significant, Chasrel's stress on femininity is the most like the profile in the *English Woman's Journal*. Promoting the genteel femininity of the artist as the crucial measure of her work, he sets up a series of associations with discourses of art and gender in which to position Browne: she is both likened to all things womanly and rescued from the possible pejorative connotations of excessive femininity; her work is delicate but not precious; it is compared to skills relegated to the lesser sphere of craft but rescued from too much diminution by the careful note that the comparison is to 'fine' needlework and the heights of accomplishment, not the labour of a common seamstress. Further, it is discreet but not inane.

If Browne is saved from the taints of excessive femininity, she is also protected from the unnatural 'search for virile energy' that 'too often' ruins women's work. Whereas numerous art critics use virile as a term of praise (Vignon worried that the harem had emasculated Browne's erstwhile virile talent), Chasrel goes to great lengths to absolve Browne from such associations. The language of the review lets the terms of description slide between their apparent object, the art work and the women who produce them. Thus we find that the 'charming' women who produce such delicate work are themselves in danger from the taints of virile energy, for 'traces' of which the critic carefully searches. The review's problem is how to encompass Browne's achievements within an ideology of art as a male activity without denying her femininity. On one hand her paintings are validated precisely because they come from a woman's sphere, but on the other she and all women artists are in danger of infection by the virility of the art world and the potency of their male counterparts whose achievements (flowing from that very virility) they no doubt might falsely wish to emulate.

The review conceptualizes Browne's Orientalism as a feminine addition to a male field. Chasrel constructs a genealogy of Orientalism in which Browne figures as cousin to the great male Orientalists without compromising her classed gentility.

> [S]ince . . . we cited the names [Fromentine, Gérôme, Delacroix] of the leaders of this line of Oriental painting we could claim a place for her beside them which they would in other circumstances not hesitate to offer her. Mme. Henriette Browne is their kinswoman and if the artist had had the time to wait to choose herself a pseudonym she could have restricted herself to the feminization of the first name of one or other of her illustrious colleagues because her painting is a cousin of theirs.[34]

The shifting status of Browne in the 'family' of Orientalism attests to the problems of locating a woman artist in this club. In order to facilitate her inclusion in the field of Orientalism Chasrel streamlines her oeuvre by de-emphasizing her role as the producer of domestic genre and portraiture which signals a woman artist. Her gender is never disguised (unlike the cross-dressing Rosa Bonheur, there is never any doubt that Browne is a woman) but is modified to produce a version of femininity that fits the concept of Orientalist art. If she figures as too feminine an artist then her status as honorary Orientalist is threatened.

USING EXPERIENCE TO CHALLENGE STEREOTYPES: WOMEN WRITE ABOUT THE HAREM

Browne's view of the harem, made possible because of her gendered access, was generally understood to be a rarity. But, as the references to Belgiojoso and Montagu suggest, her audience did know of other written accounts by women. Accordingly, in this section I am going to read Browne's images alongside written accounts (in English) of harem life by Occidental and Oriental women. This will map out a field of female experience of the Orient in which to theorize, via the different authorial positions inscribed in these texts, the type of positionalities available to Browne. To accept a gender-specific point of production does not, of course, make gendered qualities innate or legitimize claims for authorial control. As Griselda Pollock points out, the loss of the controlling author or artist does not mean the loss of the social producer of the art object.[35] Rather, by tracing the social spaces open to women artists and writers we can assess how the pictorial spaces created by Browne bear, and were made to bear, the inscription of a gendered social existence. What is more, the variety of women's representations of the Orient will allow us to speculate on the range of representational options accessible to women as they each differently resolved the contradictions of being women artists and writers.

The earliest written account I am using is Lady Mary Wortley Montagu's letters from Constantinople, published on her return from that city where her husband had been Ambassador from 1716 to 1718.[36] Another British woman writer was Sophia Poole, who travelled to Egypt in 1833 with her brother Edward William Lane, author of the famous *Manners and Customs of the Modern Egyptians* (1837). Her book, *The Englishwoman in Egypt* was published in 1844.[37] According to her Preface, he had suggested that she record and publish her impressions of the country since her access to things he was unable to observe would be a welcome supplement for his/their Western readers. Lady Anne Blunt's two-volume *A Pilgrimage to Nejd* was published, with prints after the author's drawings, in 1881.[38] It recounts her travels with her husband in Arabia and Persia and their dealings with local politics. Like Poole, Blunt was related to men associated with Orientalism (granddaughter of Lord Byron and wife of the Arabic scholar Wilfred Scawen Blunt), which no doubt contributed to the scholarly as well as popular market for her books: as with women artists, many women Orientalists benefited from an Orientalist family background.[39] Details of the exigencies of a tourist itinerary, including negotiating visits to harems, are provided by Annie Jane Harvey's *Turkish Harems and Circassian Homes* (1871).

I have also drawn upon two very different accounts of Islamic life by Oriental women: Emily Said-Ruete's *Memoirs of an Arabian Princess*, which was published in 1881 and Melek-Hanum's *Thirty Years in the Harem: or the Autobiography of Melek-Hanum, wife of H.H. Kibrizli-Mehemet-Pasha* from 1872.[40] Both these women migrated to Europe and wrote for Western audiences. But Said-Ruete, who converted to Christianity and married a German, retained fond memories of her homeland, Zanzibar, whereas Melek-Hanum, who was a Catholic Georgian by birth, never identified with the Turks or the Muslims and produces a text that is hostile to both. Their varying circumstances provide different viewpoints on the East and valuable information about the structure of Muslim women's lives in the mid-nineteenth century.

Said-Ruete, the Princess Salme bint Said ibn Sultan al-Bu Saidi, was born to a Circassian slave in the royal harem of Oman and Zanzibar. She lived in the palace harem until she eloped with her German fiancée. Melek-Hanum grew up in Constantinople and was married first to a European man (of unspecified nationality, but since he is described as Protestant and having been in the suite of Lord Byron, it is likely that he was British) for five years. During and after this time she visited Europe. There she met and fell in love with Kibrizli-Mehemet-Pasha whom she agreed to marry, despite her 'dread of the harem' and its seclusion. The marriage lasted some years and is represented, until its breakdown, as happy. Melek-Hanum who is presented throughout as

boisterous, feisty and ambitious, helped her husband to overcome reversals and obtain several important postings. When the
marriage ended he retained their only living child, a daughter,
who then fell into the power of the incalculably evil new wife.
At this point the text waxes lyrical about the evils of Islamic
society and the iniquities of Mehemet-Pasha. Eventually mother
and daughter are reunited and flee to Europe, where the narrative ends.[41] Since the period covered is the run-up to the Crimean
War, *Thirty Years in the Harem* offers an insight into the Porte's
attitude to the impending alliance with Europe.

To analyse the power relations in the production and viewing
of Browne's paintings and these women's writings we must
consider variables of class, race and religion as well as gender.
Because Western travellers like Browne, Montagu and Poole were
known to have had access to segregated Muslim spaces, their
accounts were generally seized upon as true. But their gaze in the
harem is registered both as female, since their gender gains them
entry, and as Western, since their presence is represented as
spectator and rarely participant. How do we read in women's work
the effects of the slipping of positionalities that such expeditions
provoked?

Clothes, or their absence, are frequently the means by which
such a distance is affected. Oriental clothes signify the exoticism
of the Orient, but for women, as for all Westerners, the pleasures
of cultural cross-dressing must be forfeited when Western clothes
are necessary to signal their Europeanness and inculcate respect
or discipline.[42] Lady Montagu, despite her envy of Muslim
women's financial independence, is careful to create differences
and distance between herself and the Oriental women: on a visit
to the baths she insists on remaining clothed. Sophia Poole, who
is adamant that her station as Westerner puts her above all
Oriental women, highlights the significance of dress in securing
her status. Whilst she usually wears the 'delightfully comfortable'
Turkish dress at home or when visiting Turkish 'ladies of middle
rank', when

> visiting those who are considered the noble of the land,
> I resume, under my Eastern riding costume, my English dress;
> thus avoiding the necessity of subjecting myself to any humil-
> iation. In the Turkish in-door costume, the manner of my
> salutations must have been more submissive than I should

have liked; while, as an Englishwoman, I am entertained by the most distinguished, not only as an equal, but generally as a superior. I have never given more than the usual salutation, excepting in the case of addressing elderly ladies, when my inclination leads me to distinguish them by respectfully bending . . .[43]

The careful preservation of a certain superiority and distance is complicated for women by points of possible contact and disassociation in which (scenes of) the women's quarters or of children can be both the familiar terrain of femininity and the immutable other of the Orient. For example, Poole finds that talking about children is an ice-breaker and shared interest in the harems she visits. But she is dismissive of the Oriental women's fear of the evil eye (which renders it inauspicious to praise a child outright). The actual or imagined relationship between author and Orient in these accounts is differently determined by variants of race, class and religion and personality. That Montagu is more open to playing at Turk than the snobby and frankly unlikeable Poole can be explained by their different periods, status (as wife of the British Ambassador or sister of a mere traveller and scholar), and the temperament engendered by these and other variables (wealth, contacts, etc.).

For the two non-Western writers, a different set of relations is constructed. Both Said-Ruete and Melek-Hanum contend throughout their accounts with the comments and assumptions they expect from their European readers. Said-Ruete, as a convert to Christianity, is critical of some Islamic institutions but, as a foreigner in Europe, sees the hypocrisy of Western Orientalism and defends much of Islamic life. She offers the moderated (remember, she is now dependent on European good-will) voice of the Oriental other answering back. Melek-Hanum, on the contrary, says little about Europe but is damning about Islam and the Turks. The text of *Thirty Years in the Harem* is frantic to establish a critical distance between the author and the Muslim Turks. This distance varies: depending on the heroine's ever-changing fortunes, Islam is depicted as tolerable (at times of marital harmony when the distance is minimized) and evil (where distance is maximized when she is presented as victim of the iniquities of a positively fiendish and utterly alien Islam). Whereas Said-Ruete self-consciously paints Muslim life in answer to European questions, *Thirty Years in the Harem* describes it far more in relation to the author's own changing concerns. The pleasures and familiarity of harem life are neither a problem nor a fascination. It is only when Melek-Hanum is out of favour and in danger that the image of the gullible, corrupt and cruel Turk is mobilized as negative. Prior to that the same qualities are seen as simply part and parcel of Ottoman life and she is happy to own to her successful machinations and briberies in the circles of power. The author's position as a non-Turk and non-Muslim only surfaces when she needs to assert a separation from the society around her. It is this conflict within Melek-Hanum's text that is obliterated by Melman, who cites Melek-Hanum as one of the Muslim women writers whose accounts of the harem present the oppressive realities that were edited out by Western women in their desire to see the harem in terms of the bourgeois domestic.[44] We would be very wrong not to attribute to the representational practices of those positioned as the Orientalist other the same complex of social and subjective determinants as we do to Occidental authors.

The emphasis on the 'othering' and dehumanizing of the Orient central to the critique of imperialism favoured by recent twentieth-century art historians has led to a picture of Orientalism that necessarily emphasizes the sensational and exotic aspects of the genre. But, as we have seen, the field to which Browne contributed contained conflicting images of the Orient by artists of both genders. Contemporary readings of Browne's *Interiors* structure themselves around the viewing position attributed to the artist and the authenticity of the paintings. Critics see Browne's particular cachet as being her authentic representation of an ordinary Orient – a foreign domestic – whose mundanity is charged with excitement by the exotic location and the understanding that she presents a previously unobtainable view into the harem.

Browne's version of the harem disallows some of the genre's expected pleasures; unlike the isolated sexual prison crowded with half-clothed somnolent women and desirable consumer durables, she presents a calm austere and social space, marked by relations between the female figures. She activates it as a social realm, its walls regularly penetrated by visitors, friends and musicians from outside. As such the paintings offer an alternative reading of relations of power, kinship and society in the harem. Her women are dressed and active, in clothes that have a social status and purpose in their wearers' lives instead of merely figuring as decoration or a mismatch of all things vaguely Oriental. There is no sexual intrigue in Browne's harems: the visits and entertainments seem quite above board. The dominant sense of *A Visit* is of an Oriental version of the afternoon visit which so structured European bourgeois society.

Contrary to the stereotype of the isolated forbidden harem, it was often relatively easy for Western women to visit Muslim harems. Melek-Hanum depicts Western women's visits to the royal harem in Constantinople as frequent enough to be considered commonplace in the late 1840s.[45] By the time Browne went in 1861, after the *rapprochement* of the Crimean War, the increased numbers of Western tourists in the city meant that demand for harem visits began to outstrip supply, and by 1871 Annie Harvey noted that 'every year it is more difficult for passing travellers to gain admittance to the harems'.[46] (Harvey herself had sufficient connections to ensure introductions to all the best households.) I have no evidence of where Browne visited in Turkey (nor would this conclusively prove the 'truth' of the paintings), but we can attempt to verify them with reference to representations from other sources.[47] Foreign visitors remarked on the Turks' hospitality and it is possible that Browne's paintings are based on the experience of more than one Ottoman interior.

Browne's image of the harem as a social space contradicts the two most common themes of the Orientalist fantasy harem – sex and idleness. In literary representations Western and Eastern women dispute the West's vision of the harem as a space devoted to indolence and passion. Sophia Poole notes that female 'brokers' are frequent visitors to Egyptian harems who want to shop[48] and Sarah Graham-Brown, who has traced photographic images of harems, emphasizes the number of connections the inhabitants had with the rest of the female world.[49] Poole also disputes the licentious image of harems.

> The ideas entertained by many in Europe of the immorality of the hareem are, I believe, erroneous. True, it is, that the chief ladies have much power which they might abuse; but the slaves of these ladies are subject to the strictest surveillance; and the discipline in the Eastern hareem can only be compared to that which is exercised in the convent.[50]

On the other hand, Lady Anne Blunt, who presents herself as an industrious, studious and self-disciplined traveller fearless of danger and discomfort, is convinced that Oriental women are lazy: 'They have no idea of amusement, if I may judge from what they say to me, but a firm conviction that perfect happiness and dignity consist in sitting still'.[51] Note that she itemizes dignity as one of the values placed on idleness, thus giving the women's leisure a social dimension just as it had in the West. But although European women of the middle and upper classes were encouraged to a life of leisure, it was always registered as productive – not just in the signification of the family's wealth – but also materially in the visible activities of philanthropy and cultural appreciation. For Blunt, the absolute leisure of the harem women is registered as qualitatively different to the apparent leisure of Western women. Ironically, it is Gautier who most clearly draws out the similarities between the lives of affluent women in the Orient and in Europe, highlighting the geographical mobility of Muslim women:

> 'Shopping' seems as much an amusement of the Turkish ladies as of the English; . . . contrary to the European idea, the Turkish ladies, far from remaining walled up in the harems, go out when they please, on the sole condition of remaining closely veiled; and their husbands never think of accompanying them.[52]

The power of the Orientalist stereotype of laziness is attested by Emmeline Lott, author of *The English Governess in Egypt* (1866).[53] She is no lover of Islam, and frequently bemoans the suspicion with which she is treated as an unbeliever whilst portraying the Muslims as governed by a cruel and primitively superstitious religion. In her sequel, *Nights in the Harem* or *The Mohaddetyn in the Palace* (1867) she includes a diatribe against Western assumptions about Oriental women. This is attributed to the figure of Yusuf, the *kislar agaci* (chief eunuch) of her Highness Fatimah Khaboum, wife of the recently deceased Viceroy Abuss Pacha. Yusuf, having accompanied the late Pacha to England, can compare Oriental ladies to European high society.

> 'The ladies of her Highness's suite, although unable to read, write or play on musical instruments, were not, on that account, idling away their time.'
> 'True, they were uneducated . . . but at that moment they were, or looked, patterns of industry [engaged in spinning and

sewing]. As I looked upon these sempstresses, I thought how little the few *Frenk* ladies [who have visited the *haremlik*] ... can know of how much exertion those quiet, sedate, and apparently impassive creatures are capable, whom they have only seen listlessly indulging in their cigarettes. They can work with their fingers assiduously, as you see. They can work with their *brains* also, frequently. They formerly were – ay, and many of them still are – the *profoundest* adepts in every species of political cabal or domestic intrigue; and even Machiavelli; that well-known Italian prince of diplomatists, of whom history speaks, had he possessed an Eastern harem, might have found his match – state-crafty [*sic*] and astute, as he was – in the Oriental odalisque'.[54]

Yusuf accurately sums up the characteristic Orientalist picture of the lazy, mindless, smoking odalisque and specifically challenges it in relation to the accomplishment skills expected of women in Europe. The clearest deconstruction of the stereotype of the lazy Oriental woman comes from Said-Ruete, who is obviously infuriated by its prevalence. She ignores the sexual element of the stereotype completely and deals with the Oriental's apparent leisure as an issue of work, contrasting women's work in the Orient to Europe:

How many times have I been asked: 'Do please tell me how can people in your country manage to live, with nothing to do?' I had the pleasure of answering this question six or eight times over at a large party ... coming from a person inhabiting a Northern country, the question is quite a natural one I admit, for it is hard for such to fancy a life without work, being firmly convinced, moreover, that women in the East do nothing all day but dream away their time in a shut up harem, or, for a change play with some luxurious toy.

[T]he Arab, so frequently described in books as idle and lazy, is accustomed to an abstemiousness in which perhaps a Chinaman only equals him. The climate itself, brings it about that the Southerner *may* work as he likes, while the Northerner is obliged to.

Now, I ask, is the Arab mother, who wants so very little [materially, since the 'blessed' climate decreases the dangers to the newborn] for herself or her child, to work as hard as the European housewife? She hasn't the slightest idea of what is meant by darning stockings or mending gloves, or any of those numerous trifles that a nursery entails; and as for that important and troublesome domestic item, a washing-day, it is a thing to us unknown; our linen is washed daily, and dried in little more than half an hour, smoothed flat (not ironed), and put away ... All this helps to render life to the Eastern lady, without distinction of station and rank, much less complicated.[55]

In her rebuttal of the charge of idleness, Said-Ruete produces a clearly feminine response that weaves between national and class differences. The stereotypical reference to a Chinaman's absti-nence is one of a range of national, racial and religious stereotypes that punctuates Said-Ruete's text. Whilst the existence of stereo-types and theories of racial difference in the East has often been overlooked (in the desire to see the West as the origin of all evil) they are doubtless of a different impact, depending on the status and situation of their enunciation. Her stress on the devotion of Arab mothers requires the text to prioritize the tasks of childcare as an index to Arab women's responsibilities (however much eased by the warm climate) whilst her self-presentation as royalty puts her above the menial work of a housewife. (It is quite possible that reduced circumstances, as much as the change in climate, brought Said-Ruete into contact with Northern domestic drudgery, since wealthy Western women would be equally unused to the labours described, except in the supervision of the servants performing them.)

A picture emerges from these accounts of the harem as a space governed by social and legal regulations, which is no less circum-spect or more restrictive than the European drawing room. Both Western and Eastern sources comment on the flexibility offered to women by the harem system, which is seen by some as supe-rior to the freedom enjoyed by European women. As Melman illustrates, the terms in which Muslim women's relative freedom are conceptualized vary according to the agenda of their Western observers. Thus, where the aristocratic Lady Montagu applauds Muslim women's individual (sexual) liberty in keeping with the Enlightenment concepts of personal freedom that she wants to claim for women, nineteenth-century writers stress Muslim women's freedom *from* sexual demands. They are particularly impressed by the idea that no Muslim husband entered the *haremlik* without permission, and depict the *haremlik* in terms of the middle-class concept of 'home', with all its gendered and classed connotations.

Montagu reported from rich Turkish harems that rather than 'lament the miserable confinement of Turkish ladies' as male writers were wont to do, she found them to be 'freer than any ladies in the universe'. Unlike their Western counterparts, Muslim women benefited from having control over their income and so 'are the only women in the world that lead a life of uninterrupted pleasure, exempt from cares, their whole time being spent in visiting, bathing, or the agreeable amusement of spending money and inventing new fashions'.[56] Thus, for Montagu, Islamic law ensures rather than restricts women's liberty with even the veil working to their advantage:

> [T]here is no distinguishing the great lady from her slave, and 'tis impossible for the most jealous husband to know his wife when he meets her, and no man dare either touch or follow a woman in the street. This perpetual masquerade gives them entire liberty of following their inclinations without danger of discovery.[57]

Here, Gautier's 'permanent carnival' of Islam that entrances the spectator is transformed into a string of conventions that the (independent and affluent) women participants can use to their own purpose, producing a social mode of female existence far more liberated than that of eighteenth-century Europe. In the nineteenth century Melek-Hanum paints a corroborating picture of the flexibility of harem rules. Segregated male and female worlds (which always impacted more on affluent and urban women) were not seen necessarily to deprive Muslim women of power or influence. Considering that female interest and influence in politics was precisely what the West wanted to avoid in its own women, it is not surprising that when Oriental female power is represented by men it figures as a spectre of evil. The idea of the harem as a centre of hidden patronage – despite the decline in Ottoman power the mothers and wives of royalty and high ranking officials exercised immense power through patronage networks[58] – only added to the sense of intrigue and threat that is the other side of the fantasy of the harem as a palace full of listless bimbos. Poole reports that women in the harem of the Effendi are very well informed on international affairs and discuss politics avidly;[59] Melek-Hanum is clear that women take an active and recognized part in political life and indicates that the harem system, rather than secluding women from the outside world, actively creates a central role for them in the dissemination of information.

> The women are generally the first to learn and circulate news. The men often visit each other, but they are always reserved. They speak with less restraint to their wives, and tell them for their entertainment what they have heard . . . The wives of high functionaries are on terms of close intimacy with other great ladies, and repeat to them what their husbands have said; in this way news is spread abroad with unheard-of rapidity.[60]

Women in Europe were also expected to play a part in furthering their husband's career by cultivating useful friendships. But in Turkey these subterfuges are a clearly recognized means of power. Melek-Hanum makes it quite plain that claimants knew that whilst her husband as state official could not accept 'presents' (the essential route to success and influence), his wife could. Women's communication networks were more than mere gossip circles; they constituted a recognized but unofficial part of the structure of communication and power. As even Emmeline Lott points out, women in Egypt played a considerable part in the political life of their country. Said-Ruete pointedly contrasts rich Oriental women's economic power to that of Western women.

> The household stands entirely under the control of the wife, and there she is absolute mistress. She does not receive a certain sum for housekeeping, as is customary in Europe – she has full liberty to dispose of her husband's funds. When the latter has two wives living apart, his income is equally divided between them.[61]

Her account of the questions she faced in the West shows how Islamic society was judged by the treatment of its women – who were polarized as either cruelly repressed or wantonly promiscuous. Browne's paintings which show the harem as respectably domestic destabilize the lavish fantasies projected onto Oriental women. One wonders whether the complaints about the lack of worldly goods are a transferred demand for the lush trappings of sexual excess where mirrors, fauns and carpets signify the scene, setting and satisfaction of the Orientalist fantasy.

Just like a European domestic genre scene, Browne's Orientalist painting is structured by details indicating a series of social nuances, the picture plane animated by a grid of gazes between the figures. The relations between the figures have all the marks of a ritualized social interaction: the two central figures (hostess in indoor clothes and senior visitor in outdoor clothes) greet each other with a salaam motion whilst the rest of each party prepare for their part in the visit.

The paintings accord with what is known about harem etiquette, and where they deviate there are supporting precedents. One example is the manner of greeting. Said-Ruete writes that, unlike in the painting, the hostess did not usually rise to meet her visitors. However, Melek-Hanum, aware of the significance Europeans placed on rising and, experienced in the problems of incorporating Western visitors into the harem's hierarchies, delighted her royal hosts when posted to Belgrade by going to greet them at the room's entrance.[62] Similarly, the pictures are contradictory in their use of the veil. The transparent gauze veil worn by the arrivals in *A Visit* accords with urban Ottoman fashion of the period, and corresponds to its usage as an outdoor covering – the women have presumably just arrived since they still have on their outdoor clothes (*feredge*). But the same veil in *A Flute Player*, where they are presumably staying long enough to hear a music recital, seems incongruous. It has always been assumed that veils were removed on arrival since there is no prohibition on women seeing each others' faces. It is impossible to know if Browne observed such a phenomenon or misunderstood the mix of dress visible as women arrived. But, again, evidence about the veil is conflicting according to location and culture: although Melek-Hanum observes that in Turkey veils are removed on harem visits along with the *feredge*,[63] and Poole in Egypt is evidently able to see women's faces, Said-Ruete in Zanzibar is clear that outdoor clothes are retained.[64]

Perhaps one of women writers' and artists' biggest challenges to hegemonic Orientalist versions of harem life is their representation of polygamy. A central theme of Orientalist discourse, polygamy afforded both a male fantasy of the ownership and control of multiple women and a reason to condemn Islam as heathen and barbaric. As a subject that was depraved and exciting, polygamy could be a potentially touchy subject for a woman artist. Said-Ruete, like most sources, maintains that polygamy was rare

(for economic and social reasons)[65] and compares it favourably
to the vagaries of Western marriage.

> How is it with Christians? how about wedded life in civilized
> Europe? ... Is wedlock always considered a sacred institution
> in moral Europe? Is it not bitter irony and delusion to talk of
> only 'one' wife? The Christian may, of course, marry one
> woman only, and that is the great superiority of Christianity;
> the Christian law requires the just and the good, the
> Mahometan allows the evil; but custom and practice mitigate
> to great extent in the East the evil consequences of the law,
> while sin is rampant here in spite of it. I should say the only
> difference in the position of a married woman in the East and
> in Europe to be, that the former knows the number as well as
> the characters of her rivals, while the latter is kept in a state
> of considerate ignorance about them.[66]

By presenting the harem as a domestic space whose social environment is shaped by the women who live there, Browne
minimizes the importance of the absent husband. The incorpora-
tion of a child into an utterly respectable and unremarkable
domestic scene dilutes the sexual charge of the harem location,
drawing out the parallels between the European and Oriental
domestic and challenging Western Orientalist fantasies. Unlike the
fantasy of the sexually available and interchangeable harem
women, women's accounts present us with a network of specific
kinship relations. This is basically an extended family, in which
children are clear on the various ties that link them to their
mother, their siblings, half-siblings and the foster families of their
wet-nurse. This displaces as the central force in harem relations
the all-powerful figure of the father on which Western identifications depend and thus challenges the viewing position of Western
superiority. By painting a child as part of the harem's social structure, Browne implicitly allies herself with the women's version of
harem life.

Children who are not slaves are an uncommon feature in
Orientalist painting. They were of course a staple of domestic
genre scenes where family, with woman as wife and mother, was
the mainstay of the ideological understanding of hearth and home.
Although many artists emphasized the everyday qualities of
Oriental life, few of them combined motherhood with harems.
Young children occur now and then as slaves or servants (e.g. in

Lewis' *The Reception* there is both a Black boy slave and a, fairer, girl child with the visiting party) and more rarely as the children of harem women such as in Frederick Goodall's *A New Light in the Harem* (1884, Plate 33) and Jan-Baptist Huysmans' *Tending Baby* (n.d.). Oriental women most often figure as mothers in rural settings away from the harem, particularly as Egyptian Fellahin. This helps to keep the myth of the harem as a rarefied area of sexuality and intrigue, in contrast to its more mundane function as the quarters of women and young children. Goodall's *A New Light in the Harem*, with its coy title transplants some of the sentimentality of motherhood from West to East. But unlike the upright prim young mothers of Cope's domestic (see Chapter 3), Goodall's new baby is entertained by two odalisques, their forms revealed through transparent robes as they lounge about the Oriental interior. The drape pulled back over the moucharabia emphasizes the viewer's sense of access to a private sphere. But this is not the Occidental domestic – despite the intent gaze of the mother to her child (for the logic of the painting can only allow that the white woman is the mother, thus placing the Black figure as a slave or servant); no proud Victorian mama would be leaning revealed for all to see. The tiles, nargile and animals emphasize the exotic location and key what is titularly a picture about motherhood, into the sexualized realm of racialized fantasy. The contrast between the white and Black figures here is typical of the sexualized representation of racial difference in the harem. Said-Ruete gives some idea of mothering in a harem situation, again comparing it to motherhood in the West (although this highly idealized image of harem life must be read in relation to her probable bias as the child who gained a wet-nurse, rather than the one who is displaced).

> The education of the children is left entirely to the mother, whether she be legitimate wife or purchased slave, and it constitutes her chief happiness. Some fashionable mothers in Europe shift this duty onto the nurses and by and by on the governess, and are quite satisfied with looking up their children or receiving their visits once a day. In France the child is sent to be nursed in the country, and left to the care of strangers. An Arab mother, on the other hand, looks continually after her children. She watches and nurses them with the greatest affection, and never leaves them as long as they may stand in need

of her motherly care; for which she is rewarded by the fondest filial love. Her children repay her in a great measure for all the disadvantages of polygamy, and their affection renders her life more happy and contented.[67]

The relations between women/wives/mothers in the harem and the children include not only the child's half-brothers and sisters (the children of other wives) but also the children of wet-nurses and slaves. Said-Ruete emphasizes that half-brothers and sisters are regarded as siblings. But there is no loss of distinction regarding each child's separate mother. They may share a father but each child is clear who is its mother. Said-Ruete often describes the race of the mothers and talks of childish discrimination and 'hatred of race' particularly between the children of Circassian women and the darker Abyssinians, who are generally agreed to be the next in line of beauty. Although she waxes lyrical about motherly love, it is clear that slaves act as wet-nurses and carers to harem children. This class differential is presented as also a kinship relation. Her account emphasizes the devotion of the wet-nurse and the elevation rather than loss of status for the nurses' children.

The destabilizing potential of such woman-centred accounts can still be contained within the Orientalist fantasy harem. For, although the singular relationship of each child to its mother (arguably one already split in the case of wet-nursed children) confounds the fantasy of the replaceability of women, it is upheld again by the irreplaceability of the father who has a relationship to *all* the children. For Western men, the harem rescinds the formula of marriage as the cost of secured paternity: the Oriental husband can proliferate via all the women in his harem (except his daughters) without problems of legitimacy. In the West's fantasy economy, the Oriental harem figures, as Spivak argues, as an arena to rehearse both the exploitation and subjugation of Black women by Black men (a wish-fulfilment in relation to women's social agitation at home) and the avenging of female wrongs by the morally superior West.[68] Browne offers a way in for the female viewer by depicting a suitably feminine (and maternal) space with which the female viewer can identify. This is not new: European women had been using the harem as a metaphor for their predicament for some time; in *Jane Eyre* (1847) Jane identifies with the harem against Rochester's restrictive love.

But providing a point of entry for female viewers does not necessarily mean that the harem will be seen as a positive space. It can be emptied of its local significance and charged with Western associations just as well for white women as for white men: Jane plans to save herself and the 'houris' by leading them in revolt for equality against the despot/Rochester's tyranny.[69] Here Spivak's typical formula, wherein white men save Black women from Black men, is adapted to feature a white woman as saviour – although, at least in Jane's case, the white man is also depicted as a threat and tyrant. Indeed, Joyce Zonana argues that *Jane Eyre* is part of a 'fully developed cultural code' of feminist Orientalism in which the use of Islam and the harem as a metaphor for the oppression of Western women was familiar to Charlotte Brontë and, as is evident in *Jane Eyre*, to her readers.[70] Significantly, this tradition of feminist Orientalism, whilst overtly concerned with the Islamic oppression of women, actually functions to save Western women by reforming Western men of their Orientalized sins. The Orientalization of European gender discrimination allows the Western feminist, as Zonana argues, to disarm the challenge of her words. Western women battle to purge the West of its Orientalized failings and thus return the Occident to itself, whilst simultaneously shoring up the West's Occidental primacy. What is interesting in this instance is that, whilst Zonana makes a convincing case for the familiarity of Western women writers with the traditions and tropes of feminist Orientalism, it is clear that they were equally familiar to Oriental women who wrote for a Western audience. Their writings frequently challenge feminist as well as hegemonic Orientalist assumptions. Thus Said-Ruete's defence of the apparent laziness of Oriental women stands as much against Florence Nightingale's (1849) representation of the enforced leisure of the harem as 'hellish' as it does against Western male stereotypes of indolent harem women.[71] It is within this cluster of dominant and alternative Orientalist discourse, then, that women's accounts need to be read, in order to allow for the variety of oppositional and collaborative positionalities assumed by both Occidental and Oriental women cultural agents.

Melek-Hanum, who by the end of her marriage is disenchanted with Muslim society, paints a picture of the harem system's evil effect on 'family life'. It is clear that the concept of 'family life' used here signifies the Western family model which surfaces as other and superior to the Oriental version.

Family life is, in reality, unknown amongst the Turks. The law of the Koran, which divides mankind into two distinct classes – men and women – does not admit of the existence of a family in which each member can live the same life and form part of the harmonious whole ... Thus persons who pretend to form part of one and the same family, have, in reality, nothing common amongst themselves, – neither apartments, nor goods, nor furniture, nor friends, nor even the same hours of taking rest. The selamlik (the apartments of the men) and the harem are in consequence, two separate establishments placed side by side, where each one does what pleases him or herself.[72]

Harvey, who is full of praise for the kind manners and temperament of Turkish women, sees the segregation of the harem system as an overriding evil. By the time of her visit polygamy itself was nearly obsolete in the 'best families' but the harem of course remains. In her view men and women, 'deteriorate by separation. Men who live only with other men become rough, selfish and coarse; whilst women, when entirely limited to the conversation of their own sex, grow insolent, narrow-minded, and scandal-loving'. For Harvey, the iniquities of the harem system do not compensate for its presumed benefits.

We had often heard that Eastern women enjoyed in reality far more liberty than their Western sisters, and in some respects this is certainly true ... [but these advantages] do not at all compensate for the slavery of the mind which they have to endure, from being cut off from the education and mental improvement they would gain by association with the other sex.

Mental imprisonment is worse even than bodily imprisonment, and by depriving a woman of legitimate ambition, by taking from her the wish for mental culture, she is reduced to the condition of a child – a very charming one, probably, when young, but a painful position for her when, youth having departed, the power of fascination decays with the loss of beauty.[73]

No such degradation of family life is evident in Browne's painting. Indeed, for some in the West this is just what is lacking; Browne's version of the harem becomes morally disturbing, because the apparently impeccable moral qualities of the scenes she witnessed throw into question the power relations between the Occident and Orient. Bourniol writing in the *Revue du monde catholique* in 1861 is horrified at her failure to censure Islamic law.

> One scarcely recognizes [in Browne's harem scenes] ... the place ... that the Princess Belgiojoso recently showed us in colours ... which are without doubt the truth! ... Certainly the calm of these cheerful interiors, the decent grace of the completely dressed, elegantly draped, women, scarcely recalls the shame of the moors, who are depraved, if not infamous, for the vice of polygamy. I shall restrict myself on this subject, and praise with pleasure the artist's talent and the ravishing finesse and delicacy of her fortunate pencil.[74]

The same Salon contained Gérôme's *Phryne* which Bourniol also criticized on moral grounds: 'I have the right to be severe with this artist whose talent I greatly esteem ... Unfortunately M. Gérôme seems more and more to take pleasure in a deplorable choice of morally reprobate subjects ...'.[75] Note that whilst both artists are praised for their talent, Gérôme is berated as immoral and depraved in his *choice* of subjects whilst Browne is castigated for her *treatment* of subject. In this instance the revelations of Princess Belgiojoso were preferred because the discretion of Browne's image of the harem does not appease the reviewer's proscriptive stance on the institution of polygamy. His horror at Gérôme's immoral choice of subject does not mean that a more circumspect type of Orientalism automatically finds favour. Browne's thoroughly moral and proper scene is interpreted as a canvas of implicitly lax morals because it does not overtly condemn the heathen custom of polygamy.

THE FEMALE GAZE

Whilst it is easy to accept that the gendered position from which Browne produced foregrounded certain types of representation, it is harder to ascertain whether this also produced a particular viewing position. Arguably, her harems invite us to see the Orient from a woman's point of view – but how does this gendered view relate to traditional positions of Western superiority? The Orient remains significantly different. For all that the harems have affinities with European drawing rooms, they are quite clearly not the same thing; women wear Oriental dress, loll against cushions and smoke cigarettes. However, this difference is not necessarily negative. Although reviewers are able to judge these local details as signs of Oriental deficiency (in morals, posture and work ethic) the paintings do not rule out a less judgemental stance. This is not to suggest that, because she was female, Browne in some proto-feminist manner, immediately understood the relations between misogyny at home and exploitation abroad. Rather, that, given the moral implications of subject matter, the socializing act of painting for a woman in Browne's position foregrounded a positionality in relation to the harem that was necessarily less damning and eroticized than that of her male counterparts. It is not necessarily conscious politics on her part but the position from which she paints that leads to the representation of the harem as a space respectable enough to contain the respectable lady artist persona associated with Browne. Unlike Gérôme, as analysed by Nochlin, Browne's differently detailed technique emphasizes rather than obliterates her presence at the scene. By breaking with the voyeuristic viewing position facilitated by the implied absence of the artist, Browne destabilizes the West's fantasized relationship to the Orient as other. Her sympathetic rendition of the harem theme challenges one set of artistic conventions (Orientalism) but re-affirms another (the codes of feminine art practice).

Although the paintings provide a different Western view of the Orient they are not beyond appropriation – Gautier can still revel in the beauty of the (dressed) women and Vignon can deploy stereotypes of idleness. The interpretations of race and gender that the pictures are made to bear at the point of exhibition circumscribe the radical potential of the female gaze to disrupt imperial ideologies at the point of production. Browne's pictures provide a bridge between the all-female space of the harem and the mixed gender space of the Salon. Both men and women see a female view of a female space (the harem) but within a context subject to critical meanings largely determined by a predominantly male critical community.

Contemporary criticism makes much of the active female spectatorship it associates with the paintings. We can also use twentieth-century theories of the female gaze, developed originally in film theory, to tease out the relationship between the woman artist's look and the viewing positions constructed by her paintings. The ownership of the gaze on screen and between

viewer and representation has been of significance to cultural
critics since Laura Mulvey equated being the agent of the look
with an active position of power.[76] Arguing that cinematic representation appealed to unconscious scopophilic drives (the fantasy
of control through visual mastery), Mulvey produced an explanation of pleasure in which the viewer identifies with the active
male protagonist on screen. His actions appear to drive the narrative and control the filmic space, unlike the female figures who
are subordinate and passive. Mulvey's later attempt to situate the
excluded female viewer (who can only identify sadistically with
the male character or passively and masochistically with the
female) arrived at an uncomfortable notion of transvestism,
wherein she (the viewer) slips between the two polarities of a
masculine or feminine identification.[77] Mulvey started a debate
about the nature of the female spectator and her pleasure that
lasted though the 1980s and extended beyond film to the analysis
of other forms of representation.

Though useful, developments in film theory can never be
straightforwardly applied to static visual representations like
painting. Some help is offered by the amendments made by
television theory, since television, like a visit to an art exhibition,
is viewed in circumstances where the social (in the form of inter-
ruptions, other people's opinions and the consciousness of a shared
viewing) obviously intervenes (unlike the apparently private
viewing experience of the darkened, silent cinema). Lorraine
Gamman and Jackie Stacey, working on the woman's gaze in film
and television, stress the importance of gazes (and verbal
exchanges) *between* female figures.[78] This offers a way of analysing
a desirable viewing position for the female spectator that does
not rely on Mulvey's active/passive/transvestite mode of viewing.
The active roles of, and relationship between, female protagonists
like television detectives Cagney and Lacey differ from the usual
cop show format by challenging the traditionally passive status of
woman in the narrative and therefore foreground a pleasurable
viewing position for women.

Browne's paintings differ from the generic codes of Orientalism by inserting gazes and action between women into a situation that paradigmatically relies on inactive female figures
frozen into a static space. Like narrative film, the myth of the
harem is activated by the male hero who alone has the power to
move the narrative, to be, as Teresa de Lauretis puts it, the agent

of transformation.[79] Harem women are traditionally stuck in a freeze-frame awaiting the husband's transforming presence/gaze. Browne, as the only other possible witness/viewer of the harem (symbolically, if not literally), replaces the husband as the transforming agent but, rather than simply climb into his metaphorical shoes and parody a typical harem painting, she sidesteps the myth and socializes rather than sexualizes the harem's petrified space. Browne paints the harem from a position that implies neither a sadistic identification with a male perspective nor a masochistic identification with subordinate female participants (Mulvey's original formulation), nor is she simply transvestite, hopping awkwardly between the two (Mulvey's second position). She paints from a position that *had to be female*, according to the prevailing ideas of artistic production, femininity and the harem, and that *had to be active*, according to the construction of her as the author of a text predicated on a direct viewing of an unremittingly gendered space. She thus intervenes in the dynamic of active/male and passive/female by being, and being understood to be, a female painting subject who actively looks at and represents the harem.

The active relationships she represents between the female figures counter the traditional narrative of a male-dominated harem and, like the buddy relationship of Cagney and Lacey, can facilitate a pleasurable viewing position for the women in the audience. Film theory's stress on narrative (multiple or single) is germane here not only because Browne's audience was accustomed to decoding narratives from paintings but also because to represent the harem in any form was to enter into a long-standing, well-understood narrative about the harem and the East. No representation of the harem stood on its own. As the reviews clearly show, her paintings were seen as part of an ongoing dialogue about the harem with which nearly everyone was familiar, at least in part (whether it was Decamps' paintings, cartoons, *A Thousand and One Nights* or the endless use of the harem as metaphor for slavery, servitude or sex). The paintings effectively act as another instance in an ongoing story – the painterly equivalent of the reverse shot from the woman's point of view – whose opposite (the numerous and sexualized harem scenes) is well known to the audience.

As representations of a woman's look, the *Interiors* set up a special relationship to the female spectator. They challenge the idea of women as the object, rather than owner, of the gaze by showing female figures who were looked at first by a female spectator and by representing them contrary to the generic codes of passivity. Whilst, as Mary Ann Doane highlights, 'woman' was originally conceptualized as the ideal film spectator (a passive consumer), she is generally refused the position of active looking subject in the diegesis.[80] Browne in contrast is conceptualized as doing both: she is imagined as both consumer of the scene (in this case the 'actual' scene of the harem not the represented scene) and agent of its representation. But although this allows the female viewer to stand in the artist's shoes (without resorting to cross-dressing), the distance between the artist/viewer and the subject of the picture is retained. Unlike the pathos of the 'woman's' film where weeping, a sign of over-identification with filmic characters, is a sign of the film's success, the *Interiors* cannot risk collapsing the distance between the Western observers and the Eastern observed. The insistence on the difference between women (Occidental and Oriental) effectively marks the female spectator (both Browne and the paintings' audience) as Western and other to the female subjects of the painting.

Theories of the female gaze have deconstructed the earlier tendency to a monolithic female spectator, affirming that the term refers not to any woman who watches a film but to a constructed space of viewing.[81] This textual addressee who does not equal, but whose position may be occupied by, a 'real' individual (male/female) is also subject to social differentials (race, sexual orientation, etc.) and an equally, but often differently, differentiated access to critical codes which will give various viewers a different purchase on the text.[82] Browne's demarcation of difference between Oriental and Occidental women is inscribed in the dynamics of the viewing activity rather than overtly played out in the scene itself. (Unlike the twinning of alternative female personas highlighted in Stacey's analysis of *Desperately Seeking Susan* for example.) Rather than depict herself or another Western woman in the painting as a contrast to the Oriental women, Browne's *Interiors* rely on the traditions of viewing and the codes of Orientalism to assert the difference between audience and subject. By subverting some codes and repeating others, the paintings are able simultaneously to provide points of entry and identification for women viewers and maintain the West's distance from the East. In the final analysis, the points of similarity and empathy must not override the points of difference. Browne's status as Westerner and artist requires the construction of difference at the same time as her gender allows the construction of an affinity between herself and the women's space. Browne must become not only a seeing but a differentiating agent.[83]

But the spectator who sees through Browne's eyes cannot see everything: there is still something in the harem that denies our inquisitive gaze; something signified by the intense looking activity of the two figures on the steps at the right of the painting. They twist their bodies and turn their backs to us in order to look down at something that is hidden from our view. This visual dynamic within the picture plane undercuts the visual mastery promised by the narrative and disrupts the compositional coherence of the painting. There remains a mystery in the harem that even the female gaze cannot penetrate – or, will not represent for a mixed-gender audience. There is, thus, a tension between the promise of an unimpeded vision offered by the calm, uncluttered, open spaces of the *haremlik* in Browne's painting and the signification of a residual knowledge that remains forbidden. Within the apparently transparent inscription of harem life there lurks a repressed or hidden knowledge that, as with the lesbian subtext of harem and convent imagery, could only be indirectly invoked by an artist with Browne's particularly respectable public profile.

It is evident, despite the scarcity of other examples of Orientalism by women, that women's Orientalism is as heterogeneous as its mainstream equivalent and we must not assume that Browne's version was unchallenged. For all that there are plausible reasons for her to avoid improper subjects, it does not mean that other women artists did the same. (At the same time as Browne and Mary Cassat were selecting decorous subjects to paint and behaving like nice ladies, Rosa Bonheur was rocketing to fame with her distinctly unfeminine choice of subject and self-presentation.)

We simply cannot tell why some women tried to resolve the contradictions of being a woman artist by conforming to rather than transgressing codes of femininity. It is apparent that Browne, by personality as much as upbringing, was a relatively conservative individual (using a pseudonym is indicative here). What is even more intriguing is how someone like Jerichau-Baumann could still be seen as a respectable person when she exhibited such unfeminine and potentially improper paintings. Browne's work might challenge Orientalist traditions, but it is easy to classify as feminine; yet though Jerichau-Baumann's oeuvre was far more transgressive of gender codes there is no evidence that this ever impacted badly on the artist herself: gendered codes of art and behaviour had considerable flexibility. This does not mean that the boundaries were so blurred that they ceased to be meaningful: it was their discursive ability to incorporate, or neutralize, transgressive examples like the work of Jerichau-Baumann that ensured the continued hegemony of dominant definitions of gender.

Reviewers seem to have worked hard to read Jerichau-Baumann's work as feminine. Also, it is evident from the range of work she showed that Jerichau-Baumann regularly presented herself within the parameters expected of women artists (her Royal Academy exhibits were predominantly 'feminine' genre, the picturesque or portraits). Presumably, the respectability of her social position (she was, after all, a member of the Copenhagen Royal Academy and married to its president, the eminent Danish sculptor Jens-Adolph Jerichau) also went a long way towards compensating for her more unfeminine works. But the *Art Journal*'s review of her 1871 exhibition at 142 New Bond St (possibly a one-woman show – the only other exhibits appear to have been a few by her husband) demonstrates how difficult it was to maintain critical hegemony.

> The paintings of this lady command attention as they are marked by characteristics which are by no means common to woman's work ... Madame Jerichau moves only in obedience to the purest strain of academic inspiration ... she does not yield to fascinations ['tender relations between the sexes', 'narratives of affliction'] against which the majority of female artists are not proof ... This lady is impelled upwards into the epic vein by her tastes and feelings, and, at the same time, is more pronouncedly ethnographical than perhaps any artist of the day. There is, however, one tie which her woman's heart acknowledges, and that is a love of children; at least we thus read the many studies she has so successfully endowed with the natural graces of childhood. Notwithstanding, however, the element that gives a masculine quality to Madame Jerichau's works ... she has the power of working up to the utmost refinement of feminine beauty. We instance her portrait of the Queen of Greece ... *The Favourite of the Hareem*, an oil-

picture, declares itself at once a veritable study from Oriental life. All attempts at the improvisation of Hareem beauty by painters and poets have been very wide of the truth, as we learn from this and all other genuine representations of so-called eastern beauty. There are several pictures of eastern women: what is most valuable in them is their indisputable nationality, which is brought forward without any modification or dalliance with conventional prettiness of feature ... [others afford] evidence of independent thought ... There are also one or two female studies of Fellaheen, in which truth and genuine nationality prevail over poet's dreams of matchless houris and peerless Egyptian maids ...[84]

As we shall see, ethnographic discourse was often used as a way to validate Orientalist images as scientifically authentic and thus endorse the artist's vision as objective. But in this case, the rigours of objective reality sit uneasily with the definition of feminine art. The reviewer cannot but admire Jerichau-Baumann's depiction of nationality, but would far rather see the conventional prettiness that the artist eschews. Similarly, whilst he or she is forced to applaud the assertiveness of her independent thought, the reviewer does his or her best to give her oeuvre a feminine complexion by closing with a re-affirmation of her womanly love for children. What interests me here is that her oeuvre *was* mixed and did include paintings which could be received as unproblematically womanly, but that despite this there is something about her Orientalist subjects that creates a problem big enough to destabilize the overall classification of the artist and her work, something that other women Orientalists generally manage to avoid.

That the majority of women's visual representations of the Orient, and of the harem, are morally untroubling could be either because (for those that actually travelled) they never actually saw anything immoral or that they edited it out of their accounts lest it impinge on them as witnesses of the scene.[85] In literary representation, although women writers did have to fend off charges that they were only as moral as their last novel, the conjunction of literary-critical practice and the increasing number of women writers produced a different resolution of the problem of subject than in the visual arts. Here, artists were assumed to have studied what they depicted, in a model if not in situ, and were thus tied more closely to the represented scene. For an artist like Browne, who was known for her rigorous study from life, it would have been hard, if not impossible, securely to inscribe such a disassociation from her subject. This obstructed the establishment of a morally essential distance with which a literary author might have had more chance of success. For Western women writers like Emmeline Lott it was relatively easy to disassociate themselves from any immoral acts represented by deploying an imperial distance that presumes the author's and readers' disapproval of such heathen acts. For Oriental women writing in Europe, where they presumably had to contend with racist assumptions about their own morality, it was imperative that they be dissociated from any misbehaviour in the harem. So although Melek-Hanum describes scenes of debauchery (in the apartments of Nazly-Hanum, the daughter of Mehemet-Ali, the Viceroy of Egypt) she clearly signals her disgust by telling her readers of her prompt departure from the room. The endless assumption of an isomorphic relation between Browne's pictures and her experience of the harem makes the presentation of such a split difficult.

It is clear from the response to Browne's *Interiors* that they upset dominant perceptions of the harem and of the differences between East and West. Linda Nochlin argues that the prerequisite for an art (like Manet's *Olympia*) that transgresses discursive codes is the combination of an alternative practice in both subject and technique.[86] Although the technical differences of Browne's work are not as radical as those of Manet and the French avant-garde, I think that some of the outrage aroused by the *Interiors* can be explained in relation to a similar combination of innovation in style and technique. The changes she makes in the representation of the harem may seem small, but they are not insignificant. The attention devoted to them by critics suggests that the ways which the *Interiors* differ from other (notably French) Orientalist art constitutes a challenge to generic codes. (The frequent invocation of Decamps, the symbolic father of Orientalist art, acts as a strong defence mechanism that attests to the seriousness of the threat.)

Rosemary Betterton links challenges to generic codes to the specificity of the female gaze. Writing on Suzanne Valadon, she argues that the conditions under which women view in patriarchy predispose them to look 'against the grain' and therefore subvert hegemonic codes of viewing.[87] This 'ability to move between and to acknowledge different viewing positions' is determined by the social space occupied by the painter. In Valadon's case, her specific social position (as woman, working-class, model and artist) leads to a different gaze on and resolution of her chosen subject (the female nude). This manifests itself in a subversion of the nude's generic codes. Browne, unlike Valadon or Manet, was not associated with the avant-garde but her changes to the Orientalist canon can be regarded, and were received, as similarly significant. The censure aroused by her harems is not just because she paints plain walls and austere interiors or because she claims that her subject is the actual truth about the harem, but because of the interaction of the two. Whilst the luscious surface detail of Gérôme substantiates his superior viewing position in relation to the East, the new details and austere surfaces of Browne's work transgress the ideological codes of Orientalist representation.

Her very claim to truth, that was for some the value of her painting, could also be used to downgrade her work and hence minimize its threat. Critical willingness to read the paintings' content from her entry into the harem occludes recognition of her role as active creator of the artefact and allows a discussion of the pictures as if they were transparent recordings of her experiences.[88] The tendency to read the art object as an unmediated representation of an anterior reality is common to critiques of men's and women's work. But in this case it resolves the difference between the fantasy logic of the harem and the observed truth of the woman. The tendency to accuse the paintings of technical deficiencies utilizes a language of formalism that belies its ideological function. One senses in some of the defences of Decamps the implication that hers may be more authentic but his are more artistic.

If there is a threat in her work it lies in its offer of an alternative discourse on the Orient and in its throwing into question those 'turqueries fantaisistes' of many successful male practitioners.[89] More than this, it becomes morally disturbing, because the apparently impeccable moral qualities of the scenes witnessed by Browne throw the power relations between the Occident and Orient into question. This is where the different but nearly equal stance of images of the 'ordinary' Orient (that we shall see particularly in her treatment of Oriental children) is important. Whilst it is possible to read in Browne's representations a treatment of difference that does not necessarily condemn it, the continued stress on that difference is crucial. It allows the Occident to retain its vision of the separateness of the Orient and therefore to continue to pose itself against it. The ongoing separation of the West and the East mediates any fundamental challenge to the imperial ideology that informs Orientalism. There is room within the discourse for a feminine, and perhaps less virulently xenophobic, version of Orientalism that adapts and amends but does not remove the imperial imperative.

FROM THE SUBJECTIVE TO THE OBJECTIVE: ETHNOGRAPHIC DISCOURSES OF RACE AND NATION

After 1861 Browne continued to exhibit Oriental subjects alongside portraits and the occasional genre piece. But she never returned explicitly to the harem. Her subsequent Oriental subjects were mainly ethnographic types (like *Rhodian Girl*, Salon 1867, Gambart's 1868, Plate 31[90]) and studies of Oriental children relatively unproblematic topics for a woman artist. In contrast was her painting, *Dancers in Nubia, Assouan* (Salon 1869) which, as a subject that was practically the stock-in-trade image of a sexualized Orient, was a more provocative choice for an artist with so respectable a reputation as Browne.[91]

Rhodian Girl was described by the *Athenaeum* in distinctly ethnographic terms as a 'splendid specimen of the almost Nubian-looking women of the ancient island'.[92] The fair-skinned European-looking figure in this painting bears no resemblence to a Black African Nubian, but the interpretive impact of imperial knowledge allows the review to utilize ethnography as an objective mode in which to read the painting. This type of reading was particularly effective in the case of portraits, since women artists were frequently attributed with the ability to intuit, and thus accurately represent, their subject's character. In the case of the Orientalist portrait like *Rhodian Girl*, it constructs a gaze from West to East that is immutably gendered. The review's reference to Nubia keys into the Nubians' status as an ethnic group of almost mythical beauty – conceptualized as the only beautiful Black Africans.[93] Beauty and race were important components of Orientalist art, although it required considerable juggling to fit a European vision of pale-skinned beauty into an Oriental setting. The surprising number of pale-skinned, blond-haired women represented as odalisques, slaves and concubines was frequently explained by identifying them as Circassian, an ethnic group of fair-skinned Turks who had long had a reputation as slave traders of their own people.[94]

Black female figures often appear in Orientalist paintings, but are not marked as the overt object of desire; usually the pairing of a light- and dark-skinned woman prioritizes a reading in which the white woman is the object of desire (like Jean-Jules-Antoine Lecomte du Nouy's *The White Slave Girl*, 1888, Plate 19).[95] Whilst the pale Circassians and Georgians could easily be registered as objects of desire, they could also be seen as objects of pity. Imagined as unwilling victims of Oriental despotism (as typified by the pale nude female slave in Gérôme's *Slave Market*, Plate 11) they could be conceptualized as potentially asexual and, therefore, more moral than Black women who were stereotyped as as actively sexual and, consequently, immoral. The pale harem women oscillate between being like and not like European women, i.e. as both the permitted and the forbidden object. Part of the frisson of the white odalisque comes from the projection of the white wife (the licit object) into what amounts to a brothel situation (an illicit site): she is pitied but desired as the fantasy combination of Europe's splitting of female sexuality. This is why the desire to save as well as to savour the harem woman is so significant – it allows the West to view her within a lofty Christian and abolitionist rationale, saves her from taints of the harem, but does not prohibit voyeuristic pleasure in her image.

In contrast to the *Athenaeum*'s addition of Blackness to *Rhodian Girl*, the Black figure in *A Visit* is ignored by all but Merson, and he only notices her to comment that a 'negress' accompanies the guests. None of the other reviewers pass comment on this figure, but Gautier makes much of the others' fair-skinned beauty, implicitly excluding her from this paean to Oriental beauty. I think *A Visit* deploys racial difference in a manner that is relatively unsexualized for Orientalist painting. The painting marks the Black figure as a servant or slave (the only one carrying a cushion) but does not emphasize her body or make a stereotypical contrast between the figures at all. For all that the represented bodies in the *Interiors* are mostly fair-skinned and elegant, they are clearly not European. Their foreignness is marked by their posture and dress. The critics' frequent references to 'indolence', 'leaning', and 'nonchalance' point out precisely those bodily performances that were frowned upon in Europe and, indeed, impossible for the corseted European female. There, bodily behaviour and appearance were perceived to be moral, not just aesthetic, issues. So when Gautier suggests that Eastern dress will bring crinolines into disrepute, we must take it with a pinch of salt. The beauty in the unstructured bodies on display in the *Interiors* is precisely their difference from the women at home. They are similar enough to be desirable and different enough to be exciting.[96]

Like the *Interiors*, Browne's painting *Dancers in Nubia, Assouan* tackles the sexualized image of the Orientalized other straight on. Dancing 'girls' were an early and regular feature of the (initially male) tourist itinerary and popular with painters since the subject afforded an opportunity to paint Oriental beauties in poses of abandon and sensual movement. (See for example Gérôme's *Dance of the Almah*, 1863, Plate 34.) Although some visual and written accounts gave them a status within the culture of their own community, dancers increasingly came to be fetishized into an isolated female sign of the Orient's erotic and passionate potential – a good example of the erotic potential of ethnographic detail. Like Gérôme, Browne's painting uses details of costume and instruments to authenticate the scene. So how does she negotiate the eroticism associated with the subject without compromising herself? She must have done so with some success, since no less a moralist than Bourniol praises Browne for her chaste treatment of the theme:

> *La Danse des Almés* though animated, has the merit to be perfectly chaste; the svelte and elegantly formed dancers seemed to me a little too moorish, that is to say, of a type more savage and primitive [original], than gracious.[97]

The actual title under which the painting was exhibited at the Salon was *Danseuses en Nubie, Assouan*. Just as different ethnicities were extrapolated from the portrait of *Rhodian Girl*, Bourniol redefines Browne's unspecified dancers as Almah. Like 'Nubia', 'Almah' as a category had a significance beyond its geographical and historical specificity – in this case as a signifier of the sexual display and exchange of women. The Almah were Egyptian dancers noted for their skill in improvised dancing and chanting. By the mid-century the term had come to refer to any female dancer and generally, in the West, carried sexual overtones.[98] In the East, the Almah, in common with other dancers, were often linked with prostitution: in 1834 their practice was restricted to

three cities, Qena, Esna and Assouan.[99] Bourniol uses Assouan
as a clue to reinterpret the figures as Almah, thus foregrounding
the sexual connotations of the scene, despite the lack of their
overt presence in the painting itself. Unlike other representations
of dancers, and specifically the Almah, Browne's plays down the
image of frenzy and abandon associated with the theme. Like
Bourniol, Gautier's account of Moorish dancing emphasizes the
dancers' culturally different bodies moving in 'perpetual undula-
tions'.[100] The sexual availability of the Oriental dancer is encoded
in their distinctly non-European (uncorseted) bodies. In Browne's
painting this is emphasized by posture, dress and ornament.
But, whilst her attention to movement and pose emphasizes
the unstructured body underneath the clothes, she manages, by
breaking generic codes, to minimize the sexualization of the
subject.

The painting's geographically precise title, coupled with its circulation as a female-produced artefact, help it to avoid some of the
sexual innuendo frequently associated with the subject. Of course,
the scientific claims of ethnography often helped rather than
prevented the Western objectification and fossilization of Eastern
cultures, so I am not suggesting that an ethnographic mode rescues
Browne from complicity in imperial power dynamics. But, whilst
the setting clearly signifies Orientalness, the reworking of stereotypical referents for the Oriental dancer invite the viewer to key
into the less salacious version of ethnography. Browne's dancers
dress and dance as the informed viewer would expect – but she
avoids the nudity and overt sexuality that often accompanies
images of such performances. Many of her viewers would have
been familiar with the illustrations from Lane's *Modern Egyptians*,
which pictures similarly posed and clothed women in the article
on Egyptian dancing girls (*Ghawàzee*, not Almeh, see Plate 35).
But Browne's figures do not wear revealing *décolleté*.

It is likely that the seated women in Browne's painting are part
of the troupe, not the audience, since Muslim women would not
be present (especially unveiled) at a mixed performance with male
musicians.[101] This means that the audience is placed in the viewer's
position, a non-gender-specific viewing position that is an important departure from Browne's treatment of a stereotypically
sexualized subject in the harem paintings. Where the *Interiors*
present a sight forbidden to men, prioritize a female gaze and
thus contest male fantasies, the construction of *Dancers in Nubia*,

Assouan implies a traditional viewing position. *Dancers in Nubia, Assouan* proffers a viewing position open to all (except perhaps Muslim women) and contests male representations of sights that were available to them.[102]

Although critics made much of Browne's privileged, and hence truthful, gaze on the harem, *Dancers in Nubia, Assouan* received little attention. It did not show in Britain and the British press do not pick it out in their Salon reviews. Perhaps it did not have to be taken as seriously and contested as much as the *Interiors* because men could 'verify' their rendition of the subject as well as she, once gender had no privilege. Elie Roy, writing in *L'Artiste* in 1869, can insinuate that the dancers are fake, the result of dressing up, with far more plausibility than Lagrange's attempt with the milliners' 'berquinades' in the case of the *Interiors*: 'We find, today without much surprise, but with the greatest of regret, Mme Henriette Browne in the Orientalist camp. Her *Dancers in Nubia* are of a manifest inadequacy of drawing and suggest fancy dress [*déguisement*]'.[103]

Browne's pictures of children, the most 'feminine' of her Orientalist paintings, get the least comment. Precisely because they are so easily classified as womanly and there was such a boyuant market for pleasing pictures of children, Browne's pictures of Oriental children rarely received more than a passing nod of affirmation. Where individual figures like *Rhodian Girl* could be incorporated into the critical appreciation of her existing portrait practice, the scenes of schools and children could be mapped neatly onto an extended version of women's traditional concerns with education and social welfare. One might suppose that, like the harem scenes, the pictures of children would be seen to clearly project a gendered point of production. However, pictures of Oriental children were a standard part of mainstream Orientalist art and it is hard to distinguish Browne's pictures from those of Decamps, whose numerous vignettes of Oriental children playing at home, school and in the streets, are not markedly different. No one makes much of the similarity, which is surprising, considering the outrage over her break with Decamps' depiction of the harem. In fact, no one has much to say about Browne's children at all – her reputation as a genre artist was secure by this period so most commentators simply hail the new paintings as more of the same.

Browne's scenes of children include three school scenes:

Egyptian Boys Chanting from the Qur'an (dated 1869, shown at Gambart's 1870, Plate 36); the Witt Library reproduction entitled *A Turkish Scene* (1864, Plate 37); and *Jewish School at Tangiers*[104] (Salon 1865/7, Plate 32). Individual portraits of children intersect with her other ethnographic portrait types such as *La perruche* (Salon 1875, Plate 30), *The Scribe* (possibly *Un bibliophile*, Salon 1876, Plate 38) and *A Poet: Copts in Upper Egypt* (Salon 1874, Plate 39). These paintings are evidently not diagrammatic illustrations of racial types, but the lack of details about the sitter's identity reinforces the anonymity of the figures and emphasizes the paintings' ethnographic rationale.

The scenes of children in the Orient mirror Browne's pictures of children in Europe. Followers of her career would have been accustomed to expect such paintings from her easel, from the *Catechism* of 1857 to the cutesy *The Children's Room* ten years later. The three Oriental school scenes combine the sentiment of child painting and the excitement of Orientalism. They are ethnographically respectable, with their clear demarcation of religion and region, and bear the markers of the Orient in the prominent display of the children's pointed Turkish slippers, robes and headdress. But they also tap into the market for the accurate and emotional representation of children – regardless of specific locale. These examples, together with Browne's pictures of European children, provide cameos of 'children around the world' that are facilitated rather than impeded by national barriers. On one hand, the universality of children's experience is emphasized (whether Muslim, Jewish or Christian they attend religious instruction with varying degrees of diligence), and on the other, the differences believed to exist between the Occident and Orient are endorsed through physiognomy, dress and posture. The Oriental location and suggestion of poverty is essential to demarcate these children from the rich misses and masters of domestic genre, but it does not rule them out of its range so much as link them to scenes of the European other, the poor at home and the Orientalized peasantry of Southern Europe. The distinctly classed and nationally coded body of the child in representation can be seen in Sophie Anderson's work, where her rendition of the restrained, winsome, bourgeois girl child in *No Walk Today* (n.d.) registers class and nationality quite differently from the picturesque poverty and happy dishevelement of the Southern European urchin girls of *Guess Again* (RA 1878, Plate 40).

In her paintings Browne makes a clear distinction between Oriental children and Oriental adults. Although certain similarities are suggested between children of different ethnicities, the differences between children and adults are maintained. Given that Orientals and non-Europeans (not to mention European women and the working classes) were often infantilized, this insistence on the adulthood of Oriental grown-ups is important. Her paintings of children bear all the markers of cuteness and sentiment – the overemphasized open mouths of the boys in *Chanting the Qur'an*, the fretful boredom of students in *The Catechism* and *Jewish School at Tangiers* – which allow the affinities between children to be registered as a property of childhood, whilst the insistence on generational difference refuses the paternalistic diminution of all Orientals to the status of dependent children. This leaves the adults free to signify the validity and vitality of Oriental culture. The choice of scholars and poets over other popular Oriental subjects like shopkeepers, soldiers and peasants indicates a willingness to represent the Orient as a place peopled by independent and cultured adults. As we saw with the ethnographic portraiture, the pseudo-ethnographic verisimilitude of Browne's technique is combined with a gendered reading of the pictures to presuppose an intuitive affinity with the subject of the painting. In an Orientalist context this suggests that the artist, and by implication the viewer, is engaged in a different mode of viewing. For example, Browne's pictures of scribes (*Scribe*, c. 1865, and *A Poet: Copts in Upper Egypt*, 1874) differ from the usual Orientalist stereotype. They are seen in the midst of their trade surrounded by books and papers, sitting upright on chairs, not cross-legged on the floor. Their position and posture flout conventions of representation and suggest dignity and self-possession. In each case the figures are on the viewer's eye level and in *The Scribe* the subject holds us in a clear and forthright gaze. Compare this to the positioning of the figures in Lewis' *The Arab Scribe*, where the brightly dressed scribe and his customers are set below our eye level and become, along with the ornate tiles, part of a richly exotic scene laid out for our perusal.

THE PROBLEMATIC AUTHORITY OF THE
FEMALE ORIENTALIST GAZE

As we have seen, critics generally assumed that Browne's gaze
on the Orient was different because of her gender. I have assessed
how a female gaze on the Orient can destabilize the paradigmatic
viewing, and hence power, positions of Orientalist discourse. But
we have also seen how the disruptive potential of the gendered
gaze has been minimized by appropriation and opposition. Critics
who sing the praises of Browne's specific view also confirm that
it is not the neutrally authoritative world view of male artists. The
particularity of her gaze, that on one hand marks its value, is also
the grounds of its dismissal as biased and insufficiently detached.
John Barrell has traced the pre-eminence of detachment as a mark
of authority to the eighteenth-century interest in the classical
Republics and the concept of Public Virtue wherein to qualify for
the Republic of Citizens, and hence the Republic of Taste, men
must have the ability to be self-governing and to govern others.[105]
It was the Public, or Liberal, Man's independence (financially, and
so politically and personally) that allowed the detachment needed
to make decisions for the greater good without personal motivation. Although by the nineteenth century the concept of the
Republic of Taste had been modified to include the newly rich
accultured middle classes (previously excluded because of the
coarsening effects of mercantile endeavour), the idea of disinterested objectivity lived on in art, politics and science. The classical
exclusion of women, slaves and subject peoples as unworthy,
whether by nature or nurture, from the category of citizenship
was incorporated into Enlightenment thinking and lived on in
mid-nineteenth-century ideas of femininity and race.

In relation to nineteenth-century Orientalism, woman's
gendered inability to accede to the position of the detached
scientific observer (the nineteenth-century corollary of the
Public Man) compromised her superiority as a Westerner over
the Orient. Women Orientalists tended to be positioned as
unmediated witnesses, *not* as scientifically neutral observers.
Note how Edward William Lane encouraged Sophia to publish
an account of her women-only sights in Egypt as an experiential
appendix to his scholarly research. Likewise, Browne, who is
praised for her testament about the Orient, is not constructed as
the bearer of an independent scientific look but as the transmitter

of an experiential and empathetic gaze. There is no suggestion, from even her strongest supporters, that she is learned about the East – only that she is experienced. Experience can be interpreted as good or bad: for Gautier it is an unsurpassable bonus; for Vignon it dilutes her talent.

Any authority accruing to the female gaze is grounded in its presumed (gendered) experience. Although the Romantic cult of the sublime emphasized experience, it was not a mode of engagement that correlated to the axis of female experience. The Romantic immersion in what they took to be the authentic experience of strange lands, ideally led to the loss of their contemporary Western identity in favour of a passionate over-identification with the exotic other. (Like Delacroix's paintings, Gautier's extrapolations of half-remembered previous lives is a clear example of the pathways to fantasy that the Orient offered the Romantics.) For women, the loss of identity involved in a passionate experience of the sublime threatened the boundaries of the proper femininity essential for their reputation. Only women who chose, or could afford, to risk notoriety and social ostracism could tread that path. In a period when an active female sexuality was widely conceptualized as dangerous and aberrant, female artists could only be marginally involved with the ethos and antics of Romantic life.[106] Whereas men could use passion to create art, women, if they were allowed any passion at all, were meant to subsume it into motherhood.

Browne's gendered gaze on the Orient can adopt neither the authority of disinterested science nor the over-involvement of the sublime. Instead, a position emerges in which is constructed for women a knowledge that is both particular and diminutive. It is a knowledge that has some authority because it is experiential (but that is trivialized because it rests on womanly empathy rather than the clinical detachment of the authoritative scientific gaze) and that is emotional (but petty because its emotions are merely those of feminine sympathy and intuition rather than the grand passion of the Romantics).[107] The very grounds that secure the efficacy of the female gaze also threaten to dismember it: it is caught between the inability to be disinterested and the pitfalls of over-identification. The same dynamic constrains the construction of the paintings' viewing positions. The female gaze of Browne's paintings needs to produce a viewing position that threatens neither (by an excess of feminine and insufficiently

separated identification) the West's superiority over and separation from the Orient nor (by too passionate a response) the female
spectator's femininity. Whilst over-identification for men can be
rejuvenating, for women, as Vignon points out, it is enervating
and not to be recommended. Thus, women, at best, can be
endowed with a gaze of partial authority (based on empiricism
and sympathy) which leaves unchallenged both the detachment
of science and the grand emotions of Romanticism and thus the
authority of the male gaze. This is not to deny that Browne's work
issued a challenge to the male Orientalist gaze for, as we have
seen, such a challenge was keenly felt, but to highlight how this
damage was minimized by attributing to her a knowledge that
was specific but subordinate.

Emily Apter argues that there is a counter-knowledge within
the harem genre itself.[108] She maintains that the Sapphic themes
of the harem genre are so pronounced as to constitute a veritable
'haremization' effect, in which the alleged or assumed sexual
relations between harem women construct a challenge to the patriarchal power around which the harem is understood to be
organized. Working from the position that the harem functions as
thinly disguised version of the Occidental brothel, Apter argues
that in order to understand why writers and artists took the trouble
to relocate such images in the East, we must assess the harem as
a 'cultural supplement' that offers something extra, something not
available in an Occidental setting. Seen in this light, the latent
lesbian libidinal ordering of the harem, far from being an imped-
iment to the paradigmatic male Western viewer's pleasure, actually
facilitates his voyeuristic entry. It constitutes a challenge to the
phallic interdictory power of the harem that threatens to keep
him out. It allows a scopophilic fulfilment of supplementary desires
that are suppressed in the Western context: replacing castration
anxiety with the multiple identifications of a 'more troubling vision
of bisexually coded biculturalism' (based on the pleasures of the
cultural and gender cross-dressing of the colonial *mise-en-scène*.)

The harem and its lesbian subtext thus mirror the ambivalence
of colonial discourse itself – simultaneously shoring up and challenging a vision of absolute phallic power. Apter's inference that
one of the pleasures of the harem genre is its fantastic promise
of disobeying the phallic order shares some ground with Wendy
Leeks' argument about Ingres' bathers and harem scenes. Leeks
suggests that these paintings constitute a denial of the woman's

lack (associated with the onset of the recognition of sexual difference), thus offering the viewer a loss of identity and a return to
the *jouissance* of the pre-Oedipal access to the mother's body
(before the advent of the third term). Read in this way, Apter's
haremization effect would permit an incestuous desire without the
threat of castration produced by the recognition of sexual difference. I am somewhat swayed by both these approaches, since they
seem to offer between them a possible explanation for the dialectic
between phallic power and lesbian codings that suffuses the genre.
However, I have some problems with Apter's account which
has a problematic relationship to the 'real' harem. Like me, she
reads women's accounts of the harem for traces of an alternative discourse and notes that they persistently challenge the
Orientalist fantasy account, but she sets up women's accounts
as evidence, as if they too were not the products of the self-same
discourse whose workings she has been analysing. Similarly,
whilst I am tempted by the possibilities of a feminist recouping
of the harem as an 'antiphallic, gynocentric fantasy about the
thwarting of colonial mastery', I have to argue that any attempt
that tries to reclaim the harem as a site of radical opposition
to phallic power *per se* is doomed if it does not recognize that
the phallic power that is being challenged by either the harem
women's sapphic '*mektoub*'[109] or the Western interloper is an
Oriental patriarchy that has already been constituted as impotent.
The phallic order that controls the harem is an order that in
Orientalist discourse is already understood to be, and continually
reproduced as, emasculated and de-legitimate or, at best, barbaric-
ally potent (a temporarily pleasurable identification for the
Western male viewer that has no evolutionary future). If, as Apter
emphasizes, Lacan relies on Orientalism for his metaphor that
'the phallus can only play its role as veiled', then the anti-phallic
challenge offered by the haremization effect is also one step
removed – a challenge to an already subaltern phallic order.[110]

It is here that the iconographic links between, and possible
visual pleasures of, Browne's images of convents and harems
become clearer. Both figure as sequestered communities of
women organized around the symbolic or actual power of a male
figure, cut off from the male gaze yet understood to be activated
by it. As Melman also notes (and this is particularly telling in
her sample of writings by evangelical women missionaries), we
find within the representation of the convent themes which mirror

those fundamental to the cult of the harem: repression, exclusion, despotism, punishment, sadism, exoticism, lesbianism, sexual deviancy, archaism and rescue.[111]

Just as the women in the harem rely on the bravery of a (Western) man to free them from their prison, so too do the novices in the convent either gaze helplessly out of the window or wait for men to rescue them. Both sets of women are established as passive victims of unjust regimes, rather than as active self-directing subjects formed by the praxis of both power and resistance. The repression of this play of power/s is the unconscious project of many representations of the harem and the convent. The ease with which such meanings were read into Browne's convent scenes, despite her reputation for faithful detail, pre-empted the conflictual dynamic that would greet her harem scenes. The harem paintings were understood as realistic because Henriette Browne, a woman and an artist with a reputation for factual reportage, had really been there, but they were none the less interpreted though a grid of Orientalist knowledges about the East and the harem that often over-rode the manifest content of the images. Despite her challenge to the stereotypical Orientalist fantasy, Browne's paintings obviously offered a range of alternative visual pleasures. Although she presents images of the Orient couched in realist terms we can see how, through a variety of responses, critics are able to incorporate (Gautier), provide an alternative 'truth' to (Lagrange), or simply ignore (de Callias), her challenge to the Orientalist fantasy, emphasizing the crucial flexibility of discursive definitions of the Orient.

Earlier in this chapter I suggested that we regard Browne's harems as an analogous extension of the European drawing room that offered a safe point of limited identification for female spectators. The question now arises as to whether she really did experience them as such or unconsciously projected onto them the familiar structure of the European domestic. It is a question we cannot answer and one that may not matter – we do not know what Browne observed, only what she painted, and although her representations are backed up by a number of other women's accounts, it is just as possible that they were subject to the same unconscious determinants as she. What we can deduce is that the limited viewing and painting positions available to women artists contributed in various ways to their particular framing of the Orient. This results in a series of representations of a realm generally conceptualized as innately other that, for all the exceptions like Jerichau-Baumann, display overall a remarkable structural similarity to the familiar European domestic – a similarity that tends to be affirmatively registered, rather than treated as a sexualized contrast as is the case with mainstream and men's Orientalism.[112]

I have found little in women's visual Orientalism that adopts the vigorously critical stance on harem life outlined by Zonana. So, although further investigation may reveal such works, it seems likely that women artists who wished to criticize the gender *status quo* in Europe involved themselves more directly in the representation of Occidental gender relations.[113] Whilst Browne's (apparent) lack of involvement in proto-feminist politics and cultural formations may explain why her work intervenes in Orientalist conventions without mounting an overt critique of European gender inequalities (though I do think that the presence of an implicit challenge is felt by her critical audience), I am more inclined to regard this difference as a sign of the heterogeneity of women's involvement in Orientalism. That is, that we cannot narrow down to a single strategy the ways in which Western women cultural agents represented the Orient. As Mills points out, the alternative power/knowledge relationship that prompted women Orientalists to represent the Orientalized other as individuals rather than types (what Melman calls the 'particularizing' of the harem) is the result of an experience of the Orient that was itself always structured by discourses that positioned women as emotional, empathetic and personal rather than objective, scientific and political.[114] Where Mills allows for the always-mediated nature of representation and reading, Melman retains the possibility of an innocent transcription of experience, even if viewing is acknowledged to be culturally determined (women simply 'described what they had seen. And seeing is a pre-programmed activity'[115]), that does not allow for the polysemy of the text. It is not just that Orientalism was a heterogeneous, polyglot discourse, but that each individual image was in itself polysemic and contradictory. Thus, the loss of traditional distances between self and other offered by a counter-hegemonic women's Orientalism (empathizing, particularizing, domesticating, familiarizing as it may be) is not an absence of distance but a differently inscribed distance. Although it is likely that the women's accounts I have covered bear a closer resemblance to the experience of harem life than the highly eroticized fantasies of Gérôme, they are none the less subject to the fantasy mechanisms associated with Orientalism. We can therefore regard women Orientalists as neither more pure (truthful and non-imperialist) than men, nor as more susceptible to fantasy (the dangerously gullible female tourist), but as agents whose mixture of observation and fantasy about the East is specifically gendered because of the social and psychological restraints on their experience and representation of the Orient.

NOTES

1 Billie Melman, *Women's Orients. English Women and the Middle East, Sexuality, Religion and Work 1718–1918*, Basingstoke, Macmillan, 1992, p. 101.
2 Also important here is Zonana's work on 'feminist Orientalism' discussed later in this chapter. Joyce Zonana, 'The Sultan and the Slave: Feminist Orientalism and the Structure of *Jane Eyre*', in *Signs*, vol. 18, no. 3, Spring 1993.
3 The original subtitles of Browne's paintings refer to *intérieur de harem*, which clearly indicates the generic rather than particular (intérieur *d'un* harem) status of the referent.
4 See also Lisa Tickner, 'Feminism, Art History and Sexual Difference', in *Genders*, no. 3, Fall 1988.
5 See David Scott, 'The Literary Orient', in James Thompson (ed.), *The East Imagined, Experienced, Remembered: Orientalist Nineteenth-Century Painting*, National Gallery of Ireland and National Museums and Galleries of Merseyside, 1988.
6 Thus, women missionaries worked with Oriental women and children, aiming to civilize Oriental men via the feminine sphere, in an Orientalized reproduction of women's moral mission at home. Melman, *Women's Orients*, p. 42.
7 See Chapter 3.
8 The *Art Journal*, May 1862, p. 126.
9 The *Athenaeum*, April 1862, p. 514.
10 The English titles given to these paintings varied slightly but included most, or different versions, of the geographical detail. For example, *Les oranges; Haute Égypte* was shown at Gambart's under the title *Children with Oranges; Nubia*.
11 Guilloche refers to ornamentation that imitates braided ribbons.
12 The Koran requires women to cover their breasts and ornaments, but not faces. The veil was not a religious Islamic ruling, but a social institution based on secular and religious ideas of modesty which impacted most on affluent and urban women. Rural women were far less likely to observe it, since the economic imperative which required their agricultural labour made more than a cursory attempt

at observance impossible. See Ian C. Dengler, 'Turkish Women in the Ottoman Empire: The Classical Age', in Lois Beck and Nikki Keddie (eds), *Women in the Muslim World*, Cambridge, MA., Harvard University Press, 1978; Emily Said-Ruete, *Memoirs of an Arabian Princess: Princess Salme bint Said ibn Sultan al-Bu Saidi of Oman and Zanzibar*, (1888) London, East-West Publications, 1981, p. 149; Lynn Thornton, *Women as Portrayed in Orientalist Painting*, Paris, Edition ACR, 1985, p. 54.

13   Théophile Gautier, *Abécédaire du salon de 1861*, Paris, Libraire de la Société des Gens de lettres, 1861, pp. 72–7.

14   Gautier, *Abécédaire*, p. 75.

15   Gautier, *Abécédaire*, p. 76.

16   See, for example, the treatment of Eliza Fox Bridell's Algerian scenes as topography when other location shots like Robert's are dealt with as mainstream Orientalism, or Gautier on the Princess Mathilde's *Une Fellah* which is read as a picturesque portrait. Gautier, *Abécédaire*.

17   This phrase about the cigarette also occurs in Gautier's *Constantinople of Today*. It is apparent in this, and other, reviews of Orientalist work that Gautier frequently drew on his Turkish experience to read Orientalist paintings. Some phrases are repeated almost verbatim.

18   See Robert Snell, *Théophile Gautier: A Romantic Critic of the Visual Arts*, Oxford, The Clarendon Press, 1982, pp. 61–4.

19   Claude Vignon, 'Une visite au salon de 1861', in *Le Correspondent*, vol. 18, 25 May 1861, pp. 137–60.

20   See Chaper 3.

21   Hector de Callias, 'Salon de 1861', in *L'Artist*, vol. 11, no. 11, 1 June 1861, pp. 241–8.

22   Olivier Merson, *Exposition de 1861: la peinture en France*, Paris, Libraire de la Société des Gens de lettres, 1861, pp. 275–6.

23   Princess Belgiojoso is sometimes referenced as a woman who wrote about travels in the East. The Italian-born princess lived part of her life in Paris and was noted for her nationalism, her literary and political salon and her frequent *belles-lettres* publications on subjects as diverse as Catholic dogma and travel. Larrouse, p. 491.

24   Léon Lagrange, 'Salon de 1861', *Gazette des beaux-arts*, vol. 11, 1 July 1861, pp. 49–73.

25   See Theresa Ann Gronberg, 'Femmes de Brasserie', in *Art History*, vol. 7, no. 3, September 1984.

26   Lagrange, 'Salon de 1861'.

27   Rani Kabbani, *Europe's Myths of Orient*, London, Macmillan, 1986, p. 70.

28   Said-Ruete, *Memoirs*, p. 20.

29   Gautier, *Constantinople of Today*, (1953) trans. Robert Howe Gould, London, David Bogne, 1854, pp. 106–7, 187, 203–7.

30   Harvey confirms that the walls of reception rooms were generally painted plain cream with 'Turkish' sentences from the Koran as a

border. Annie Jane Harvey, *Turkish Harems and Circassian Homes*, London, Hurst and Blackett, 1871, p. 56.

31   Charles Newton (personal communication).

32   T. Chasrel, 'Henriette Browne', in *L'Art revue hebdomadaire, illustré*, vol. 2, 1877, pp. 97–103.

33   Chasrel, 'Henriette Browne', pp. 97–103.

34   Chasrel, 'Henriette Browne', pp. 97–103.

35   See Griselda Pollock, 'Agency and the Avant-garde: Studies in Authorship and History by Way of Van Gogh', in *Block*, no. 15, 1989.

36   Lady Mary Wortley Montagu, *The Complete Letters*, (1763) (ed.) Robert Halsand, Oxford, The Clarendon Press, 1967.

37   Sophia Poole, *The Englishwoman in Egypt: Letters from Cairo, written during a residence there in 1842, 3 and 4 with E.W. Lane Esq, Author of 'The Modern Egyptians', by His Sister*, 2 vols, London, Charles Knight and Co., 1844.

38   Lady Anne Blunt, *A Pilgrimage to Nejd: The Cradle of the Arab Race. A Visit to the Court of the Arab Emir, and 'Our Persian Campaign'*, 2 vols, London, John Murray, 1881.

39   See Jane Robinson, *Wayward Women: A Guide to Women Travellers*, Oxford, Oxford University Press, 1990. See also Melman, *Women's Orients*, p. 31.

40   Melek-Hanum, *Thirty Years in the Harem: Or, the Autobiography of Melek-Hanum, Wife of H.H. Kibrizli-Mehemet-Pasha*, (London, 1872) second edition, Calcutta, Lewis and Co., 1888.

41   Melek-Hanum subsequently published *Six Years in Europe: Sequel to Thirty Years in the Harem*, London, Chapman and Hall, 1873.

42   See Gail Ching-Liang Low, 'White Skins/Black Masks: The Pleasures and Politics of Imperialism', in *New Formations*, no. 9, Winter 1989.

43   Poole, *Englishwoman in Egypt*, vol. 1, p. 209.

44   Melman, *Women's Orients*, pp. 308–10.

45   Melek-Hanum, *Thirty Years*, p. 13.

46   Harvey, *Turkish Harems*, p. 8.

47   Neither is it known whether Browne worked from props in her Paris studio as well as from direct observation. Certainly, some of the later Orientalist subjects like *La perruche* (Salon 1875) could quite easily have been done in the studio.

48   Poole, *Englishwoman in Egypt*, vol. 2, p. 18.

49   Sarah Graham-Brown, *Images of Women: The Portrayal of Women in Photography of the Middle East 1860–1950*, London, Quartet, 1988.

50   It is unclear whether the surveillance is intended to discipline the slaves or control the wives' movements via their slaves. Poole, p. 79.

51   Blunt, *A Pilgrimage*, vol. 2, p. 232.

52   Gautier, *Constantinople*, pp. 121–90.

53   Emmeline Lott, *The English Governess in Egypt: Harem Life in Egypt and Constantinople*, London, Richard Bentley, 1866.

54   Lott, *Nights in the Harem* or *The Mohaddetyn in the Palace*, London,

79 Teresa de Lauretis, 'Aesthetic and Feminist Theory: Rethinking Women's Cinema', in Deidre Pribham (ed.), *Female Spectators: Looking at Film and Television*, London, Verso, 1989.

80 See Mary Ann Doane, *The Desire To Desire: The Woman's Film of the 1940s*, Bloomington, Indiana University Press, 1987.

81 See Mary Ann Doane and Janet Bergstrom (eds), 'The Spectatrix', Special Issue *Camera Obscura*, no. 21, 1989.

82 On the specificities of the Black female gaze and its implications for cultural studies see Jaqueline Bobo and Ellen Seiter, 'Black Feminism and Media Criticism: *The Women of Brewster Place*', in *Screen*, vol. 32, no. 3, 1991; Jane Gaines, 'White Privilege and Looking Relations: Race and Gender in Feminist Film Theory', in *Screen*, vol. 29, no. 4, 1988.
    On the interrelationship between (socially determined) critical and spectatorial positionings see Deborah Cherry, *Painting Women: Victorian Women Artists*, London, Routledge, 1993, pp. 115–16.

83 The phrase is adopted from Rosalind Coward, who uses it in relation to sexual difference. Rosalind Coward 'Rereading Freud: The Making of the Feminine', in *Spare Rib*, no. 70, 1978.

84 'The Works of Madame Jerichau', in the *Art Journal*, 1871, p. 165.

85 Melman claims that they edited out evidence of Muslim women's oppression in order to preserve the 'domesticated' image of the harem as a forum in which to bemoan Western women's oppression. Melman, *Women's Orients*, pp. 308–9.

86 See Nochlin, 'Women, Art and Power', in *Women, Art and Power and Other Essays*, London, Thames and Hudson, 1988, pp. 12–13.

87 Rosemary Betterton, 'How Do Women Look? The Female Nude in the Work of Suzanne Valadon', in Betterton (ed.), *Looking On: Images of Femininity in the Visual Arts and Media*, London, Pandora, 1987.

88 Melman's emphasis on women Orientalists' tendency to construct intersubjective relationships with Oriental women, operating as 'participant observers' rather than as distant onlookers, also runs into the problem of seeing their texts as the straightforward transcription of that experience. Whilst I agree that women were often more inclined to position themselves as participants, this positioning is itself presented to us through a series of textual strategies that simultaneously emphasize the intersubjectivity of the represented encounter and strive to differentiate between the text's Occidental and Oriental subjects. Melman, *Women's Orients*, pp. 62–3.

89 The phrase is from Chasrel.

90 In the Salon catalogue the painting is entitled *Jeune fille de Rhodes* and was exhibited at Gambart's as *A Young Rhodian Girl*.

91 For a more detailed analysis of these paintings see Reina Lewis, 'Women Orientalists: Diversity, Ethnography, Interpretation', in *Women, A Cultural Review*, vol. 6, no. 1, 1995.

92 The *Athenaeum*, April 1868, p. 531.

93 See Sander Gilman, 'Black Bodies, White Bodies; Towards an

Iconography of Female Sexuality in Late Nineteenth-Century Art, Medicine and Literature', in *Critical Inquiry*, vol. 12, 1985–6.

Nubians were also widely identified in the nineteenth century with the slave trade, as both slaves and slavers.

94 See Thornton, *Women*, p. 183; Bernard Lewis, *Race and Slavery in the Middle East: An Historical Enquiry*, New York, OUP, 1990. See also Said on Lewis' 'traditionally' Orientalist attitudes, in Edward W. Said, *Covering Islam: How the Media and the Experts Determine How we See the Rest of the World*, London, Routledge, 1981.

95 Lynne Thornton in her extensively researched volume *Women* reaches the same conclusion. The absence of such images even in her vast sample suggests that Black women were never placed as the acknowledged object of desire, or that if they were we must look to other media for such representations. One possibility in a non-High Art category of Orientalism would be the picture post-card which often verges on the pornographic in its depiction of Oriental women in provocative and semi-clothed poses, and also images of Black and Oriental women in European pornography. See Malek Alloulah, *The Colonial Harem*, Manchester, Manchester University Press, 1987.

96 Kabbani notes that like Munby and his Pre-Raphaelite peers who re-educated, re-moulded and married working-class British women, Lane repeated the process in the Orient, this time purchasing a female slave whom he educated and subsequently married. Kabbani, *Europe's Myths*, p. 79.

97 Bathild Bourniol, 'L'Amateur au Salon 1869', In *Revue du monde catholique*, vol. 25, no. 28, 25 May 1869, pp. 516–45.

98 However, Edward Lane in the 1830s had been careful to distinguish between the respectable and educated Almah and other dancers, identified as *Ghawàzee*, who were prepared to perform unveiled in public.

99 See Metin And, *A History of Theatre and Popular Entertainment in Turkey*, Ankara, Forum Yayinlari, 1963–4.

100 Gautier quoted in Thornton, *Women*, p. 136.

101 Women did attend mixed performances in the country, where religious codes were more relaxed, but Assouan is a town.

102 It is possible that by the late 1860s the exiled dancers performed to mixed-gender audiences of Western tourists and that Browne's party attended such a display, or hired dancers for a private performance.

103 Elie Roy, 'Salon de 1869', in *L'Artiste*, June 1869, p. 91.

104 Jews function as both a specific and generic Oriental population in Orientalist discourse. Jewish women in particular being so frequently used as unveiled female models that they often serve as an unidentified stand-in for the Oriental Islamic woman. See also Thompson, p. 70. Melman suggests that European women artists, unlike their male counterparts, were able to persuade Muslim women to pose for them. Melman, *Women's Orients*, p. 117.

105 John Barrell, *The Political Theory of Painting From Reynolds to Hazlitt: The Body of the Public*, New Haven, Yale University Press, 1986.
106 In contrast, Romanticism in literature did provide a forum in which women writers could encode explorations of fantasy and sexuality. I am unable here to pursue this comparison.
107 See also Sara Mills, *Discourses of Difference: An Analysis of Women's Travel Writing and Colonialism*, London, Routledge, 1991, p. 99.
108 Emily Apter, 'Female Trouble in the Colonial Harem', in *Differences*, vol. 4, no. 1, 1992.
109 '*Mektoub*' is an Arabic term denoting a passive acceptance in the face of destiny. It is taken by Apter as a way to reconceptualize what the West characterizes as harem women's passive docility in response to the tyranny of the harem. She rereads '*mektoub*' as a 'kind of fatal, voluptuous, sapphic masochism pegged to an originary self-generating feminine libido'. Apter, 'Female Trouble', p. 219.
110 I also wonder if a haremization effect would be possible in a Western setting. One might fruitfully explore the significance of contemporaneous representations of lesbianism in Occidental locations. See also Thaïs-Morgan, 'Male Lesbian Bodies: The Construction of Alternative Masculinities in Courbet, Baudelaire, and Swinburne', in *Genders*, no. 15, Winter 1992.
111 Melman also finds that similarities are registered in relation to the communal living arrangements of the convent and the harem, where inhabitants live, sleep and eat *en masse*. In contrast the bourgeois home was an increasingly divided space. Melman, *Women's Orients*, pp. 158–9.
112 See Kabbani, *Europe's Myths*, on the Oriental interior as transplanted Occidental interior.
113 See, for example, Deborah Cherry on Rebecca Solomons in *Painting Women*.
114 See also Satya P. Mohanty, 'The Epistemic Status of Cultural Identity: On *Beloved* and the Postcolonial Condition', in *Cultural Critique*, Spring 1993.
115 Melman, *Women's Orients*, p. 308.

Chapter 5

Aliens at home and Britons abroad
George Eliot's Orientalization of Jews in *Daniel Deronda*

This chapter sets out to examine how George Eliot's representation of Jews and Judaism in *Daniel Deronda* relates to the Orientalist paradigm. *Daniel Deronda*, published by Blackwoods in eight parts from February to September 1876,[1] was George Eliot's eighth and final novel. It offered a devastating critique of English society, seen as degenerating and regressive, by holding up a Jew, the Daniel of the title, as an emblem of an ancient but thriving Jewish culture to which England should look for inspiration. Whilst the earlier 'English' half was uniformly well received (despite some early disapproval of Gwendolen as a role model for the female readership)[2] the 'Jewish' half provoked strong reactions in Gentile critics. However, the book was taken up gratefully by Jewish critics in Britain who were desperate for a positive image in mainstream culture. George Eliot's oft-quoted letter to Harriet Beecher Stowe makes it clear that the book was primarily aimed at a Gentile readership and that she had anticipated some of the hostility it provoked.

> As to the Jewish element in 'Deronda', I expected from first to last in writing it, that it would create much stronger resistance and even repulsion than it has actually met with. But precisely because I felt that the usual attitude of Christians towards Jews is – I hardly know whether to say more impious or more stupid when viewed in the light of their professed principles, I therefore felt urged to treat Jews with such sympathy and understanding as my nature and knowledge could attain to. Moreover, not only towards the Jews, but towards all oriental peoples with whom we English come in contact, a spirit of arrogance and contemptuous dictatorialness

is observable which has become a national disgrace to us.
There is nothing I should care more to do, if it were possible,
than to rouse the imagination of men and women to a vision
of human claims in those races of their fellow-men who
most differ from them in customs and beliefs. But towards
the Hebrews we western people who have been reared in
Christianity, have a peculiar debt and, whether we acknowledge it or not, a peculiar thoroughness of fellowship in
religious and moral sentiment. Can anything be more dis-
gusting than to hear people called 'educated' making small
jokes about eating ham, and showing themselves empty of
any real knowledge as to the relation of their own social and
religious life to the history of the people they think themselves
witty in insulting? They hardly know that Christ was a Jew.
And I find men educated at Rugby supposing that Christ spoke
Greek.[3]

In this chapter I will be arguing that, despite the novel's generally positive portrayal of Judaism and Marian Evans' evident
desire to challenge prejudice, *Daniel Deronda* replicates many of
the fundamental Orientalist tropes of difference and otherness
that are modulated if not challenged by Henriette Browne's paintings.[4] In keeping with those critics who have claimed that *Daniel
Deronda* is a novel whose apparently split plot is driven by a
concern with heredity, race and degeneration, it will be further
argued that the deployment of Jews as a signifier of otherness for
English society reinforces, despite its attempts to challenge, naturalized ideologies of racial difference. Nineteenth-century readings
of *Daniel Deronda* will be used to explore how fluctuating theories of racial identity were read into the book by both Gentiles
and Jews. It will be asserted that for both it was an important
factor in the conception of Anglo-Jewry and that for Jews it was
a central moment in the formation of Diaspora identities: the
British Chief Rabbi wrote to George Eliot praising the novel;
Rabbi David Kauffman from the Budapest Yeshiva published a
series of articles (*George Eliot and Judaism: An Attempt to
Appreciate Daniel Deronda*, 1878) in defence of the novel that
were immediately translated into English; Jews wrote reviews in
the *Jewish Chronicle* and the mainstream press (Joseph Jacobs
in *Macmillan's Magazine* and James Picciotto in *Gentleman's
Magazine*).

Accordingly, this chapter concentrates on the meanings ascribed to *Daniel Deronda* in the years immediately after its publication, rather than entering into the field of twentieth-century George Eliot scholarship. Her other work and the corpus of the George Eliot letters will be used as auxiliary material to trace the development of the concepts (notably of Englishness, the familiar and the alien) that pre-empt and structure *Daniel Deronda*. Although Jews throughout Germany and Eastern Europe responded to *Daniel Deronda* (in the Yiddish, Hebrew and vernacular Jewish press) I shall be concentrating mainly on the responses of British Jews (or rather of Jewish critics in the English or Anglo-Jewish press), in order to focus my analysis on the interpenetrative discourses of Englishness and Jewishness that suffuse the novel and its reception.[5]

EVOLUTION, ORGANICISM, FICTION AND JEWS: CONTEMPORARY RESPONSES TO *DANIEL DERONDA*

Because *Daniel Deronda* was published serially, every month for eight months, critics were able to develop their opinions as the novel unfolded.[6] This accounts for the immediacy of some of the reviews where readers speculate on characters' future actions and possible plot outcomes, just as we would today over a soap opera or television drama serial. Several critics wrote more than one review, changing their views as the narrative, and the controversy it provoked, developed. Critics were also trying to adapt to the changes that *Daniel Deronda* signalled in George Eliot's oeuvre. By no means all the general press were hostile to the Jewish elements of *Daniel Deronda*, but to many, its intellectualism was overdone – either in its scientificity (of language and sentiment) or its irrevocable distance from the bucolic realism of *Adam Bede* (for which many of her fans were nostalgic). Critics might admire her research and be in awe of *Daniel Deronda*'s intellectual capacity, but they often regarded such intellectualism as an ungainly addition to the romance or, more xenophobically, as a foreign intrusion into an English narrative. George Eliot did not complete the final volume of *Daniel Deronda* until June 1876 (five months after publication began) and, despite Lewes' well-known censorship of criticism, was not unaware of responses to the novel as it emerged; the tenor of which she had correctly anticipated.

One of the most overtly anti-Semitic and jingoistic responses
was paraded in an unattributable review in the *Saturday Review*
in September 1876 as publication of *Daniel Deronda* came to a
close. The elements of this review, with its mix of outright anti-
Semitism and the very high-handed arrogance that George
Eliot had criticized in the letter to Beecher Stowe, encapsulate
the main themes found in objections to *Daniel Deronda*: namely,
that English readers would not be interested in Jewish concerns;
that it was too foreign; that it lacked religious sentiment; that it
was too intellectual; and that the plot was incredible by realist
standards of reading.

> The reader ... has to ask himself whether the conviction that
> the author has fallen below her usual height is owing to any
> failure of power in herself, or to the utter want of sympathy
> which exists between her and her readers in the motive and
> leading idea of the story ... Some resolute readers may indeed
> endeavour to adjust their sympathies to this supreme effort,
> but there can be no class of sympathizers. Jew and Christian
> must feel equally at fault ... the fact is that the reader never
> – or so rarely as not to affect his general posture of mind –
> feels at home. The author is ever driving at something foreign
> to his habits of thought. The leading persons – those with whom
> her sympathies lie – are guided by interests and motives with
> which he has never come into contact ...
>   And not only are these personages outside our interests, but
> the author seems to go out with them into a world completely
> foreign to us. What can be the design of this ostentatious
> separation from the universal instinct of Christendom, this sub-
> sidence into Jewish hopes and aims? ... It might be explained
> if it were the work of a convert, but *Daniel Deronda* may be
> defined as a religious novel without a religion ... Nobody seems
> to believe in anything in particular. Nobody has any prejudices
> ... Nobody expects a novel to contain a religious confession,
> and the reader of strictest personal faith may pass over latitude
> in this matter in an author whose legitimate work of delin-
> eating human nature is well executed; but when a young man
> of English training and Eton and University education, and, up
> to manhood, of assumed English birth, so obliging also as to
> entertain Christian sympathies, finishes off with his wedding in
> a Jewish synagogue, on the discovery that his father was a Jew,

the most confiding reader leaves off with a sense of bewilderment and affront – so much does definite action affect the
imagination, and we will add the temper ...

... She must know her public too well ... [not to] have been
fully aware that Mordecai would be caviare to the multitude,
an unintelligible idea to all but an inner circle.

Of course in the design of *Daniel Deronda* we are reminded
of the part played by Fedalma in the *Spanish Gipsy* [*sic*].
Fidelity to race stands with this author as the first of duties and
virtues, nor does it seem material what the character of the
race is. Fedalma feels her gipsy [*sic*] blood, as soon as she is
made aware of her origins, to be as strong and imperious a
chain as his Jewish descent is with Deronda.[7]

The link to *The Spanish Gypsy* (George Eliot's epic poem of 1868
in which the heroine Fedalma, though raised as a Spanish noble-
woman, renounces the affective and social ties of her upbringing
for the blood ties of her gypsy blood) is not lost on other critics.
Indeed, several maintain that the subject of 'hereditary race
feeling'[8] is best suited to poetry and should stay there. George
Saintsbury's review for the *Academy* in September is explicit about
the difficulty of aligning such subjects with the 'English' novel.

We do not in the slightest degree feel 'imperfect sympathy'
with Jews, and we hold that Shylock had the best of the argument. But the question here is whether the phase of Judaism
now exhibited, the mystical enthusiasm for race and nation, has
sufficient connection with broad human feeling to be stuff for
prose fiction to handle. We think that it has not ... Poetry
could legitimately treat [Daniel and Mordecai's beliefs]; indeed,
many of Mordecai's traits may be recognised, – as we think,
more happily placed – in the Sephardo of *The Spanish Gypsy*.
They are, no doubt, interesting historically; they throw light on
the character and aspirations of a curious people, and supply
an admirable subject for a scientific monograph. But for all this
they are not the stuff of which the main interest or even a
prominent interest, of anything but a very carefully reduced
side interest, of prose novels should be wrought.[9]

The accusation that, though appropriate for intellectual activity,
such investigation of contemporary Judaism has no place in fiction,
is an extension of his dislike of the scientific slant in George Eliot's

later work. Whilst he cannot but admit that, '[i]f the thing was to be done, it could hardly have been done better', he cannot accept the 'singular way in which the characters are incessantly pushed back in order that the author may talk about them and about everything in heaven and earth while the action stands still'.[10] He reads technique as a sign of intellectual allegiance, citing phrases like 'emotive memory', 'dynamic quality', 'hymning of cancerous vices' and 'keenly perceptive sympathetic emotiveness'[11] as proof of George Eliot's worrying support for new sciences, not only as digressions from the plot.

Like Saintsbury (whose opposition to Darwin was well known),[12] Henry James and Richard Holt Hutton also take exception to George Eliot's introduction of scientific language and values to a novel. Henry James published a dialogue about *Daniel Deronda* in the *Atlantic Monthly* of December 1876 that encapsulates the split response to the novel. The three characters Theodora, Pulcheria and Constantius respectively defend, deplore and dither about the book. Pulcheria displays all the tropes of upper-class anti-Semitism. She muses on the likelihood of Daniel's nose ('I am sure he had a nose, and I hold that the author has shown great pusillanimity in her treatment of it. She has quite shirked it') and the odiousness of Jews – whom she sees as either priggish or dirty.[13] Further, George Eliot is accused of a 'want of tact' in bringing scientific language into a novel and, moreover, of corrupting English literature with language that, whether it be German or Latin, is definitely 'not English'. George Eliot is defended by Theodora who, in contrast to Pulcheria's patronage of Austen and Thackeray, cultivates a taste for French novelists like Balzac and George Sand and other 'impure writers'.[14]

> Theodora: [S]o long as she [George Eliot] remains the great literary genius that she is, how can she be too scientific? She is simply permeated with the highest culture of the age ... It shows a very low level of culture on the world's part to be agitated by a term [dynamic] perfectly familiar to all decently-educated people.[15]

The foreignness of *Daniel Deronda*, associated with Theodora's taste for French novels, is registered here at one remove, since the author and his characters are Americans reviewing the English literary scene.[16] But it is a pointed reminder of the way that the Gentile reviewers subsume other intrusions under a dislike of the

Jewish content. The problem of foreignness that is made so explicitly by the *Saturday Review* is about more than Jews – it is about the way that the novel distances itself from the concerns of the 'English' half (and presumably the familiar concerns of the English readership) that should by rights provide its setting and focus.

The criticism of George Eliot's technique, like those of Browne's changes to the vocabulary of Orientalist painting, are fuelled by the defence of the values they both implicitly or explicitly attack. Hutton, in a series of reviews in the *Spectator*, characteristically attempts to find a moral message and belief in a 'higher order' in a book that implicitly challenges a Christian world view. He cannot like her scientific technique but, unlike others, who see its scientificity as proof of its flawed character, Hutton finds *Daniel Deronda* to be George Eliot's most successfully structured narrative. This is because he is able to find evidence that George Eliot really does (despite earlier doubts or indications to the contrary) believe in an order higher than Man. Although he is at first worried about her challenge to established principles, by July (six volumes on) he is convinced that the novel has a clearly moral, if not godly, message.

> There is in this tale more of moral presentiment, more of moral providence, and more of moral subordination to purposes higher and wider than that of any one generation's life, than in any previous story of this author's . . .[17]

In this case the coalition of Judaism and science denotes not intrusive threats but the long-awaited proof of George Eliot's traditional Christian devoutness.

> It is true that so far as this book conveys the author's religious creed, it is a purified Judaism, – in other words, a devout Theism, purged of Jewish narrowness, while retaining the intense patriotism which pervades Judaism; and that the hero . . . evidently sees nothing in the teachings of Christ which raises Christianity above the purified Judaism of Mordecai's vision. But however much we may differ from her here, it is not on such a difference that our estimate of the power or art of this fine tale can turn . . . The art of this story is essentially religious.[18]

Judaism is both evoked and denied: like the fetish, it exists to prove that loss does not occur, that George Eliot has not challenged God and Englishness. Hutton imagines that *Daniel*

Deronda's representation of Judaism provides sufficient evidence of George Eliot's abiding interest in religion to save her from the other evil of atheistic positivism. By emptying Judaism of its specific meaning, he is able to abstract a universal of faith which is implicitly re-registered as proto-Christian.

Although Hutton manages to make a pro-Christian element out of *Daniel Deronda*, in general, both its representation of Jews and its scientific language are interpreted as signs of a foreign intervention into English literature, alien to the English imagination and unfit subjects for literature. Like science, the representation of Jews would be more manageably placed in poetry or, better still, as the object of scientific investigation. Despite the obvious differences between a positivist scientific framework and Jewish mysticism, both are understood as variously out of place, immigrant, inappropriate and impossible to empathize with. The displacement from Judaism to science indicates a disavowal by reviewers (who do not want to identify as anti-Semitic) in which the negative value of Jews as interlopers and aliens in the English body politic is projected onto the inappropriate incursion of scientific language into the body of English literature. The English state and the English literary imagination must both be defended from an alien force that threatens to change characteristics held dear as natural, ancient and moral by overthrowing naturalized boundaries between Jew and Gentile, science and art. This attempt to segregate Judaism into another field (from literature to poetry to scientific observation) marks a process of fetishistic disavowal. This denies the reality of loss (here of Englishness) either by displacing the anxiety-producing (Jewish) object into a more comfortable form (Judaism as the object of science), or by disavowing its existence altogether (Judaism purified into Christianity).[19] This desire to remove Judaism from English literature and segregate it into another field is reminiscent of Joel Kovel's description of the aversive racist as one who, unable to reconcile racist feelings with his/her superego, represses them into a fantasy life and avoids contact with the object of hate.[20] This is in contrast to the dominative racist who enacts violent feelings about racial difference and therefore requires intimacy with the object of hate (notably found in the plantation slavery system). The aversive racist needs the object of hatred to be at a distance. If it comes too close (by moving in next door or wanting to marry the white daugter or, in this instance, by intruding into English literature) then the aggressive feelings that are normally sublimated will be reactivated, with a corresponding problem of self-image for the subject who believes that s/he is 'not racist but . . .'.

Despite the concern evinced by critics about the particular amalgamation of science and fiction in *Daniel Deronda*, scientific ideas frequently found their way into fiction. Scientific thought had a wide circulation among the educated public and fiction not only reflected but actively promoted the lay interest in science, with many novels being published whose intention was an explication of one theory or another.[21] The publication of Darwin's *On the Origin of Species* in 1859 and then *The Descent of Man* in 1871 prompted a flurry of novels dealing specifically with the evolutionary debate. *Daniel Deronda* is a novel that unites evolutionary theory with concerns about degeneration, taking the project of *Silas Marner* and *Adam Bede* (which looked at the best of old England) further to assess the future of the nation. That Jews were held up as a healthier alter ego offended readers even more than the unfavourable analysis of Englishness itself. To understand this we must understand the situation of Jews in England and their significance in an intellectual framework dominated by evolutionary theory – whether accepted or rejected, Darwin's ideas could not be ignored.

George Eliot was a novelist particularly interested in science. She and Lewes were associated with positivist circles and her interest in evolutionary theory and organicism was well known.[22] Organicism, a theory of the interdependent growth and development of organisms (individual and collective, plant and human), stresses the interdependence of the parts on each other and on the whole. No organism can be assessed outside the role of its constituent parts or the parts in isolation from each other. When transposed to an analysis of society, the ratio of individual rights/will to civic duty is contested by the theory's exponents, but all writers (from Mills to Comte, to Spencer and Lewes) agree on the importance of historical specificity to an analysis of the social organism. Of all George Eliot's novels, *Daniel Deronda* most overtly incorporates scientific theories. In many ways it is the culmination of her vision of organicist development as the solution to the theme of personal will versus social and moral responsibility that structures her fiction over a number of years.

In *Daniel Deronda* organicist ideas about the healthy development of the individual and society are based on a concept of a

nation-specific and racialized social unit in which the two key identifications are Jewish and English. This brings together organicism,
evolution and theories of racial identity. Indeed, for Darwin's
public the very idea that some species evolved more successfully
than others (the survival of the fittest) was extended to differences within species to argue, notably by Herbert Spencer, that
some humans had evolved better than others. Darwinian theory
was thus linked to discourses of class, gender and race identity.
Current social problems (be it the poor standard of army recruits
scrutinized by the army reforms of the early 1870s, nascent feminism or criminality and insanity) were analysed in relation to the
evolution and possible degeneration of different sections of
society.[23]

On the Origin of Species displaced man from the centre of the
universe and challenged the traditional anthropocentric view of
the world. By the time *Daniel Deronda* was written, Darwin's
Descent of Man had defined man as part of the animal kingdom,
which further threatened the already destabilized image of man
as born leader. This had implications for theories of racial and
national identity that saw white man as the natural ruler of the
world.[24] The *Descent* also included a section on the role of sexual
selection in evolutionary survival, thus giving an evolutionary
significance (of heredity and descent) to the novel's typical themes
of marriage, sex and beauty. In *Daniel Deronda*, for example, the
ethos of civic responsibility for women is one that centres around
marriage and lineage. Gwendolen's inner conflicts and romances
become more than a matter of individual preference. The women
in the novel have a moral and civic duty to select worthy mates
and produce offspring who will benefit the polity and, in the case
of Catherine Arrowpoint, maintain the family fortune.

At the time of *Daniel Deronda*'s publication, theories of degeneration were increasingly influential, and intersected with
evolutionary thought. Definitions of degeneration stemmed
from concern with the opposite to progress and evolution – the
aberrations of illness, insanity and criminality that threatened
the body politic and the progress of the race.[25] To medical and
scientific commentators in the nineteenth century the Western
model of industrial progress that was meant to be the apotheosis
of evolution appeared to bring with it a perplexing increase in
devolution and social unrest. Like the debate over evolution,
degeneracy theory was a heterogeneous formation with numerous

applications (educational, medical, military). Of most relevance here is its stress on heredity and the fear of hidden threats to the social fabric that were thrown up by changes in the concept of degeneration. It shifted from being understood as something that threatened the individual to something that threatened society and, correspondingly, from being an illness (that anyone could contract) to a congenital inheritance (to which some groups were more prone). Indeed, it has been argued that the growth of national identities in the late eighteenth century was a crucial prop for the emergent definitions of normality and abnormality that structured degeneracy theory.[26] The threats perceived to reside in the working class, the insane and criminals were exactly those projected onto Blacks and the colonies. As Daniel Pick argues, the imperial concept of the inferior but dangerous racial other is bound up in, and relies on, a sense of the other at home.

DANIEL DERONDA AND THE FORMATION OF AN ANGLO-JEWISH IDENTITY

If, as I have argued, Jews are positioned as England's Orientalized other in *Daniel Deronda*, then Jewish responses to *Daniel Deronda* will be indicative of the third movement in Said's three-way process of Orientalism. That is, if *Daniel Deronda* is the product of the West (England) looking at and writing up the Orient (Jews) with an agenda of Western (English) concerns, then Jewish responses testify to the impact of Orientalist representation on the self-image of the represented. The haste and enthusiasm with which Jews rallied *Daniel Deronda* to their cause (Joseph Jacobs in retrospect characterized his review as 'gushing')[27] shows the desperate quest of the Orientalized to modify and improve their self-image and the inflated significance accorded to Occidental representations. Jewish responses to *Daniel Deronda* not only contain traces of the processes by which Anglo-Jewry constructed and contested a series of self-identifications; when placed alongside Gentile criticism, they reveal the reading of *Daniel Deronda* to be an arena in which Jewish and Gentile writers struggled to control the classification, meaning and identity of Anglo-Jewry.[28]

By 1880 there were 60,000[29] Jews in Britain. This figure had risen from 35,000 in 1850, but Jews remained a small percentage of Britain's population, being 0.01 per cent in 1850, 0.17 per cent in 1880 and 0.38 per cent in 1900.[30] In Europe as a whole there were

4,100,000 Jews out of a population of 266,000,000. Their numbers in Europe increased in the nineteenth century from 1.1 per cent of Europe's total population at the start of the century to 2.2 per cent at its close.[31] Throughout Europe Jews were still subject to restrictions on their movements and occupations: in Russia the Pale of Settlement was not revoked until the 1917 Revolution, whilst political emancipation was achieved in Austria–Hungary in 1867 and in Germany in 1871. In France, although Jews were enfranchised along with the rest of the population in 1789, their rights to be counted as citizens were questioned throughout the nineteenth century and conspiracy theories thrived in Catholic, secular and socialist circles.[32] Jews were not officially allowed into Britain after the expulsion of 1290 until 1656.[33] From then until the 1860s Jewish immigration was never above 8,000 a century (less than the corresponding figures for other immigrant groups like the Hugenot refugees who fled to Britain and Ireland). Jewish emancipation in Britain came in 1835 when the removal of the requirement to swear the Christian Abjuration Oath effectively gave Jews access to parliamentary representation.[34]

The first Jewish immigrants to England were Sephardim (largely skilled business families) who, as the most established section of Anglo-Jewry, were at the core of the struggle for emancipation. The Sephardim (Jews of Spanish and Portuguese descent who had emigrated to Protestant Northern Europe or the Ottoman Empire after the inquisitions) tended to be seen as having a culture that was sophisticated and unassimilated but not ghettoized and isolated. Although by 1700 there were as many Ashkenazim as Sephardim in Britain,[35] the first wave of significant Ashkenazi immigration did not occur until the mid-nineteenth century when Western European Jews who fled after involvement, or implication, in the European revolutions of 1848–9 were augmented by Russian and Polish Jews fleeing pogroms and persecution. This challenged the balance of power in the Anglo-Jewish community and is the backdrop against which *Daniel Deronda* was read. In contrast to the Sephardic image of dynastic wealth and learning, Ashkenazim from Eastern and Central Europe were seen as illiterate peasants (albeit with a tradition of spiritualism and piety), although Western European Ashkenazim tended to be seen as highly educated and politically radical.[36]

In retrospect, the 1870s were a period of calm and consolidation for Jews in Britain prior to the upheaval caused by the mass

migration of Russian Jews after the renewed pogroms of 1881–
1904. When *Daniel Deronda* was written the Jewish community
in Britain was relatively stable and increasingly well organized,[37]
and enjoying increased legal rights despite continued anti-
Semitism. But this does not mean that George Eliot's contemporary Jewish readers did not have pressing concerns about
their status in Britain and the development of their own community. Although the turmoil leading up to the Aliens Act of 1905
has tended to take precedence in twentieth-century histories, the
1840s–60s was a period in which the older Jewish communities
were already being challenged and changed by the influx of
Ashkenazi migration. The resultant frictions were not just (as is
sometimes understood) because of Ashkenazi or Sephardi cultural
differences, but over political and religious affiliations too.

   Daniel Deronda was reviewed by Jews in the Jewish and Gentile
press and on the whole greeted with acclaim.[38] Whilst Jewish
writers praised George Eliot's literary skill, they made no bones
that their main interests lay in her sympathetic portrayal of Jews
and the realism of *Daniel Deronda*'s Jewish characters as well
as the related issues of assimilation, anti-Semitism and the rise of
Jewish nationalism. In contrast to what, as we shall see, was an
overwhelmingly positive response to *Daniel Deronda* in the organs
of the Anglo-Jewish communities, the response from Jews in
Germany and Eastern Europe was far more mixed. *Daniel
Deronda* was published in German in 1876, almost simultaneously
with its British publication, and sections of it translated into
Russian, Lithuanian and Hebrew over the next decade. Indeed,
for many Jewish readers, the novel only existed in the form of a
series of translated passages (notably Mordecai's speeches),
elements of which were mobilized almost instantaneously by
Zionists. Like their Gentile counterparts who concentrated only
on the Christian half of the novel, reviews and debates in the
European Jewish press focus mainly on the Jewish characters and
the Zionist narrative. But unlike Britain, the response of Eastern
European Jewish writers was far less a consensus: some were
opposed to the Zionist slant; others, whilst supporting the ethic
of a national heritage, stopped short of the Zionist dream of actually settling in Palestine; others criticized readers for concentrating
only on the representation of Jews and advocated an artistic appreciation of the novel as a whole. George Eliot, it seems, whilst
pleased to be informed of positive Zionist attitudes to the book,

declined to be actively involved or lend her support to the political campaigns of Zionists like Chaim Geudallia, with whom she
had some correspondence.[39]

In Britain *Daniel Deronda* was seen as an answer to the dearth
of literary portraits of Judaism and an antidote to unbalanced
stereotypes.[40] Joseph Jacobs writing in *Macmillan's Magazine* in
1877 asserts that

> Hitherto the Jew in English fiction has fared unhappily: being
> always represented as a monstrosity, most frequently on the
> side of malevolence and greed . . . [or] still more exasperatingly
> on the side of impossible benevolence. What we want is truth,
> not exaggeration, and truth George Eliot has given us . . . The
> gallery of Jewish portraits contained in *Daniel Deronda* gives
> in a marvellously full and accurate way all the many sides of
> our complex national character.[41]

Picciotto (in *Gentleman's Magazine* of November 1876) is keen
to treat the book as a novel rather than a political tract, as
which it was dismissed by critics. He can thus validate George
Eliot's representation of Jews as disinterested realism, rather than
political posturing. He applauds Daniel as a realistic portrait –
a Jew who is 'perceived to be neither a Sidonia nor a Fagin, neither
a Shylock nor a Riah'.[42]

Jewish supporters of *Daniel Deronda* confront its critics by
insisting that Jews and Judaism are a suitable subject for fiction.
They defend Daniel and Mordecai as convincing characters
and insist on Daniel's suitability as an emblem for the race in the
face of Gentile critics' dismissal of him as unrealistic, weak and
unlikeable. Picciotto rescues Daniel from charges of sainthood,
perfection and effeminacy ('ideal men, drawn by feminine hands')
by stressing how George Eliot's consummate artistry allows Daniel
to develop into a real man – flaws and all. This transforms Daniel
into a realistic young man and, most importantly, into a romantic
but credible figurehead for Judaism.[43] It is important to establish
Daniel as a believable character, so that his 'conversion' cannot
be invalidated as implausible. The issue of his conversion to
Judaism, which so horrifies the English press, is to Jewish readers
a central feature of the book's validation of heredity and race
identity and a welcome reversal of counter-conversion scenarios.
Faced with internal disputes over assimilation and reform,
the Jewish writers place themselves firmly against assimilation and

welcome *Daniel Deronda*'s Messianic schema of redemption, nationalism and, above all, religious and cultural vitality.

Both Picciotto and the anonymous reviewer in the *Jewish Chronicle* (15 December 1876) hold up anti-Semitism as the root of assimilationist tendencies. This even extends to the Princess Halm-Ebstein's denial of Judaism. Picciotto recognizes that as a rejecting and unloving mother she is 'scarcely likely to inspire much sympathy or attachment', but still presents her as an ultimately maternal woman. The Princess' revolt against the institutions of orthodoxy that *Daniel Deronda* represents as being motivated by her own (gender-specific) desire for self-expression and fame is transformed into a (maternal) revolt against Judaism *per se*; thus, her motivation in denying her son his Jewish identity is to protect him from the pain of persecution in an anti-Semitic society. Picciotto thus minimizes the potential damage of a Jew's conscious denial of Judaism. The *Jewish Chronicle* also ignores the Princess' campaign against the institutions of orthodoxy and reads her as a victim of anti-Semitism. She becomes a representation of

> ... the class of Jews who despair of the future because borne down not by legal persecution, which no longer exists, but by social ostracism ... by which the bigotry of the past has warped the Jewish character; and which like the scars of wounds continue to disfigure and impede movement long after the original wounds have been healed. They are therefore anxious to save their offspring the pangs of the struggle they had to endure themselves ...[44]

These Jews are chastised for sending their children to Christian schools at impressionable ages and thereby diminishing the strength of their Jewish identity. Whether this identification is constructed as religious and/or historico-cultural or racial or national it is perceived to be under threat from assimilation. Jacobs, writing for a mixed audience in *Macmillan's Magazine*, provocatively extends the discussion of anti-Semitism to analyse the signs of contemporary prejudice in the reviews by Gentile critics. He agrees with the book's critics that the Jewish half fails 'in reaching and exciting the interest and sympathy of the ordinary reader' because of the difficulty of accepting the new idea that 'Judaism stands on the same level as Christianity'. He imagines the

jar most readers must have felt in the omission of any explanation of the easy transition of Deronda from the Christianity
in which he was bred to the Judaism in which he had been
born.[45]

But he proceeds to demolish such objections by claiming that if
critics experience difficulty in sympathizing it is because their
suppressed anti-Semitism has prompted them to deny their familiarity with the very concepts (of hereditary determinism and
evolution) that would allow them to make sense of the book.

> English critics, however, seem not to believe in hereditary
> influences: they have unanimously pronounced him [Mordecai]
> an impossibility ... We do not remember a single critic who
> seemed to think that Mordecai's fate was in any way more
> pitiful than that of any other consumptive workman with mystic
> and impossible ideas. What reasons can be given for this defect
> of sympathy? In addition to the before-mentioned assumption
> that Mordecai does not possess artistic reality, there has been
> the emotional obstruction to sympathy with a Jew, and the intel-
> lectual element of want of knowledge about modern Judaism.
> If Mordecai had been an English workman laying down his life
> for the foundation of some English International with Deronda
> for its Messiah Lassalle, he would have received more atten-
> tion from the critics. But a Jew with views involving issues
> changing the future history of Humanity – 'impossible, vague,
> mystic.' Let us not be misunderstood: the past generation of
> Englishmen has been so generous to Jews that we should be
> ungrateful if we accused cultured Englishmen of the present
> day of being *consciously* repelled by the idea of a poor Jew
> being worthy of admiration. But fifteen centuries of hatred are
> not to be wiped out by any legislative enactment. No one can
> say that the fact of a man's being a Jew makes no more differ-
> ence in other men's minds than if he were (say) a Wesleyan.
> There yet remains a deep unconscious undercurrent of preju-
> dice against the Jew which conscientious Englishmen have often
> to fight against as part of that lower nature, a survival of the
> less perfect development of our ancestors, which impedes the
> Ascent of Man.[46]

Jacobs uses current scientific theory to undercut the myopia of
the Gentile critics, pointing out again and again how unconscious

resistance to experiencing any affinity with Jews causes them to de-skill themselves as readers. This turns the evolutionary tables on the English who in other accounts see themselves as the ultimate in evolution. Jacobs pictures them hovering on the brink of devolution in which repressed anti-Semitism threatens to cause an atavistic throwback to ancient, uncivilized prejudice and thus a national regression to a previous and inferior incarnation. Thus, where Gentile critics fulminate against the inappropriate incursion of science into literature in an attempt to protect a national culture from intruders, Jacobs reads their exclusion of modern science as a sign of the arrested growth and hence potential degeneration of the very culture they seek to protect.

The Jewish reviews I have come from a culturally hegemonic section of the Jewish population. None the less, they are structured by the limitations that constrain the subordinate discourse of an ethnic minority whose exploration of identity is couched in terms of their racialized representation in the dominant culture. We have no evidence of how *Daniel Deronda* was received by less powerful sections of the Jewish community – although George Eliot and *The Times* note that Dr Herman Adler lectured on *Daniel Deronda* to 'the Jewish Working Men'.[47] Both George Eliot and Lewes emphasize that the Jews who wrote in praise of *Daniel Deronda* were 'learned'.

> ... we have both been much gratified at the fervent admiration of the Chief Rabbi and other learned Jews, and their astonishment that a Christian should know so much about them and enter so completely into their feelings and aspirations.[48]

GEORGE ELIOT AND JEWISH SOURCES

Despite the evident approval of her Jewish readers, George Eliot's selection of Jewish material highlights the Orientalist structure of *Daniel Deronda*. For all that she addresses contemporary Jewish concerns, she presents a picture that is edited according to Judaism's role as other, not centre, of the text. There was considerable Jewish research available to George Eliot (she read nine Jewish historians in all) and many of their ideas are espoused by characters in *Daniel Deronda*. Given that the ethical and political differences within contemporary Jewish scholarship would have been clear to her, the way she uses these sources and decides which version of Judaism will be legitimized by the narrative, indicates her sympathies.[49] Basically, nineteenth-century Jewish historiography was divided into two camps – assimilationist and nationalistic – and George Eliot read several authors in each. Those most heavily referenced in the novel are Zunz and Geiger (assimilationist) and Graetz and Munk (nationalist). Despite their differences, these four were united against the picture of contemporary Judaism as culturally sterile popularized by Jost (with whom George Eliot was also familiar). Their books, written in the 1820–70s, must be understood, like all history writing, as bound up in the contemporary debates and dilemmas of their authors' worlds.[50] Although Marian Evans knew some Jews in Britain, most of the information in *Daniel Deronda* comes from written sources in Jewish history and philosophy. She also translated Spinoza's *Ethics* in 1854 and shared with Lewes an enthusiasm for the poetry of Heinrich Heine, whose positive attitude to being Jewish and emphasis on the common humanity of man sat well with their humanism and organicism.[51] It was Heine who authored an epic poem on the medieval mystic and philosopher Jehuda ben Halevi (c.1075–c.1141), the philosopher and poet whose major work the *Kusari* is quoted directly in *Daniel Deronda*.[52]

George Eliot's research on Jewish religion and history was based on her visit to Germany in 1854 and she drew on German rather than British Jewish scholarship. However, her emphasis on the spiritual Sephardi period of the Spanish–Arabic Renaissance ignores one of the main developments in nineteenth-century German Judaism – the Jewish Reform Movements. Like the Anglo-Catholic Revival's interest in Eastern Churches as the living embodiment of ancient patristic religion rather than as a contemporary and developing faith, George Eliot represents Judaism as a living example of an ancient culture that owes more to developments in its past than its present. (Although Zionism was a contemporary concern it is conceptualized in relation to ancient and Renaissance traditions rather than to, for example, contemporary socialism.) Thus, British Jewish scholarship is ignored in favour of German Jewish scholarship, and research into the Spanish Renaissance is preferred to contemporary German Jewish developments in theology and liturgy. Although the existence of a Jewish Reform Movement is referenced in the novel, particularly in the scene in the Hand and Banner, the narrative and the plot endorse Mordecai's vision over all – not only his Zionism but his allegiance to Sephardi spiritualism and orthodox religion.

This minimization of Reformism in British Jewry does not accord with its actual support at the time of writing. (And all reviewers understood the novel's setting to be the recent past.) Although the Jewish Reform Movement initiated by Moses Mendelssohn in the late eighteenth century was never as popular in nineteenth-century Britain as it was in Germany and North America, there was a discernible body of Reform Jews in Britain. It is clear from their struggle to be included in the English state's liaison with Anglo-Jewry that they regarded themselves as an alternative to the Orthodox. (When the government wished to designate a statutory representative body of Anglo-Jewry in 1846, Reform Jews fought unsuccessfully against the Orthodox Board of Jewish Deputies. Similar campaigns continued throughout the century.)[53] The battle against the ascendancy of the Orthodox in the specific situation of state recognition indicates the fierce struggle for the definition and public image of Jews in Britain. Like the government, *Daniel Deronda*'s validation of Orthodoxy as *the* valid form of Jewish expression and identity supports the claims of the Board of Deputies to define being Jewish in England. The increasingly hegemonic status of this organization (and the fears of criticizing one's own in public) presumably account for the lack of criticism about this in the reviews. Certainly, the *Jewish Chronicle* supported the Board of Deputies and Picciotto was no opponent.

Daniel Deronda's disapproval of Reform Judaism may seem an unlikely choice for the author who popularized Methodist Non-Conformist Christianity. The Jews in *Daniel Deronda* are often of a sort calculated to stay strange, unlike the Methodists in *Adam Bede* who, though strange to the villagers, are found to be familiar (homely to the point of fulfilling a family role, like Dinah as surrogate daughter to Adam's grieving mother). By choosing to emphasize Orthodox Judaism and marginalize Reform, *Daniel Deronda* bars access to precisely that section of the Jewish population that most vociferously advocated adaptation to English social mores. (Not that Reformism was assimilationist *per se*.) For a writer who might be expected to support a more rationalist version of religion, and an author who demystified Methodism as England's religious other (though never the ultimate other of

Roman Catholicism), *Daniel Deronda*'s mystical Judaism is an anomaly.

The exclusion of Reformist philosophy from the narrative's sympathy also closes off an avenue of Judaism that might allow more fulfilment to the female characters. Judaism is not represented as a liberatory force for women in the same way as it is for mankind and Jewish national interests: the only heroism open to the *ayshet chayil* (woman of worth) is the quiet, determined, understated support of her menfolk for which Picciotto praises such 'daughters of Israel'. The thriving organic development of Judaism comes to a halt in relation to its women: it is the prison from which the Princess flees and the haven that Mirah craves, but it is never represented as changing in response to their actions. As usual in George Eliot's fiction it is the exceptional woman, Alchirisi, who most approaches fulfilment in her own terms. She is able to move out of the bounds of respectability (this time Jewish Orthodox) because of her talent; ' "I had a right to be an arist ... My nature gave me charter" '. [728]

Although evidence shows that Halevi was a significant figure in nineteenth-century Jewish thought, we have to explore why *Daniel Deronda* gives his ideas such prominence when other equally influential writers are ignored.[54] Why does *Daniel Deronda* support a form of Jewish identification that is Sephardi, that is based on the highly esoteric traditions of the Kabbalah and that propounds a Jewish nationalism in both rational and spiritual terms, when we know that George Eliot also read Spinoza and the writers of German Reformism? The answer lies, I think, in the book's mission to spread tolerance and understanding among the English readership and suggest a way forward for English society. Thus, Mordecai's Kabbalistic vision not only offers a way to reconstruct society but conveniently relocates nineteenth-century Jews in a spiritually glowing medieval past, thereby bypassing any of the difficulties associated with contemporary Jews with all their flaws.

Apparently, *Daniel Deronda*'s vision of a thriving medieval culture (in spite of the horrendous persecution of that period) was as attractive to representatives of Anglo-Jewry as it was appropriate and expedient for *Daniel Deronda*. Jewish reviewers do not reject *Daniel Deronda*'s endorsement of mysticism, even though it was not a predominant feature of Anglo-Jewish life. The status accorded to Sephardi spiritualism had changed in the mid-century prior to the writing of *Daniel Deronda*. It shifted from being disparaged as a defensive reaction to Spanish anti-Semitism to being hailed as a golden age of cultural achievement and spiritual integrity. *Daniel Deronda*, therefore, presents the Kabbalistic past, which for nineteenth-century Jews has come to function as a mythical prior moment; to Gentile readers as a contemporary phenomenon. It is hardly surprising that Jews were pleased – *Daniel Deronda* wraps nineteenth-century Anglo-Jewry in the glow of a long-gone halcyon past and offers a fantasized return to glory (manifestly Zionism, but latently medieval Sephardi Diaspora) at the same time as it offers Gentiles a route to regenerate England.

Daniel Deronda places Daniel as a direct heir to learned Sephardi traditions in two ways: firstly as Mordecai's spiritual heir (a position he is seriously considering even before his Jewish origin is known to him), and secondly, through the dynastic heritage revealed to him by Kalonymos. His grandfather, Daniel Charisi, is represented to him as a doctor who, 'mingled all sorts of learning ... like our Arabic writers in the golden time' and as someone who insisted 'that the strength and wealth of mankind depended on the balance of separateness and communication, [but] was bitterly against our people losing themselves among the Gentiles'.[791]

Daniel's Sephardi heritage is presented as one of learning and aristocracy. His association with the substitute patriarch Kalonymos links him to a dynasty of *hofjuden*, or court Jews. [790] If the Ashkenazim could lay claim to a tradition of, often impoverished, mystics and martyrs (as epitomized in the modern-day figure of Mordecai) the Sephardim gloried in a proud heritage as scholars, statesmen and nobility, with a corresponding stress on dynastic continuity and reputation, into which Daniel can be inserted. Picciotto's derision of that 'certain class' who change their names is in contrast to his emphatic praise of the Sephardim who 'have carefully preserved through generations and ages their ancient family names, and are proud of them'.[55] It is thus significant for both Jewish and Gentile readers that Daniel is identified as a particular sort of Jew – Sephardi, learned and aristocratic.

SHIFTING STEREOTYPES: ORIGINS, HEREDITY, IDENTITY

Daniel's descent, upbringing and 'conversion' are central to the narrative's construction of both Englishness and Jewishness, for he is the linchpin of a new identity for both. George Eliot complains at those readers who 'cut the book into scraps and talk of nothing in it but Gwendolen. I meant everything in the book to be related to everything else there'.[56] This is the other much quoted statement about *Daniel Deronda* and is taken to refer both to her organicist beliefs and the desire to make readers confront their anti-Semitism. Sally Shuttleworth, who sees *Daniel Deronda* as a profoundly organicist novel, argues that for George Eliot the Jews represent 'the virtues of organic growth without the attendant disadvantages of the corruption of the English social organism'.[57] Typically, the discussion about Jewish identity in the Hand and Banner is framed in evolutionary terms. Against arguments that post-emancipation Jews should assimilate and refrain from their 'superstitions and exclusiveness' or that 'as a race [the Jews] have no development in them' Mordecai retaliates that the faith that has survived centuries needs only to be revitalized in a new organic state.

> Revive the organic centre: let the unity of Israel which has made the growth and form of its religion be an outward reality. Looking towards a land and a polity, our dispersed people in all the ends of the earth may share the dignity of a national life which has a voice among the peoples of the East and the West – which will plant the wisdom and skill of our race so that it may be, as of old, a medium of transmission and understanding.
>
> The divine principle of our race is action, choice, resolved memory . . . choose our full heritage, claim the brotherhood of our nation and carry it into a new brotherhood with the nations of the Gentiles.[592–8]

But the Orientalist construction of Jews as other (albeit positive), overrides the purity of George Eliot's organicist theory. The construction of Judaism as a healthy organicist alternative to stultifying Britain relies on an anachronistic image of medieval Jewry that is out of keeping with the relativism of its own organicist drive. George Eliot invokes Judaism as an unbroken continuum of practically unchanging spiritual development. By giving narrative endorsement to Mordecai's transhistorical hopes for the transmigration[58] of his soul into a union with Daniel's, she suggests a romantic affiliation with the imagined past rather than any heroicization of the average modern-day Jew. Despite organicist and evolutionary stress on the ever changing state of an organism, Judaism is represented as a curious mix of adaptation (physical/economic) and stasis (spiritual): successful adaptation has enabled it to survive centuries of persecution and landlessness, whilst a tenacious clinging to ancient traditions has maintained its spiritual life. Judaism is no longer seen by Daniel, and hence the reader, as 'a sort of eccentric fossilised form . . . [but as] something still throbbing in human lives, still making for them the only conceivable vesture of the world'.[411]

Daniel's gradual accession to his Judaic heritage acts as an antidote to his personal aimlessness (conceptualized as an unhealthy remoteness from the rest of the social organism) and as a model for the revitalization of English society. His Judaism provides a solution to the plot's requirement that he marry Mirah and continue Mordecai's mission, and the narrative's *Bildungsroman* of his inner life. (Gwendolen, who acts as the representative of English society with her vacuous introspection and lack of meaningful social interaction, is moved by Daniel towards a will to live that breaks her out of her narcissistic isolation but never approaches the state of moral plenitude achieved by Daniel.) The pre-Judaic Daniel labours under a

> too reflective and diffusive sympathy [that] was in danger of paralysing in him . . . the conditions of moral force . . . [He] longed for . . . some external event, or some inward light, that would urge him into a definite line of action and compress his wandering energy . . . the influence that would justify partiality, and making him what he longed to be yet was unable to make himself – an organic part of social life, instead of roaming in it like a yearning disembodied spirit, stirred with a vague social passion, but without fixed local habitation to render fellowship real.[413]

His need for a role in the social organism, a moral purpose and his quest for his origins are all structured *a priori* to be fulfilled by the eventual revelation of his Jewish birth. The shock of this conversion/transition makes sense in relation to contemporary attitudes to comparative religion, evangelism and Empire. The horror and denial revealed in the press is produced by the spectre of the imperial English gentleman undergoing precisely the process of influence through example and eventual conversion that was being propounded in the colonies by Empire and Church. Missionary and popular colonial literature is awash with examples of natives converting not only to Christianity but also to a (lowlier) version/imitation of British life.[59] If a Briton is represented as 'going native' it is rarely applauded. Note in *Daniel Deronda* that the instant response to meeting or hearing about Mirah from both the Meyricks and Lady Mallinger is to speculate on the possibility of converting her.

This desire to convert Jews into Christians adumbrates the aversion to Christians converting into Jews that was to be articulated by Gentile critics. At the heart of the critics' outrage is a curious fantasy of cultural miscegenation, for Daniel – though raised a Christian – was *born* a Jew: his move to Judaism in adult life cannot technically be called a conversion, it is really a discovery. Although the responses to *Daniel Deronda* display all the tropes associated with discourses of racial purity, there is no mixed blood. Even within the discourse's own fantastical definitions of pure blood and stable originary identities, Daniel's biological and intellectual heritage comes directly from both his natural parents. He receives his Jewishness through the matrilineal line (the fact of being born of a Jewish mother). From his father (a patriarchal endowment unwillingly passed on by the Princess) derive the traditions and heritage that sustain him and offer the 'fixed local habitation' and 'definite line of action' that he craves. Yet, nevertheless, Daniel is never really a whole Jew. Rather, he will be a new hybrid Jew as George Eliot fuses blood with sympathy-through-experience to advocate a heredity that is socially as well as biologically derived. This is the miscegenation or cross-breeding of the text. It mixes the social with the biological and thus recognizes both origins – the English and the Jewish. Daniel is able, in terms of plot and narrative, to go forth as the new Messiah who will symbolically revitalize English society and inspire Europe's Jews *because* he is both Jew and Gentile.[60]

> 'The effect of my education can never be done away with. The Christian sympathies in which my mind was reared can never die out of me,' said Deronda, with increasing tenacity of tone.

'But I consider it my duty – it is the impulse of my feeling – to identify myself, as far as possible, with my hereditary people, and if I can see any work to be done for them that I can give my soul and hand to, I shall choose to do it.'[724]

'I will not say that I shall profess to believe exactly as my fathers have believed. Our fathers themselves changed the horizon of their belief and learned of other races.'[792]

George Eliot has Kalonymos greet this last quotation with respect and benediction. The cultural interface becomes one of exchange, where the novel's vision of a Judaic enrichment of English life is offset by Daniel's stress on his allegiance to his English Christian heritage. The emphasis laid on Daniel's attachment to his English upbringing attempts to retain the reader's support and the narrative's credibility. But the threat of his conversion and the spectre of the trappings of English aristocratic civilization dropping from him outweigh such structural concessions. The press response, from incredulity to fury, suggests the severity of such a disruption.

The anger over Daniel's 'conversion' is typical of the English in *Daniel Deronda*, who are marked by their refusal to accept their connections with other races and nations. It is this narrow-mindedness, unlike the fertile cross-influences of the Jewish Diaspora, that accounts for their petrified culture. The English assumption of imperial power is challenged by Klesmer's attack on Mr Bult, which highlights the disavowal (of relations with other nations and of imperial brutality) at the heart of England's autarky. This is criticized again in the colonial characterization of Grandcourt's tyrannous rule over Gwendolen.

He knew the force of his own words. If this white-handed man with the perpendicular profile had been sent to govern a difficult colony, he might have won reputation among his contemporaries. He had certain ability, would have understood that it was safer to exterminate than to cajole superseded proprietors, and would not have flinched from making things safe in that way. [655]

The sense of difference and superiority experienced in relation to the colonies underlies the perceived difference and distance between England and mainland Europe, and between the English and the Jews. Grandcourt's standoffishness in Genoa culminates

in a theatrical display of such stereotypical English arrogance and
eccentricity that it leads to death.

> This handsome, fair skinned English couple manifesting the
> usual eccentricity of their nation, both of them proud, pale, and
> calm, without a smile on their faces, moving like creatures who
> were fulfilling a supernatural destiny – it was a thing to go out
> and see, a thing to paint.[745]

Whilst *Daniel Deronda* criticizes the ethos of imperialism on
several occasions, it does not relate it to Mordecai's plans in the
East.[61] However, by choosing to represent Jews George Eliot
unleashes the latent anti-Semitic aggressions that were otherwise
camouflaged or side-lined by a series of periodically more overt
hostilities towards the more distant and more successfully
'othered' peoples of the colonies.[62] The assertion that Jews are
not only similar enough to be a role model but also are already
present in the English bosom was just too much – reviewers'
hostility was in direct proportion to the psychic importance of
keeping Jews separate from the self. The link between Jews and
English imperialism is not only thematic. At times Jews were
perceived to have very specific potential for England's imperial
development: in 1840 Palmerston's government considered
supporting Jewish colonization in Palestine as a solution to
conflicting imperial interests in the region. His letter to the British
ambassador in Constantinople advised that the Sultan should be
persuaded of the

> very great benefit [that] would accrue to the Turkish
> Government if any considerable number of opulent Jews
> could be persuaded to come and settle in the Ottoman
> Dominions, because their wealth would afford employment
> to the People, and their Intelligence would give an useful
> direction to Industry . . .[63]

Palmerston's letter brings the Jews into play as an envoy group
of Europeans to the Orient; they count as aliens at home and
Britons abroad. But where Palmerston in 1840 depicts Jews as
agents of British imperial interest, the Bulgarian Horror the year
before *Daniel Deronda* was published (when Disraeli continued
to support the Turks despite their massacre of Bulgarian
Christians) led many to see Jewish links abroad as a threat
to British interests.[64] The idea of Jews as a nation within a nation

persistently stressed that their contacts and alliances abroad allowed them a loyalty to the British state that was, at best, tenuous. In this light, the efforts of Jewish institutions to prove their loyalty and their Englishness can be seen as a defence mechanism as well as a desire for national identity. Mordecai's vision of Israel as a buffer state in the East constructs Jews as civilized Westerners and able statesmen in much the same way as had Palmerston's communiqué to Constantinople thirty years earlier.

> There is a store of wisdom among us to found a new Jewish polity, grand, simple, just, like the old – a republic where there is an equality of protection, an equality which shone like a star on the forehead of our ancient community, and gave it more than the brightness of Western freedom amid the despotisms of the East ... And the world will gain as Israel gains. For there will be a community in the van of the East which carries the culture of every great nation in its bosom; there will be a land set for a halting of enmities, a neutral ground for the East as Belgium is for the West ... Let our wise and wealthy show themselves heroes. They have the memories of the East and West, and they have the full vision of a ... new Judea, poised between East and West – a covenant of reconciliation.[594–7]

Here, Jews as a race are constructed as a 'medium of transmission and understanding' that relies on their similarities to Europe rather than to the East (though they will benefit from their knowledge of both). Where the letter to Beecher Stowe links Jews and Orientals as recipients of English prejudice, Mordecai's speech clearly differentiates between Jews (here presented as ersatz Westerners) and Orientals (presented as despotic). In their construction as Western envoys, as stand-in European Christians, Jews come to occupy a space comparable to the category of the 'not quite not white' that Homi Bhabha analyses in his work on colonial mimicry.[65] Compared to the ultimate other of 'despotic' Orientals, the Jews become like Europeans, offering in their democratic (republican) state a repeat or mimicking of England that bridges the gap between the Oriental/colonized and the English. The Jewish state will fulfil England's desire for a 'reformed, recognizable Other', that is 'a subject of a difference that is almost the same but not quite'.[66] Like the constitutions given to colonies, the 'almost but not quite', other of colonial mimicry is not meant to have any power. The constitution appears real, but is only pretend. Likewise, the new Jewish state can only mimic the power of the colonizers to whom it will owe its being; it is not intended to have its own efficacy.

But the Jew, who does function as 'not quite not white', is not the mimic man. The mimic man is a translator, a go-between, who looks native but thinks and feels English. Bhabha's mimic man only retains his place by filling an always partial subjectivity that relies on him, despite appearances, *'emphatically'* not being English. *Daniel Deronda*, on the other hand, presents Judaism, the new Danielic Judaism, as an authentic and complete identity. There is nothing lacking in Daniel's subjectivity – now all is made whole, he will be the best of both. The shifting significance of Jews in discourses of nation and race mirrors the ambivalence in colonial discourse necessary for the creation of mimicry. It is the Jew's symbolic not quite not whiteness that, like the fetish, testifies to the fear that it is its function to disavow. The desire to place the Jewish state as a mimic state of nearly but not quite Europeanness in the East displays a disavowal of racial difference (between Orientals and Occidentals) that reveals, to borrow Bhabha's phrase, the 'phobic myth of the undifferentiated whole white body'[67] at the heart of colonial and Orientalist discourse. Because Jews are in between Black and white, are in themselves the signifier of a problematically unspecifiable difference,[68] the Jewish state occupies a different space to the mimic states of puppet colonial principalities. The Jewish state has more chance of being more properly white than any other and is, therefore, both more useful and more dangerous.

George Eliot's letters and her essays construct another representation of Jews. In this, the differences between Jews and Gentiles are minimized (so extensively as to allow her a partial identification with Jews) and replaced with a stress on the differences *between* Jews. The correspondence divides Jews into good and bad Jews, with education as the differentiating sign of the special/good Jew.

> [W]e have both been much gratified at the fervent admiration of the Chief Rabbi and other learned Jews, and their astonishment that a Christian should know so much about them and enter so completely into their feelings and aspirations.[69]

Had not learned Jews and impassioned Jewesses written to her from Germany, Poland, France, as well as England and America, assuring her that she had really touched and set vibrating a deep chord, Mrs. Lewes would have been very despondent . . .[70]

Whereas *Silas Marner* or *Felix Holt* invite us to empathize with the common people, it is impossible in the George Eliot letters to contemplate such an alliance of sympathy with the common Jew. That only the learned (and acculturated) Jew can break across the inbuilt barriers of prejudice is borne out in George Eliot's recipe to David Kaufman for the perfect Jewish reader.

Certainly, if I had been asked to choose *what* should be written about my book and *who* should write it, I should have sketched . . . an article which must be written by a Jew who showed not merely sympathy with the best aspirations of his race, but a remarkable insight into the nature of art and the processes of the artistic mind. Believe me, I should not have cared to devour even ardent praise if it had not come from one who showed the discriminating sensibility, the perfect response to the artist's intention . . .[71]

The emphasis on the specialness of the educated mind sets up a meritocracy in which the educated Jew can be a social equal. Moreover, George Eliot's alignment with good Jews allows the disavowal of the bad Jew (the one who deserves to be the object of discrimination – like the unexceptional woman who does not deserve liberation). This permits revulsion from common Jews to stand unchallenged and shifts the disapproval of (some) Jews from an unacceptable basis in race discrimination to a more acceptable basis in class discrimination. George Eliot is content to pass as a Jew (although only the best sort – a learned Rabbi[72]) but not as working class. The pleasures of going native, in this case a sort of intellectual cultural cross-dressing, are predicated on the security of knowing one is really English. So although George Eliot can be flattered to be accepted as a quasi-Jew, the letters construct her as emphatically non-Jewish, thereby allowing the fantasy of passing for native without the risk of being judged as one.

The emphasis on education is not only a euphemism for class (the educated working class appearing cultured enough to pass as middle class), but a specific category of social validation that had biographical significance for Marian Evans and Lewes. The repeated reference to learning and special intellectual qualities suggests the elevated currency of intellect for Marian Evans who, herself of modest class origin and choosing to occupy a marginal and transgressive social position as Lewes' common-law wife, relied on her profession as an intellectual for finance and social status. George Eliot may risk diluting her religious and national identity in the affiliation with Jews, but the stress on education serves to maintain a sufficiently distinct class identification to underwrite these transitions. In the corpus of her work it is clear that, whereas Christianity and nationality can be criticized, and even disowned, class remains stable. Once Marian Evans had given up her ardent Non-Conformist Christian belief, her work betrayed little difficulty in criticizing Christianity. Likewise, she is a frequent critic of the English national character, not only for the regressive degeneration seen in *Daniel Deronda* but particularly for its xenophobic small-mindedness.

> To my feeling . . . this inability to find interest in any form of life that is not clad in the same coat-tails and flounces as our own lies very close to the worst kind of irreligion. The best that can be said of it is, that it is a sign of the intellectual narrowness – in plain English, the stupidity, which is still the average mark of our culture.[73]

But despite her illuminating studies of class relations and the sympathy for the rural working class espoused in *Adam Bede* and *Silas Marner*, the letters and essays have no problem enunciating a genteel 'we'. The letters are peppered with requests for servants with good 'characters' and accounts of hiring 'help'. George Eliot's essay 'Servants' Logic' in the newly established *Pall Mall Gazette* of March 1865 dwells ironically, but with an air of longsuffering familiarity, on the problems of communication between mistress and servant, without ever challenging the terms of class difference.

> . . . the fellow-mortals we most need to involve, and whose minds we find ourselves the most incapable of grasping, are our servants, and especially our cooks . . . When reasoning with servants we are likely to be thwarted by discovering that our axioms are not theirs . . . A mild yet firm authority which rigorously demands that certain things be done, without urging motives or entering into explanations, is both preferred by the servants themselves, and is the best means of educating them into any improvement of their methods and habits.[74]

DISTANCE AND DIFFERENCE: THE PROBLEMS OF READING *DANIEL DERONDA*

Despite her sympathy for the working class, George Eliot maintains a distance from them that avoids a compromise of her, or her readers', class position. The empathy between reader and working-class object in the earlier works relies on the successful implementation of a distance that is lacking in relation to the racialized Jewish object of *Daniel Deronda*. In *Adam Bede* and *Silas Marner* the spatial and temporal distance of narratives set in the long-gone but dimly remembered (and already mythologized) rural past allows a nostalgic and safely remote sense of affiliation. This, like *Felix Holt*'s careful differentiation between the good, worthy, working-class radical and the terrifying spectre of an uncontrolled mob, permits an association that will not compromise middle-class readers' sense of self.[75] But in *Daniel Deronda* the closeness of the contemporary Jews threatens to close down the reassuring distance necessary for the empathy she apparently intends. If *Daniel Deronda* is to fulfil George Eliot's aim of reconciling Christians to their Jewish compatriots, then a distance between the Christian reader and the Jewish object must be established. But this is where the book sets up its own self-destruction: it is impossible to bring Christian readers to a recognition of their 'debt' to Jews without collapsing the psychically essential distance between reader and textual other that is successfully maintained in the earlier novels.

If, as many critics suggest, *Daniel Deronda* is a failure, it is because the success of the plot relies on Daniel being accepted as both Jewish and Christian and this, because it requires the loss of distance and a recognition of the Judaic roots of Christian culture, is more than many can stomach. The difficulty of accepting Daniel's hybridity disrupts the narrative and intervenes in the pleasure of reading to such an extent that it prompts a denial – of Daniel, the novel and the existence of anti-Semitism. Like Freud's description of the uncanny – the shock of seeing the familiar (*heimlich*) in an alien guise (*unheimlich*) – Jews contain elements of the familiar in a form that is strange.[76] Daniel, who is recognizable as the ultimate English gentleman (or is he? Is he not always strangely looking for something more – to the bewilderment of Sir Hugo?) is now a Jew, something alien, and the horror of this explains the denial we see in the reviews.

The reason the uncanny is familiar is because it is elements of the self that have been repressed and displaced. According to Otto Fenichel, it is the projections of anti-Semitism that render the Jew uncanny.[77] The revulsion readers feel for Daniel as a Jew is based on the unpleasantness of being confronted with repressed elements of their own unconscious. The expectations readers have of George Eliot novels, where the development of individual characters often stands in for a larger generic (individual and social) development, leave them particularly open to empathize and identify with the lead characters. This explains the level of shock when characters like Daniel turn out to be Jewish. The misrecognition, as self blurs with other, is cumulative, as Jews, who previously were alien, are revealed to be the 'man next door' and seem increasingly to populate the novel.

For Freud, displacement in the uncanny is normally of negative qualities. *Daniel Deronda* turns this on its head by presenting Jews as the uncanny, but claiming that they represent favourable qualities of Englishness (faith, vision, integrity, organic purpose) that have been lost from the English self. The Jew in *Daniel Deronda* becomes the sum total of the repressed elements of the English psyche. The Jew personifies qualities that are debased and forgotten in Englishness – qualities that were present in another form in the pre/early industrial rural society of *Adam Bede* and *Silas Marner* – but sadly lacking by the time of *Daniel Deronda*. The uncanniness of the Jews is that they represent a displaced version of Englishness itself, embodying the positive elements of the English character that were, it is implied, sacrificed in the construction of the industrial and imperial subject. Thus, Klesmer, a sensitive, Jewish musician outside the industrial order, retains elements of humanity and creativity that are lacking in the party man Mr Bult.

This is the tension that unhinges the narrative of *Daniel Deronda* – that the Jews are simultaneously produced as a projection of the self and something alien to the self. It thus naturalizes the very dynamic it tries to challenge. This distance between reader and textual other threatens to collapse and bring with it a clash with repressed elements of the self that, whether negatively or positively valued, can only result in trauma. Therefore, the divisions established between good Jews and bad Jews are essential to rearticulate the distinctions between self and other, like and not like, that are challenged by the closeness (uncanniness) of the

Jews' dangerously partial otherness. The assumptions about class difference in the letters underpin its role as substitute in *Daniel Deronda* for the race bias it endeavours to challenge. Although the narrative is critical of the Arrowpoints' snobbery in finding Klesmer too foreign to be their heir, and ostensibly counteracts prejudice about 'vulgar' Jews, it none the less requires that Daniel himself be revealed as coming from noble and learned stock. In order for Daniel to function as the representative of the Judaism that is going to inspire and invigorate Britain his class status must be secured, by the attribution to him of those elements of Jewish stereotypes that might find most favour with its British Gentile audience: he is represented as educated, learned, independently wealthy, sensitive to the plight of others and, importantly, from an impeccable dynastic heritage. In addition to this, he is healthily athletic (all that rowing!), which, in combination with his qualities of sportsmanship and platonic loyal friendship, presents a form of Judaism that pre-empts the advent of muscular Judaism in the 1890s. (This alternative to the cerebral ghetto Jew propounded an Anglicized upper-class model of masculinity following the ideals of muscular Christianity.)[78]

The problem with reclaiming the more acceptable elements of any racial stereotype is that it will also invoke its other components. George Eliot herself, in a review of Beecher Stowe's *Dred* in *Westminster Review*, is adamant that unrealistically positive images can be counterproductive.[79] To what end, then, does *Daniel Deronda* represent negative qualities in Jews? The component parts of the Jewish stereotype are present in *Daniel Deronda*'s Jewish characters but not always brought to the fore. Avarice, for example, recurs in different ways: whereas Kalonymos, who is presented as all things noble, is not denigrated on account of his occupation as a banker, Cohen's occupation as a pawnbroker definitely drags him down. He is described as distastefully 'fat' and 'glistening', not to mention money-grabbing, and although the family are represented as common but not unlikeable (they are after all invited to the wedding), it is clear that they are mercenary. Their charity in housing Mordecai is tempered by his use value: 'he's an encumbrance; but he brings a blessing down, and he teaches the boy. Besides he does the repairing of the watches and jewellery'.[452] In a pro-Jewish novel, popular anti-Semitic financial conspiracy theories (reactivated by the crashes of the 1860s) are not advocated – but cannot be excised.[80] Mrs Davilow explains their reversal of fortune to her daughter thus, blaming the loss on one person alone, who bears a distinctly Jewish-sounding name.

> You know nothing about business and will not understand it; but Grapnell & Co. have failed for a million and we are totally ruined . . . we must resign ourselves to God's will. But it is hard to resign oneself to Mr. Lassman's wickedness, which they say was the cause of the failure.[43–4]

George Eliot's comments about *Dred* are borne out by Lewes and Kaufman, who both feel that her treatment of negative qualities in Jews is fundamental to the book's task of making Jews real.

> . . . [*Daniel Deronda*] will rouse all the Jews of Europe to a fervor of admiration for the great artist who can – without disguising the ludicrous and ugly aspects – so marvellously present the ideal side of that strange life.[81]

> I am far from imagining that a thinker and poetess of George Eliot's calibre would ever have attempted to represent Judaism as the only source of high-mindedness, and Jews as the sole and hereditary possessors of all morality . . . The specifically Jewish virtues may go along with the specifically Jewish vices, concerning which hatred has invented so many fables.[82]

Kaufman is clear that it is the anti-Semitic interpretation of vice in Jews that is of interest.

> While all the world is satisfied that avarice is congenital among the Jews, and their special inheritance rather than the inheritance of all mankind, George Eliot expresses a very different opinion. She says of Ezra Cohen: 'He was not clad in the sublime pathos of the martyr, and his taste for money getting seemed to be *favoured with that success* which has been the most exasperating difference in the greed of the Jews during all ages of their dispersion.' To be greedy, then, is human; it is successful greed that seems to be peculiarly Jewish.[83]

Despite her criticisms of Beecher Stowe, George Eliot does hero-icize the Jews in *Daniel Deronda*: like Fedalma in *The Spanish Gypsy*, Daniel also beatifies himself by giving up a privileged place in his foster culture to join his hereditary people in their oppression. But although Fedalma gives up all for her old ties and Daniel at least does not reject his English Christianness, critics writing on *Daniel Deronda* suggest that *The Spanish Gypsy* was easier to stomach. One might imagine that this could be explained by the obvious difference of affiliation – English critics are less likely to be personally afronted by the renunciation of a Catholic Spanish identity than by the dilution of a cherished Englishness – but the initial responses to *The Spanish Gypsy* were startlingly similar to those that met *Daniel Deronda*. The unwelcome elements (of hereditary determinism and scientific theory) made it a bad poem and a failed romance just as they were held to blight *Daniel Deronda*. We see the same sense of personal outrage displayed in response to Fedalma's rejection of her affective ties as we do to Daniel's amendment of his.

> [I]n our opinion, the cultured Fedalma should live, and not the untutored Zincala who pays the mere barbarian's homage to authority ... The doctrine of authority preached in this fashion is nothing higher than the unmeaning loyalty of a savage.[84]

> We are inclined to maintain that when the conduct of a hero of romance is such that to expound it you must have recourse to physiological phenomena, your romance is a failure [like] [p]oetry that is unintelligible till it is subjected to scientific demonstration ...
>
> Fedalma is a woman of gypsy blood: but at three years old she is taken into the home of a great lady and reared as a Christian gentlewoman: as a Spanish gentlewoman. So secluded is she from the coarser accidents of life that she is described as having been 'nurtured as rare flowers are ...'
>
> Does anybody believe that being born of a certain family of human creatures is sufficient to account for the apparition of a high bred young woman – always delicately nurtured – dancing in the midst of a mob on the highway?[85]

How is it that by the time *Daniel Deronda* was published eight years later, *The Spanish Gypsy* seemed a more acceptable treatment of the theme? To some extent the intersection of romance and the exotic helps to remove the scene from the reader's everyday life, unlike the contemporaneity of *Daniel Deronda* which more overtly threatens the *status quo*. But the strength of feeling evinced about *The Spanish Gypsy* in 1868 pre-figures rather than dilutes the shock of 1876 when the terms of comparison are brought closer to home.

... moreover, she is a Christian gentlewoman (do not let us forget that) ... And in an hour, in her bridal dress, with that kiss by which she pledged herself still on her lips, she is persuaded by a gypsy father whom she has never before known in her life to go away with him for ever. And why? because Zarca's political aspirations demand her help, after he has sacked the city in which his daughter has been cherished so tenderly, and has slaughtered or overthrown those who have ministered to her all her days. Is that quite a credible thing? ... [only if we assume] that in gypsy blood there is so much loyalty that the moment it is appealed to it overcomes every other feeling, and levels the edifice of a whole life's education and circumstance.[86]

Daniel, like all Gentiles who have not knowingly met a Jew, knows the stereotype ('he had lately been thinking of vulgar Jews with a sort of personal alarm'[414]) and it is this familiar stereotypical knowledge about Jews that *Daniel Deronda* seeks to make strange. The alternative (stereo)type that emerges is a preferred image of Jews that disarms their dangerous generic strangeness by making them individually knowable to the reader (we, like Daniel, overcome our initial prejudice) but that also retains the sense of the Jews' difference crucial to their function as the text's other. Whereas George Eliot often uses emblematic characters to great success, the Jewish characters in *Daniel Deronda*, particularly Daniel, cannot but remain strange: unlike, for example, Eppie in *Silas Marner* who (despite her obvious symbolic role) can be realistically familiar because she evokes what readers recognize as their collective past. The difficulty of associating with the persistent alienness of the (now) *heimlich* Jews disallows, for George Eliot's nineteenth-century Gentile readers, a comfortable reading position and is what prompts the (critics') splitting of the text. *Daniel Deronda* insists that the Jews are both familiar and alien (their strangeness remains even as their familiarity and acceptability increases) but attempts to reverse the value of their difference: what was once the sign of their inferiority is now the mark of their superiority, the signifier of the new life. But it does not work; for *Daniel Deronda*'s contemporary readers the psychical risks of giving up the separation between self and projected other are too high. It is clear in the critical response that, like the inviolable division between George Eliot and her working-class servants, the very alienness that makes the Jew work as the text's other, makes it practically impossible for Gentile readers – those to whom the book was ostensibly addressed – to achieve an empathetic positionality. It becomes a case of either splitting the text or splitting the self.

Anita Levy has argued that the project of British domestic fiction was, broadly, to naturalize the middle-class nucleated family as a unit based on affective ties rather than on aristocratic demands of dynasty and the mystification of blood.[87] This helped develop both middle-class hegemony and the form of social reproduction required by industrial capitalism. Whilst, in some ways, this is indeed the project of *Daniel Deronda* – where Gwendolen's hopeless marriage to preserve a decaying aristocratic title is contrasted to Mirah's affective relationship to Daniel – the Jewishness of the romantic hero sets it up to fail. The modal middle-class English audience cannot accept an affective tie with a subject so stubbornly Jewish. For Jewish readers, on the other hand, this combination of blood and affection is perfect, since the Jewish identity relies on a blood lineage. Parodoxically, the novel is able to provide for Jewish readers the confirmatory narrative arguably expected from fiction (via a combination of future fulfilment and a naturalized past) that it cannot provide for the Gentile audience.

George Eliot's social and subjective position allows only a partial identification with the version of Christian Englishness defended by her detractors. For her, identification with the vilified Jewish other is made possible because the emphasis on Daniel's learnedness and dynastic heritage maintains the class identifications which, as we have seen, were the crucial underpinnings of her oppositional gender positioning. Thus, like the paradigmatic woman traveller who, as a representative of white colonial power, could accede to an ersatz male authority once displaced into the bush, George Eliot is able, through the transmogrification of class into learning, to enunciate an alternative (masculine) English identity. That this appears to offer little to the female characters in the novel is in keeping with her usual refusal to provide redemptive narratives of gender. Unlike Henriette Browne's work, which appears to offer an improved range of viewing positions for Western women spectators, the textual spaces of *Daniel Deronda* are shifted through the interposition of a class opposition. The emphasis on class (sublimated as learning) that secures Daniel as a viable identificatory position for George Eliot is never enough for her critics. Although, as I have argued, her representation of Daniel and the other Jews from whom he is differentiated, is reliant on an imperial and Orientalist notion of difference, her departures from, or challenges to, the value systems of these discourses is too much for her Gentile critics; they cannot accept the newly modelled re-presented Jew (who is anyway too much of a woman's fantasy of the ideal man) as one who lurks uncannily in their midst without facing a terrifying destabilization of the sovereign subject and the imperial privileges and pleasures on which it depends.

How is it, then, that a representation of Jews that is arguably determined by an Orientalist construction and valorization of them as other, nonetheless appeared to offer them something they craved? George Eliot received

> testimonies ... from Jews and Jewesses in Germany, France, America and England – especially the learned Rabbis who seem to think 'Deronda' will instruct, elevate, and expand the minds of Jews no less than modify the feelings of 'Christians' towards the Jews.[88]

In contrast to *Daniel Deronda*'s picture of Judaism as a vibrant, spiritually rich entity with a path into the future, the contemporary Jewish press construct Judaism as being under threat from anti-Semitism, assimilation and Reformism. George Eliot's representation of Judaism, whilst more positive and less overtly anti-Semitic than others, is still one that fantasizes the state of contemporary Judaism in relation to the concerns of dominant English society. Her desire to challenge prejudiced stereotypes of 'Jews [and] all oriental peoples',[89] whilst no doubt of potential benefit to Jews as the victims of persecution, is really addressed to the Gentile reader. Jewish reviewers were not unaware of the problems in *Daniel Deronda*, for example, its glossing over of the Ashkenazi/Sephardi divide, but generally declined to criticize the resultant homogeneity.

It is clear that for Jews there is a productivity to Daniel's hybridity which counterweighs the inherent problems of an Orientalist representation. Robert Young argues that although Bhabha solves the problem of Said's unified and monolithically repressive colonial subject by pointing to the splits and anxieties that undercut the colonizer's subjectivity (and hence offer the possibility of resistance), the same theory must imply similar splits in the subjectivity of the colonized with the attendant problems for the formation of an effective resistance.[90] But this need not be a problem since resistance, like power, need not be monolithic to be effective. In *Daniel Deronda*, the split nature of Daniel's identity works for Jewish readers *because* it speaks to the split subjectivity of the represented within Orientalism rather than attempting to be a discrete totality that can only be couched in the terms of distinct otherness. The vision of Daniel as the ultimate Jew, cast in the mould of all that is best about Englishness *and* Judaism is acceptable because it is in keeping with the nascent project to be like the Christian English and maintains the separateness of Mordecai. The reality of anti-Semitism is in keeping with, not opposed to, the fantasy of resolving both parts of the immigrant experience by being both Jew and English. Kaufman is clear that Daniel's acculturation is essential for the success of plot and narrative in *Daniel Deronda*.

> Hence it is peculiarly characteristic that he [Mordecai] cannot conceive the fulfiller of his ideas and the hero of his race as other than a noble, prosperous, and cultivated man of the world.[91]

Daniel's enhanced separateness (being the best of Jew and Gentile) is why *Daniel Deronda* appeals to Jewish readers. The hook of *Daniel Deronda* is that whilst one could argue that it opportunistically deploys Jews (and uses contemporary debates about Jewish national identity) to suggest how English society might be revitalized, it also offers Jews a chance to see themselves represented in a positive light and validates a national identity they crave. The crumbs from the Orientalist table have a *hamishe* [Yiddish: home-made] flavour. *Daniel Deronda* relies on its realistic appropriation of Jewish concerns in the hope that for Gentile readers this will make strange the old stereotype and familiarize a new one, but in this it largely fails, creating a disturbance where it seeks to produce harmony. But it does succeed in contibuting to a modified self-identity for Jews. They seek a unified and unifying identity in order to combat assimilation but cannot deny the power of the divisions within the Jewish population. *Daniel Deronda* offers Jews the fantasy of a unified identity – even if the proffered identity only partially accords with their own agenda.

NOTES

1 All references are to the Penguin edition, page references hereafter given in brackets in the text. George Eliot, *Daniel Deronda*, (1876) Harmondsworth, Penguin, 1987.
2 See also Bonnie Zimmerman, 'Gwendolen Harleth and the "Girl of the Period" ', in Anne Smith (ed.), *George Eliot: Centenary Essays and an Unpublished Fragment*, London, Vision Press, 1980.
3 George Eliot to Harriet Beecher Stowe, 29 October 1876 in Gordon S. Haight, *The George Eliot Letters: Vol. 6, 1874–1877*, London, Oxford University Press, 1956, pp. 301–2.
4 On the distinctions between Marian Evans and George Eliot see Chapter 2.
5 On the European Jewish response to *Daniel Deronda* see Shmuel Werses, 'The Jewish Reception of *Daniel Deronda*', in Alice Shalvi (ed.), *Daniel Deronda: A Centenary Symposium*, Jerusalem, Jersualem Academic Press, 1976.
6 Twentieth-century research into literary (as distinct from art) criticism means that more reviews in this part of the book can be identified. Therefore this chapter will use the names of critics wherever possible and signal those that cannot be identified.
7 Unattributable review in, *Saturday Review*, 23 September 1876, quoted in John Holmstrom, and Laurence Lerner (eds), *George Eliot and Her Readers. A Selection of Contemporary Reviews*, London, The Bodley Head, 1966, pp. 146–8.
8 Unattributable review in the *Academy* 5 February 1876 in Holstrom and Lerner, pp. 126–7.
9 George Saintsbury in the *Academy* 9 September 1876, in David Carroll (ed.), *George Eliot: The Critical Heritage*, London, Routledge, 1971, pp. 374–5.
10 Saintsbury, in the *Academy*, 1876, in Carroll, *George Eliot*, p. 374.
11 Saintsbury, in the *Academy*, 1876, in Carroll, *George Eliot*, p. 374.
12 See Harold Orel, *Victorian Literary Critics*, London, Macmillan, 1984.
13 Henry James, '*Daniel Deronda*: A Conversation', in *Atlantic Monthly*, December 1876, in Carroll, *George Eliot*, p. 420.
14 James, in Carroll, *George Eliot*, p. 419.
15 James, in Carroll, *George Eliot*, p. 427.
16 On the significance of James' relationship to European culture as an American, Perkin points out that though for the English literary scene George Eliot was avant-garde in the French realist style ('low' subjects, that challenged the existing social and literary orders), for James, who was versed in French literature, her changes were minimal. This explains his accusations elsewhere that her work was conformist. In this light, Pulcheria's comments are a snide aside on the narrowness of the English literary imagination. J. Russell Perkin, *A Reception-History of George Eliot's Fiction*, Ann Arbor, Mich., UMI Research Press, 1990, p. 88.
17 Hutton, in the *Spectator*, 29 July 1876, in Holmstrom and Lerner, *George Eliot and Her Readers*, p. 135.

18 Hutton, in the *Spectator*, 9 September 1876, in Carroll, *George Eliot*, p. 366.

19 Sigmund Freud, 'Fetishism', in *On Sexuality*, Pelican Freud Library, Harmondsworth, 1977, vol. 7.

20 Joel Kovel, *White Racism: A Psychohistory*, London, Free Association Books, 1988.

21 See Leo Henkin, *Darwinism in the English Novel 1860–1910. The Impact of Evolution on Victorian Fiction*, New York, Russell and Russell, 1940.

22 Her essay 'The Natural History of German Life' (1856), based on a review of Riehl's work is generally cited as the clearest explanation of her organicist views. See Gillian Beer, *Darwin's Plots: Evolutionary Narrative in Darwin, George Eliot and Nineteenth-Century Fiction*, London, Routledge, 1983, ch. 4; Sally Shuttleworth, *George Eliot and Nineteenth-Century Science. The Make-Believe of a Beginning*, Cambridge, Cambridge University Press, 1984.

23 Jews were a moot point within nineteenth-century classification of race and nation. They were used to prove (opposing) evolutionary arguments by both polygenists and monogenists. See Beer, *Darwin's Plots*, p. 203.

24 On Darwin's attitudes to race, see Beer, *Darwin's Plots*.

25 See Daniel Pick, *Faces of Degeneration. A European Disorder c.1848–c.1918*, Cambridge, Cambridge University Press, 1989.

26 George L. Mosse, 'Nationalism and Respectability: Normal and Abnormal Sexualities in the Nineteenth Century', in *Journal of Contemporary History*, vol. 17, no. 2, 1982.

27 'I had written an enthusiastic – I fear I must add gushing – defence of *Daniel Deronda*, from a Jewish point of view in the June number of *Macmillan's Magazine . . .*' Joseph Jacobs, *Literary Studies*, London, 1895, p. xv.

28 For twentieth-century examples of the impact of Orientalist representations on the Orientalized reader, see Edward W. Said, *Covering Islam: How the Media and the Experts Determine How We See the Rest of the World*, London, Routledge, 1981; Zakia Pathak *et al.*, 'The Prisonhouse of Orientalism', in *Textual Practice*, vol. 5, no. 2, Summer 1991.

29 V.D. Lipman, *Social History of the Jews in England, 1850–1950*, London, Watts, 1954, p. 65.

30 Colin Holmes, *Anti-Semitism in British Society 1876–1939*, London, Edward Arnold, 1979, pp. 4–5.

31 Figures in Salo W. Baron, 'The Jewish Question in the Nineteenth-Century', in *The Journal of Modern History*, vol. 10, no. 1, March, 1938.

32 Jacob Katz, *From Prejudice to Destruction: Anti-Semitism, 1700–1933*, Cambridge, MA., Harvard University Press, 1980, chs. 8 and 9.

33 See Holmes, *Anti-Semitism*, p. 3.

34 See M.C.N. Salbstein, *The Emancipation of the Jews in Britain: The Question of the Admission of Jews to Parliament, 1825–1860*, Rutherford, N.J., Fairleigh Dickinson University Press, 1982.

35 See Lipman, *Social History*, p. 5.
36 See Salbstein, *Emancipation*, and Cecil Roth, *A History of the Jews in England*, Oxford, The Clarendon Press, 1941.
37 Jewish schools were established by the early nineteenth century and by 1850 the Board of Jewish Deputies had persuaded the government to grant aid to Jewish schools in keeping with other denominations; by 1859 the Jewish Board of Guardians was established to oversee relief work. Lipman, *Social History*, pp. 41–64. Note that Lipman sees the main period of change as running from the 1880s to 1905.
38 The Anglo-Jewish press also began during the period of legal reform and mass immigration of the 1840s. The first to be published was the Reform-minded *Voice of Jacob* (1841–8) but the later Conservative Orthodox *Jewish Chronicle* (est. 1841) proved to be longer lasting. The Yiddish press did not take off in England until the 1870s and 1880s brought a large Yiddish and bundist (Jewish Trade Union) readership over from Eastern Europe. See *The Jewish Encyclopedia*, New York and London, Funk and Wagnalls, 1904.
39 See Werses, 'Jewish Reception'.
40 See also Montagu Frank Modder, *The Jew in the Literature of England: To the End of the Nineteenth Century*, Philadelphia, The Jewish Publication Society of America, 1939; Michael Ragussis, 'Representation, Conversion and Literary Form: *Harrington* and the Novel of Jewish Identity', in *Critical Inquiry*, vol. 16, no. 1, Autumn 1989; Linda Gertlin Zatlin, 'High Tea and Matza Balls: Religion in the Victorian Jewish Novel', in *Victorian Newsletter*, Spring 1979.
41 Joseph Jacobs, 'Mordecai: A Protest Against the Critics', in *Macmillan's Magazine*, June 1877, p. 100.
42 James Picciotto, 'Deronda the Jew', in *Gentleman's Magazine*, November 1876, in Carroll, *George Eliot*, p. 408.
43 On the difficulty of constructing Daniel *and* Gwendolen as credible characters in relation to the rest of George Eliot's work see Baruch Hochman, '*Daniel Deronda*: The Zionist Plot and the Problematic of George Eliot's Art', in Shalvi, *Daniel Deronda*.
44 Unattributed review, the *Jewish Chronicle*, 15 December 1876, in Holmstrom and Lerner, *George Eliot*, p. 151.
45 Jacobs, *Macmillan's Magazine*, p. 103.
46 Jacobs, *Macmillan's Magazine*, p. 104–7 (original emphasis).
47 George Eliot, letter to Charles Bray, 21 December 1876, in Haight, *Letters. Vol. 6*, p. 320.
48 George Henry Lewes to Elma Stuart, 12 October 1876, in Haight, *Letters. Vol. 6*, p. 294.
49 Ruth Raider, who is concerned with how the mix of literary styles in *Daniel Deronda* works against the credibility of its narrative, relates George Eliot's selection of Jewish material to the highly theatrical manner in which they are represented. Ruth Raider, ' "The Flash of Fervour": *Daniel Deronda*', in Ian Gregor (ed.), *Reading the Victorian Novel: Detail into Form*, London, Vision Press, 1980.
50 See William Baker, ch. 7, for details, but briefly: of the assimilationists

Zunz and Geiger, Zunz (whom Daniel is represented as reading in ch. 42) stresses poetry of lament and suffering, plays down nationalism and hopes that a knowledge of Jewish culture and intellectual traditions would increase Jewish and Christian understanding, while Geiger values Diaspora culture's contribution to humanity as a whole. The nationalist writer Graetz presents Jewish history as a history of great individuals who act as transmitters of the faith and keep the religion alive. (It is from Graetz that George Eliot probably derived the Berenice story of Hans Meyrick's paintings.) William Baker, *George Eliot and Judaism*, Salzburg, Institut für Englische Sprache und Literatur, Universität Salzburg, 1975.

51 George Eliot wrote four essays on Heine in 1855 and 1856 for the *Saturday Review*, the *Westminister Review* and two for the *Leader*. See Thomas Pinney (ed.), *Essays of George Eliot*, London, Routledge, 1968.
52 See Baker, *George Eliot*, ch. 3; also Gershom Scholem who disputes that Halevi was a mystic. Gershom G. Scholem, *Major Trends in Jewish Mysticism*, third edition, London, Thames and Hudson, 1955.
53 Salbstein, *Emancipation*, pp. 47–50.
54 Baker, *George Eliot*.
55 James Picciotto, *Sketches of Anglo Jewish History* (1875) in Carroll, *George Eliot*, p. 412.
56 George Eliot to Barbara Bodichon, 2 October 1876, in Haight, *Letters*. *Vol. 6*, p. 290.
57 Shuttleworth, *George Eliot*, p. 184.
58 Kabbalistic traditions (most notably from the post-expulsion Sephardi community in Safed) speak of the transmigration of souls in need of support into a union with a stronger 'mother' or host soul. See also Scholem, *Major Trends*, pp. 250–83; Beer, *Darwin's Plots*, pp. 182–190; Shuttleworth, *George Eliot*, p. 180; Hani al-Raheb, *The Zionist Character in the English Novel*, London, Zed Books, 1985, p. 90.
59 See Brian Street, *The Savage in Literature: The Representation of 'Primitive' Society in English Fiction 1858–1920*, London, Routledge, 1975.
60 See also Patrick Brantlinger, 'Nations and Novels: Disraeli, George Eliot, and Orientalism', in *Victorian Studies*, vol. 35, no. 3, Spring 1992.
61 See Edward W. Said, 'Zionism From the Standpoint of Its Victims', in *Social Text*, vol. 1, 1978.
62 Indeed, Horkheimer (in 1946) suggests that the apparent decrease in anti-Semitism in the nineteenth century is due to the substitution of colonized peoples as the recipient of the aggression previously (and subsequently) directed at the Jews. Max Horkeimer, 'Sociological Background of the Psychoanalytic Approach', in Ernst L. Simmel, *Anti-Semitism: A Social Disease*, New York, International Universities Press, 1946.
63 Palmerston quoted in Baron, 'Jewish Question', p. 63.
64 Holmes, *Anti-Semitism*, pp. 10–14.

65 Homi Bhabha, 'Of Mimicry and Man: The Ambivalence of Colonial Discourse', in *October*, no. 28, Spring 1984.
66 Bhabha, 'Of Mimicry and Man', p. 126.
67 Bhabha, 'Of Mimicry and Man', p. 133.
68 Daniel fulfils the Jew's role as the perennial other, the outsider on the inside who is alien at the same time as he is included.
69 George Henry Lewes to Elma Stuart, 12 October 1876, in Haight, *Letters. Vol. 6*, p. 294.
70 George Henry Lewes to Edward Dowden, February 1877, in Haight, *Letters. Vol. 6*, p. 336.
71 George Eliot to David Kaufman, 31 May 1877, in Haight, *Letters. Vol. 6*, p. 379, original emphasis. According to Werses, George Eliot read Kaufman's book in its original German form and was instrumental in getting it translated and published in England. Werses, 'Jewish Reception', p. 14.
72 George Henry Lewes to Blackwood, 1 December 1875, in Haight, *Letters. Vol. 6*, p. 196.
73 George Eliot to Harriet Beecher Stowe, 29 October 1876, in Haight, *Letters. Vol. 6*, p. 302.
74 George Eliot, 'Servants' Logic', in *Pall Mall Gazette*, no. 1, 17 March 1865, in Pinney, *Essays*, pp. 392–5.
75 On George Eliot's splitting of the working class, see Raymond Williams, *Culture and Society 1780–1950*, second edition, Harmondsworth, Penguin, 1963.
76 Sigmund Freud, 'The Uncanny', in James Strachey (trans. and ed.), *The Standard Edition of the Complete Psychological Works of Sigmund Freud*, London, The Hogarth Press and the Institute of Psycho-analysis, 1955, Vol. 17.
77 Otto Fenichel, 'Elements of a Psychoanalytic Theory of Anti-Semitism', in Simmel, *Anti-Semitism*, pp. 20–22.
78 See Richard Voeltz, '. . . A Good Jew and a good Englishman: The Jewish Lads' Brigade', in *Journal of Contemporary History*, vol. 23, no. 1, January 1988, pp. 119–29. On the different ways in which this was incorporated into the new figure of the pioneering Zionist Jew see al-Raheb, *Zionist Character*; and Said, *Orientalism*, Harmondsworth, Penguin, 1978, p. 286.
79 George Eliot, 'Three Novels', in *Westminster Review*, October 1856 in Pinney, *Essays*, pp. 323–34.
80 See also Baker, *George Eliot*, pp. 124–30. See also Ellen Rosenman's analysis of how *Daniel Deronda*'s narrative of financial collapse re-inscibes a normally absent female perspective. Ellen Rosenman, 'The House and the Home: Money, Women and the Family in the *Bankers' Magazine* and *Daniel Deronda*', in *Women's Studies*, vol. 17, nos. 3–4, 1990.
81 George Henry Lewes to Blackwood, 1 December 1875 in Haight, *Letters. Vol. 6*, p. 196.
82 David Kaufman, *George Eliot and Judaism: An Attempt to Appreciate Daniel Deronda*, London, Blackwood and Sons, 1877, pp. 55–6.
83 Kaufman, *George Eliot*, pp. 76–7 (original emphasis).

84 Unattributed review, *Westminister Review*, July 1868, p. 189.
85 *Pall Mall Gazette*, 27 June 1868, p. 12.
86 *Pall Mall Gazette*, 27 June 1868, p. 12.
87 Anita Levy, *Other Women: The Writing of Class, Race and Gender, 1832–1898*, Princeton, Princeton University Press, 1991.
88 George Henry Lewes to Elma Stuart, 23 December 1876, in Haight, *Letters. Vol. 6*, p. 322.
89 George Eliot to Harriet Beecher Stowe, in Haight, *Letters. Vol. 6*, pp. 301–2.
90 Robert Young, *White Mythologies: Writing History and the West*, London, Routledge, 1990, ch. 8.
91 Kaufman, *George Eliot*, p. 69.

Afterword
Gendering Orientalism

The research on which this book is based was sparked off by a hunch that if I could find proof of women's involvement in Orientalist culture I would be able to challenge masculinist assumptions about women and imperialism. Indeed, the excavation of a woman Orientalist artist like Browne in itself appeared initially to offer a new paradigm for the study of Orientalism. The mere existence of a woman's representation of the harem's forbidden spaces undercut the characteristic homogeneity, intentionality and omnipotence that Said had ascribed to the Orientalist gaze. Her view of the Orient as respectable and domestic could not but challenge some of Orientalism's key sexualized myths. But, as the research went on, I kept unearthing clues to other female versions of the Orient and the harem. Scraps of information, faded catalogue illustrations, elusive references in reviews, all pointed to a previously unimaginable number and range of images by women. All of a sudden, the apparently neat counter-discourse that I had set up around Browne began to fragment and fray at the edges. Yes, there were indeed substantial numbers of women artists enngaged in Orientalist representation, but they did not all follow the same route as the eminently respectable Henriette Browne. At the very moment that I proved my hypothesis of women's involvement in visual Orientalism, the stability of its constituent categories began to crumble. The alternative female Orientalism indicated by the likes of Elisabeth Jerichau-Baumann, with her semi-nude monumental odalisques, undercut the determining imprint of gender that appeared to operate so smoothly in the case of Browne. The female Orientalist gaze became a far more fluid and contested entity than I had previously suspected.

Orientalism emerged as a diverse field in which meanings were always and already contested and shifting. It is clear from the reviews of Browne's work that whilst her images provided a challenge to dominant Orientalist conventions, they were in themselves already understood to be one among a number of competing alternative discourses. The heterogeneity of nineteenth-century Orientalist discourse simultaneously produced spaces from and in which women could represent whilst developing strategies to contain, appropriate or minimize the threat of their alternative voices. The hegemonic knowledges about the East that Said sees as fundamental to imperialism are still there – but the emphasis now is on the fluidity essential to the maintenance of that hegemony. Orientalism is never static, but perpetually fending off or responding to challenges from within and without: challenges that are not simply an unavoidable burden, but that are themselves productive of dominant and alternative definitions of not only race or Orientalism, but also gender, class and nation. Thus, we are able to consider women's relationship to Orientalism and imperialism as a series of identifications that did not have to be either simply supportive or simply oppositional, but that could be partial, fragmented and contradictory.

The position that I arrived at through the analysis of women's visual culture illuminated the complexities of female positionings within the intersecting discourses that made up Orientalism and gave me another way to approach women's written culture. By re-introducing Orientalism into the analysis of *Daniel Deronda* I was able to demonstrate how the book's self-consciously anti-discriminatory project is itself reliant on an Orientalist construction of the Jewish other. It is this that permits its 'pro-Jewish' stance and facilitates its author's partial identification with the ethnic subject matter of her novel. This approach is in keeping with developments in feminist literary criticism that can acknowledge the discursive constraints on women's writing without needing to save or condemn them. This re-situates Eliot (who now occupies a senior position in the feminist literary canon) as a figure whose gendered authorial voice and social identities could not but be shaped by the classed imperial power relations of her day. The conditions of possibility for the pursuance of her literary career in general, and the construction of the positive Jewish stereotype of *Daniel Deronda* in particular, rely on interconnecting ideologies of racial, class and sexual difference. Thus, it becomes impossible to separate out the achievements of a subject like George Eliot from the figure of the 'other woman' so clearly demarcated by Spivak and Levy (see Chapter 1). It is not just that George Eliot's fiction simply contributes to the overwhelming displacement of other women into the structural monolith of the other woman – but that, by focusing on the otherness of the Jews (and by dividing the Jewish other into a series of knowable characteristics) – she effectively proliferates and re-inscribes the otherness she seeks to make familiar. The positive portrayal of Daniel reproduces, in a differently gendered but structurally identical setting, the projection and displacement that Levy describes: 'precisely that talking about other women, historically, has been the source of their displacement'.[1] In George Eliot's case, the tragedy of this prevalent dynamic is that *Daniel Deronda* cannot avoid displacing 'those members of a different race, class and sexuality in a negative relation to the rational, middle-class, white Englishman'[2] even as it tries to talk about them. George Eliot's fiction and her construction of a professional and tolerant self cannot operate without the strategic displacement of a range of (feminized) others at the same time as she tries to combat those very forms of projection and denial.

Where Levy argues that it is impossible to talk about other women without re-enacting their displacement, Eve Kosofsky Sedgwick worries that the topos of otherness has become naturalized, institutionalized even, within liberal analysis.[3] Whilst she agrees that a theory of othering is often initially necessary to make the oppressed visible, she raises two questions about its efficacy: firstly, that it tends to ignore the variability of forms of othering and, secondly, that it cannot explain how those that Orientalism, for example, creates as other, 'those whom *it* figures simply as relegated objects', engage and act, even where this agency also figures in their own relegation.[4] When we look at European women's representation of and participation in processes of othering, we are looking at representations made by agents who are themselves partially othered (as the symbolic feminized other of men in Europe) and whose actions may add to both the relegation of themselves *and* of other women. There is work to be done (and, indeed, being done) on the forms of representation enunciated by the Orientalized others of nineteenth-century imperialism and the contradictory positionalities they construct.[5] It remains to be seen whether the field can move beyond a theory of othering as Sedgwick demands; I hope that I have shifted the debate forward by destabilizing the dominant terms of that critical formation.

The previous chapters have, hopefully, repositioned Orientalism as a discourse that, riding above the specificities of imperialism and colonialism, but reliant on the forms and relations they produce, functioned through contradiction rather than despite it. Orientalism thus had room within it for a diversity of women's voices. It could allow the articulation of knowledges and subjectivities outside of its dominant orders that were in themselves constitutive of both liberatory and relegatory positionings. The myriad ways in which middle- and upper-class European women positioned themselves in relation to the various possible others of Orientalist discourse indicate both the flexibility of imperial power and the contingency of resistance. That resistance is in various ways contingent does not mean that it is not, or cannot be, effective. Rather, this line of enquiry, by focusing on the critical meanings circulated about the texts, underlines the tensions inherent in the Orientalist project in order to reveal the always conflicted nature of the identifications that the criticism seeks to produce for the text, its author and its audience.

This also has implications for new historicist[6] discussions about the role of representation and the problematic of the category 'woman' in women's studies. We need a form of history writing that is able to find the missing female object *at the same time* as it disaggregates the category 'woman'. This does not lead us into some nihilistic deconstructionist void, nor to the impossibility of a gendered analysis; instead, it offers us the opportunity to understand the necessarily conflicted nature of our subjects without having to reduce all to a single determinant. This means that we can research how women as women – since their gendered socialization affected the conditions of production, reception and circulation of their work – contributed to the culture of imperialism and to the imperial project itself. Some advocates of women's history take an anti-theoretical stance, unable to tolerate losing the object of their study (and identification) to critical theories. My approach allows us to retain a version of the object (as indeed we must retain versions of identification) without having to resort to essentialism or a naive belief in the purity of the archive.

I hope to have shown that, whilst all archives are imprinted with the ideological matrix of their production, we can find within those patternings the gaps and stresses that, like the near impossibility of the woman Orientalist, reveal the constituent tensions of the discourse. We do not lose the woman in history, therefore, but are able to locate her as a nodal point at the intersection of a variety of different determining discourses. She appears as a subject who is overdetermined but not without agency: the variety of women's responses to the exercise of representing the Orientalized other cannot be explained without some allowance for the vagaries of personality and individual psychology.[7] This, to my mind, opens up rather than closes down the possibilities for feminist research. It provides a way to think about gender and empire that can allow for the different modes of female creativity signified by Browne or Jerichau-Baumann or George Eliot and for the structural significance of all of them for the formation of identities in the distinct but relational fields of culture, empire, gender, domesticity and nationality.

This book, like all history writing, is driven by the needs of its present; in this case by my need to develop an understanding of the relationship between gender and empire that can contribute to the understanding of late twentieth-century postcolonial power relations and move beyond the assumed polarities of identity politics. I wanted to be able to think beyond simple binary analyses of culpability and innocence towards an understanding of how we are variously interpellated into the types of complex positionings that can lead to racism in the name of feminism, or homophobia in the name of Black nationalism or anti-intellectualism in the name of class. The very anxiety associated with using such a universalistic 'we' is a sign, not of the tyranny of so-called Political Correctness, but of the efficacy of those postcolonial structural differences that make it almost impossible for anyone to articulate the realities of their experience without simultaneously grappling for the words to describe the forms of othering that it produces. Unless we can find a way to acknowledge the myriad and convoluted balance of subjective and social payments instituted by imperialism, to talk of the possibility of opposition without requiring proof of absolute purity or absolute oppression and without resorting to blaming and silencing, we will not be able effectively to shift the discursive paradigms that structure our existence. It is also to this debate that I hope this book has contributed.

NOTES

1 Anita Levy, *Other Women: the Writing of Class, Race and Gender, 1832–1898*, Princeton, Princeton University Press, 1991, p. 5.

2 Levy, *Other Women*, p. 5.

3 Eve Kosofsky Sedgwick, 'Nationalisms and Sexualities in the Age of Wilde', in Parker *et al.*, *Nationalisms and Sexualities*, London, Routledge, 1992.

4 Sedgwick, 'Nationalisms', in Parker *et al.*, 1992, pp. 238–9 (original emphasis).

5 See for example Patricia Rooke, 'Slavery, Social Death and Imperialism: The Formation of a Christian Black Elite in the West Indies 1800–1845', in Mangan (ed.), *Making Imperial Mentalities: Socialization and British Imperialism*, Manchester, Manchester University Press, 1990; Spivak, 'Can the Subaltern Speak? Speculations on Widow Sacrifice', in *Wedge*, nos 7/8, Winter/Spring 1985; Hazel Carby, *Reconstructing Womanhood: The Emergence of the Afro-American Woman Novelist*, New York, Oxford University Press, 1987; Ziggi Alexander and Audrey Dewjee (eds), *The Wonderful Adventures of Mrs Seacole in Many Lands*, Bristol, Falling Wall Press, 1984; Mervat Hatem, 'Through Each Other's Eyes: The Impact on the Colonial Encounter of the Images of Egyptian, Levantine-Egyptian and European Women, 1862–1920', in Chaudhuri and Stobel (eds), *Western Women and Imperialism: Complicity and Resistance*, Bloomington, Indiana University Press, 1992; Sylvia M. Jacobs, 'Give a Thought to Africa: Black Women Missionaries in Southern Africa', in Chaudhuri and Strobel (eds), *Western Women*. Particular attention has been paid to the changing role and signification of the veil in North Africa. See, for example, Winifred Woodhull, 'Unveiling Algeria', in *Genders*, no. 10, Spring 1991; Lama Abu Odeh, 'Post-Colonial Feminism and the Veil: Thinking the Difference', in *Feminist Review*, no. 43, Spring 1993.

6 One cannot ignore the category new historicism, but I must admit I agree with Judith Newton's attitude that it seems to be a posh new title for what some of 'us' (feminist, socialist, cultural materialist) critics have been doing all along. Judith Newton, 'History as Usual?: Feminism and the "New Historicism"', in *Cultural Critique*, no. 9, Spring 1988.

7 On the importance for art history of making a 'pragmatic' allowance for a version of the social even outside, or at the edges of, discourse, in so far as it structures women's experience of themselves and their agency as women see Janet Wolff, 'Excess and Inhibition: Inter-disciplinarity in the Study of Art', in Grossberg *et al.* (eds), *Cultural Studies*, New York, Routledge, 1992.

Select bibliography

SOURCES PUBLISHED BEFORE 1925

Alexander, Ziggi, and Dewjee, Audrey (eds), *Wonderful Adventures of Mrs Seacole in Many Lands*, (1857) second edition, Bristol, Falling Wall Press, 1984.

Blunt, Lady Anne, *A Pilgrimage to Nejd: the Cradle of the Arab Race. A Visit to the Court of the Arab Emir, and 'Our Persian Campaign'*, 2 vols, London, John Murray, 1881.

Bøgh, Nicholaj, *Elisabeth Jerichau-Baumann: En Karakteristik*, Copenhagen, Trykt hos J. Jørgenson and Co., 1886.

Bryan's Dictionary of Painters and Engravers, London, George Bell and Sons, 1903.

Champlin, John Dennison, *Cyclopedia of Painters and Paintings*, London, Bernard Quaritch, 1888.

Clayton, Ellen, *English Female Artists*, London, Tinsley, 1876.

Clement, Clara Erskine, *Women in the Fine Arts. From the 7 Century BC to the Twentieth Century AD*, New York, Houghton Mifflin, 1904.

Gautier, Théophile, *Constantinople of Today*, (1953) trans. Robert Howe Gould, London, David Bogne, 1854.

——, *Abécédaire du salon de 1861*, Paris, Librairie de la Société des Gens de lettres, 1861.

Graves, Algernon, *A Century of Loan Exhibitions*, London, Algernon Graves, 1913–15.

Harvey, Annie Jane, *Turkish Harems and Circassion Homes*, London, Hurst and Blackett, 1871.

Jameson, Anna, *Sisters of Charity and the Communion of Labour: Two Lectures on the Employment of Women*, (1855) London, Longman, Brown, Green, Longmans and Roberts, 1859.

Jerichau-Baumann, Elisabeth, *Brogede Rejsebilleder*, Copenhagen, Thieles Bogtrykkeri, 1881.

Jacobs, Joseph, *Literary Studies*, (1894) second edition, London, David Nult, 1895.

The Jewish Encyclopedia, New York and London, Funk and Wagnalls, 1904.

Kaufmann, David, *George Eliot and Judaism: an Attempt to Appreciate Daniel Deronda*, London, Blackwood and Sons, 1877.

Kingsley, Charles, *Yeast, a Problem*, London, 1860.

Lane, Edward William, *An Account of the Manners and Customs of the Modern Egyptians*, (1837) 2 vols, third edition, London, Charles Knight and Co., 1842.

Larouse, Pierre, *Grand dictionnaire universel du XIXe siècle*, Paris, 1864–76.

Lott, Emmeline, *The English Governess in Egypt: Harem Life in Egpyt and Constantinople*, 2 vols, London, Richard Bentley, 1866.

——, *Nights in the Harem or The Mohaddetyn in the Palace*, 2 vols, London, Chapman and Hall, 1867.

Melek-Hanum, *Thirty Years in the Harem: or the Autobiography of Melek-Hanum, Wife of H.H. Kibrizli-Mehemet-Pasha*, (London, 1872) second edition, Calcutta, Lewis and Co., 1888.

— —, *Six Years in Europe: Sequel to Thirty Years in the Harem*, London, Chapman and Hall, 1873.

Merson, Olivier, *Exposition de 1861: la peinture en France*, Paris, Libraire de la Société des Gens de lettres, 1861.

Montagu, Lady Mary Wortley, *Embassy to Constantinople: the Travels of Lady Mary Wortley Montagu*, (1763) ed. Christopher Pick, intro. Dervla Murphy, London, Hutchinson, 1988.

de Nerval, Gérard, *Journey to the Orient*, (1851), trans. Norman Glass, London, Peter Owen, 1972.

Picciotto, James, *Sketches of Anglo Jewish History*, London, Trübner and Co., 1875.

Poole, Sophia, *The Englishwoman in Egypt: Letters From Cairo, Written During a Residence There in 1842, 3 and 4 With E.W. Lane Esq, Author of 'The Modern Egyptians', by His Sister*, 2 vols, London, Charles Knight and Co., 1844.

Said-Ruete, Emily, *Memoirs of an Arabian Princess: Princess Salme bint Said ibn Sultan al-Bu Saidi of Oman and Zanzibar*, (1888) London, East-West Publications, 1981.

Thieme, Ulriche and Becker, Felix, *Allgemeines Lexikon der Bildenden Künstler von der Antike bis zur Gegenwart*, Leipzig, Verlag von E.A. Seemann, 1907.

Tourneux, Maurice, *Salons et expositions d'art à Paris 1801–70*, Paris, Jean Schemit Libraire, 1919.

Woolf, Virginia, 'George Eliot', in *The Times Literary Supplement*, 20 November 1919.

JOURNALS AND PERIODICALS CONSULTED

L'Artiste
L'Art revue hebdomadaire
The *Art Journal*
The *Athenaeum*

Chronique des arts et de la curiosité
Le Correspondant
The *Englishwoman's Journal*
The *Fine Arts Quarterly Review*
Gazette des beaux-arts
Gentleman's Magazine
L'Illustration
The *Jewish Chronicle*
Journal des desmoiselles
Macmillan's Magazine
Magasin des desmoiselles
Le Moniteur universel
Musée universel
Pall Mall Gazette
Quarterly Review
Revue catholique
Revue chrétienne
Revue d'économie chrétienne
Revue du monde catholique
The *Saturday Review*
The *Westminster Review*

SECONDARY SOURCES

Abel, Elizabeth, 'Race, Class, and Psychoanalysis? Opening Questions', in Hirsch and Fox Keller 1990.

Abu Odeh, Lama, 'Post-Colonial Feminism and the Veil: Thinking the Difference', in *Feminist Review*, no. 43, Spring 1993.

Alexander, Sally, 'Women's Work in Nineteenth-Century London: A Study of the Years 1820–50', in Mitchell and Oakley 1983.

Alloula, Malek, *The Colonial Harem*, (1986) Manchester, Manchester University Press, 1987.

And, Metin, *A History of Theatre and Popular Entertainment in Turkey*, Ankara, Forum Yayinlari, 1963–4.

Anderson, Benedict, *Imagined Communities: Reflections on the Origin and Spread of Nationalism*, (1983) second edition, London, Verso, 1991.

Andrews, Malcolm, 'A Note on Serialization', in Gregor 1980.

Anson, Peter F., *The Call of the Cloister: Religious Communities and Kindred Bodies in the Anglican Communion*, London, S.P.C.K., 1964.

Apter, Emily, 'Female Trouble in the Colonial Harem', in *Differences*, vol. 4, no. 1, Spring 1992.

Arac, Jonathan and Ritvo, Harriet, *Macropolitics of Nineteenth-Century Literature: Nationalism, Exoticism, Imperialism*, Philadelphia, University of Pennsylvania Press, 1991.

Baker, William, *George Eliot and Judaism*, Salzburg, Institut für Englische Sprache und Literatur, Universität Salzburg, 1975.

——, 'George Eliot and Zionism', in Shalvi 1976.

Baron, Salo W., 'The Jewish Question in the Nineteenth Century', in *Journal of Modern History*, vol. 10, no. 1 March 1938.

Barrell, John, *The Political Theory of Painting From Reynolds to Hazlitt: The Body of the Public*, New Haven, Yale University Press, 1986.

Barthes, Roland, 'The Death of the Author', (1968) in Barthes 1977.

——, 'From Work to Text', (1971) in Barthes 1977.

——, *Image Music Text*, trans. Stephen Heath, London, Fontana, 1977.

Beck, Lois and Keddie, Nikki (eds), *Women in the Muslim World*, Cambridge, MA., Harvard University Press, 1978.

Beer, Gillian, *Darwin's Plots. Evolutionary Narrative in Darwin, George Eliot and Nineteenth-Century Fiction*, London, Routledge, 1983.

——, *George Eliot*, Brighton, Harvester Wheatsheaf, 1986.

Bellanger, Claude, *Histoire générale de la presse française*, Paris, Universitaires de France, 1969.

Bénézit, E., *Dictionnaire critique et documentaire des peintres, sculpteurs, dessinateurs et graveurs de tous les temps et de tous les pays par un groupe d'écrivains spécialistes français et étrangers*, (1911–26) third edition, Paris, Librairie Gründ, 1976.

Betterton, Rosemary, 'How Do Women Look? The Female Nude in the Work of Suzanne Valadon', in Betterton 1987.

—— (ed.), *Looking On: Images of Femininity in the Visual Arts and Media*, London, Pandora, 1987.

Bhabha, Homi, 'The Other Question', in *Screen*, no. 24, vol. 6, 1983.

— —, 'Of Mimicry and Man: The Ambivalence of Colonial Discourse', in *October*, no. 28, 1984.

Birkett, Dea, *Spinsters Abroad: Victorian Lady Explorers*, Oxford, Blackwell, 1989.

Bivona, Daniel, *Desire and Contradiction: Imperial Visions and Domestic Debates in Victorian Literature*, Manchester, Manchester University Press, 1990.

Blake, Susan L., 'A Woman's Trek: What Difference Does Gender Make?', in *Women's Studies International Forum*, vol. 13, no. 4, 1990.

Bland, Lucy, 'The Domain of the Sexual', in *Screen Education*, no. 39, 1981.

Bobo, Jacqueline, '*The Colour Purple*: Black Women as Cultural Readers', in Pribram 1989.

—— and Seiter, Ellen, 'Black Feminism and Media Criticism: *The Women of Brewster Place*', in *Screen*, vol. 32, no. 3, 1991.

Boime, Alfred, *The Academy and French Painting in the Nineteenth Century*, London, Phaidon, 1971.

——, 'The Case of Rosa Bonheur: Why Should a Woman Want to be More Like a Man?', in *Art History*, vol. 4, no. 4, December 1981.

Bolt, Christine, *Victorian Attitudes to Race*, London, Routledge, 1971.

Brantlinger, Patrick, 'Nations and Novels: Disraeli, George Eliot, and Orientalism', in *Victorian Studies*, vol. 35, no. 3, Spring 1992.

Brownfoot, Janice N., 'Sisters Under the Skin: Imperialism and the Emancipation of Women in Malaya, c.1891–1941', in Mangan 1990.

Burton, Antoinette M., 'The White Woman's Burden: British Feminists and The Indian Woman, 1865–1915', in *Women's Studies International Forum*, vol. 13, no. 4, 1990.

Bury, J.P.T., *France 1814–1940*, (1949) fifth edition, London, Methuen, 1985.

Cain, P.J. and Hopkins, A.G., *British Imperialism: Innovation and Expansion 1688–1914*, London, Longman, 1993.

Callaway, Helen, *Gender, Culture and Empire. European Women in Colonial Nigeria*, Basingstoke, Macmillan, 1987.

Carby, Hazel V., *Reconstructing Womanhood: The Emergence of the Afro-American Woman Novelist*, New York, Oxford University Press, 1987.

Carpenter, Mary Wilson, 'The Apocrypha of the Old Testament. *Daniel Deronda* and the Interpretation of Interpretation', in *PMLA*, vol. 99, 1984.

Carroll, David (ed.), *George Eliot. The Critical Heritage*, London, Routledge, 1971.

Casteras, Susan P., 'Virgin Vows: The Early Victorian Artist's Portrayal of Nuns and Novices', in *Victorian Studies*, vol. 24, no. 2, Winter 1981.

——, *Images of Victorian Womanhood in English Art*, London, Associated University Press, 1987.

de Certeau, Michel, *Heterologies: Discourse on the Other*, trans. Brian Massumi, Minneapolis, University of Minnesota Press, 1986.

Chadwick, Whitney, *Women, Art, and Society*, London, Thames and Hudson, 1990.

Chase, Cynthia, 'The Decomposition of Elephants: Double Reading *Daniel Deronda*', in *PMLA*, vol. 93, 1978.

Chaudhuri, Nupur and Strobel, Margaret (eds), *Western Women and Imperialism: Complicity and Resistance*, Bloomington, Indiana University Press, 1992.

Cherry, Deborah, *Painting Women: Victorian Women Artists*, London, Routledge, 1993.

—— and Pollock, Griselda, 'Woman as Sign in Pre-Raphaelite Literature: A Study of the Representation of Elizabeth Siddall', in *Art History*, June 1984.

Clarke, T.J., *The Painting of Modern Life: Paris in the Art of Manet and His Followers*, New York, Alfred A. Knopf, 1984.

Clifford, James, *The Predicament of Culture: Twentieth-Century Ethnography, Literature and Art*, London, Harvard University Press, 1988.

Codell, Julie F., 'Marian Henry Spielman and the Role of the Press in the Professionalization of Artists', in *Victorian Periodicals Review*, vol. 22, no. 1, Spring 1989.

Coombes, Annie E., 'Museums and the Formation of National and Cultural Identities', in *Oxford Art Journal*, vol. 11, no. 2, 1988.

Coward, Rosalind, 'Re-Reading Freud: The Making of the Feminine', in *Spare Rib*, no. 70, 1978.

Cox, R.G., 'The Reviews and Magazines', in Boris Ford 1958.

Dale, Peter Allan, *In Pursuit of a Scientific Culture: Science, Art and Society in the Victorian Age*, Madison, University of Wisconsin Press, 1989.

Dale, Peter, 'Symbolic Representation and the Means of Revolution in *Daniel Deronda*', in *Victorian Newsletter*, no. 59, Spring 1981.

Dabydeen, David (ed.), *The Black Presence in English Literature*, Manchester, Manchester University Press, 1985.

Davidoff, Leonore, *The Best Circles: Society, Etiquette and the Season*, London, Croom Helm, 1973.

——, 'Class and Gender in Victorian England: The Diaries of Arthur Munby and Hannah Cullwick', in *Feminist Studies*, 1979.

—— and Hall, Catherine, *Family Fortunes: Men and Women of the English Middle Class 1780–1850*, London, Hutchinson, 1987.

Dawkins, Heather, 'The Diaries and Photographs of Hannah Cullwick', in *Art History*, vol. 10, no. 2, June 1987.

Dengler, Ian C., 'Turkish Women in the Ottoman Empire: The Classical Age', in Beck and Keddie 1978.

Diamond, Irene and Quinby, Lee, *Feminism and Foucault: Reflections on Resistance*, Boston, North Eastern University Press, 1988.

Diawara, Monthia, 'Black Spectatorship: Problems of Identification and Resistance', in *Screen*, vol. 29, no. 4, 1988.

Dictionnaire de biographie française, Paris, 1982.

Doane, Mary Ann, *The Desire to Desire: the Woman's Film of the 1940s*, Bloomington, Indiana University Press, 1987.

—— and Bergstrom, Janet (eds), 'The Spectatrix', Special Issue *Camera Obscura*, no. 21, 1989.

Doughan, David and Sanchez, Denise, *Feminist Periodicals 1855–1984*, Brighton, Harvester Wheatsheaf, 1987.

Drummond, A.L., *The Churches in English Fiction*, Leicester, Backus, 1950.

Dyer, Richard, 'Believing in Fairies: the Author and the Homosexual', in Fuss (ed.), 1991.

Eagleton, Terry, Jameson, Fredric and Said, Edward W., *Nationalism, Colonialism and Literature*, Minneapolis, University of Minnesota Press, 1990.

Easthope, Antony, *Literary into Cultural Studies*, London, Routledge, 1991.

Eldridge, C.C., *Victorian Imperialism*, London, Hodder and Stoughton, 1978.

Ellegård, Alvar, 'The Readership of the Periodical Press in Mid Victorian Britain. Vol. II. Directory', in *Victorian Periodicals Newsletter*, vol. 13, September 1971.

Errington, Lindsay, *Social and Religious Themes in English Art 1840–1860*, New York, Garland, 1984.

Fanon, Frantz, *Black Skin, White Masks*, (1952) London, Pluto Press, 1986.

Fawcett, Trevor and Phillpot, Clive, *The Art Press: Two Centuries of Art Magazines*, London, 1976.

Fenichel, Otto, 'Elements of a Psychoanalytic Theory of Anti-Semitism', in Simmel 1946.

Ford, Boris (ed.), *The Pelican Guide to English Literature*, vol. 6, *From Dickens to Hardy*, Harmondsworth, Penguin, 1958.

Foucault, Michel, *The Archaeology of Knowledge*, (1969) London, Tavistock Publications, 1972.

——, *The History of Sexuality: vol. I. An Introduction*, (1976) Harmondsworth, Penguin, 1978.

——, 'What is an Author?', (1969) in *Screen*, vol. 20, no. 1, Spring 1979.

——, *Power/Knowledge: Selected Interviews and Other Writings 1972–1977 by Michel Foucault*, ed. Colin Gordon, Hemel Hempstead, Harvester Wheatsheaf, 1980.

Freud, Sigmund, 'Fetishism', (1927) in Pelican Freud Library vol. 7, Harmondsworth, Penguin, 1977.

——, 'The Uncanny', in James Strachey (trans. and ed.), *The Standard Edition of the Complete Psychological Works of Sigmund Freud*, London, The Hogarth Press and the Institute of Psycho-analysis, 1955, Vol. 17.

Fuss, Diana (ed.), *Inside out: Lesbian Theories, Gay Theories*, London, Routledge 1991.

Gaines, Jane, 'White Privilege and Looking Relations: Race and Gender in Feminist Film Theory', in *Screen*, vol. 29, no. 4, 1988.

Gamman, Lorraine, 'Watching the Detectives: The Enigma of the Female Gaze', in Gamman and Marshment 1988.

—— and Marshment, Margaret (eds), *The Female Gaze: Women as Viewers of Popular Culture*, London, The Women's Press, 1988.

Garb, Tamar, ' "L'Art Féminin": the Formation of a Critical Category in Late Nineteenth-Century France', in *Art History*, vol. 12, no. 1, March 1989.

Gilman, Sander L., 'Black Bodies, White Bodies: Towards an Iconography of Female Sexuality in Late Nineteenth-Century Art, Medicine and Literature', in *Critical Inquiry*, vol. 12, 1985–6.

——, *Difference and Pathology: Stereotypes of Race, Sexuality and Madness*, Ithaca, Cornell University Press, 1985.

Graham-Brown, Sarah, *Images of Women. The Portrayal of Women in Photography of the Middle East 1860–1950*, London, Quartet, 1988.

Graver, Suzanne, *George Eliot and Community: A Study in Social Theory and Fictional Form*, Berkeley, University of California Press, 1984.

Green, Nicholas, *The Spectacle of Nature: Landscape and Bourgeois Culture in Nineteenth-Century France*, Manchester, Manchester University Press, 1990.

Greenhalgh, Paul, *Ephemeral Vistas: The Expositions Universelles, Great Exhibitions and World's Fairs 1851–1939*, Manchester, Manchester University Press, 1988.

Gregor, Ian (ed.), *Reading the Victorian Novel: Detail into Form*, London, Vision Press, 1980.

Gronberg, Theresa Ann, 'Femmes de Brasserie', in *Art History*, vol. 7, no. 3, September 1984.

Gross, John, *The Rise and Fall of the Man of Letters: Aspects of English Literary Life Since 1800*, London, Weidenfeld and Nicolson, 1969.

Grossberg, Lawrence, Nelson, Cary and Treichler, Paula A. with Linda Baughman (eds), *Cultural Studies*, New York, Routledge, 1992.

Haggis, Jane, 'Gendering Colonialism or Colonising Gender? Recent Women's Studies Approaches to White Women and the History of

British Colonialism', in *Women's Studies International Forum*, vol. 13, nos. 1/2, 1990.

Haight, Gordon S. (ed.), *The George Eliot Letters. Vol. 4: 1862–1868*, London, Oxford University Press, 1956.

—— (ed.), *The George Eliot Letters. Vol. 6: 1874–1877*, London, Oxford University Press, 1956.

——, *George Eliot. A Biography*, Oxford, Oxford University Press, 1968.

Hall, Catherine, 'The Economy of Intellectual Prestige: Thomas Carlyle, John Stuart Mill, and the Case of Governor Eyre', in *Cultural Critique*, no. 12, Spring 1989.

Hatem, Mervat, 'Through Each Other's Eyes: The Impact on the Colonial Encounter of the Images of Egyptian, Levantine-Egyptian, and European Women, 1862–1920', in Chaudhuri and Strobel 1992.

Henkin, Leo, *Darwinism in the English Novel 1860–1910: the Impact of Evolution on Victorian Fiction*, New York, Russell and Russell, 1940.

Hennessy, Rosemary and Mohan, Rajeswari, 'The Construction of Woman in Three Popular Texts of Empire: Towards a Critique of Materialist Feminism', in *Textual Practice*, vol. 3, 1989.

Henriques, Julian, Hollway, Wendy, Urwin, Cathy, Venn, Couze and Walkerdine, Valerie, *Changing the Subject: Psychology, Social Regulation and Subjectivity*, London, Methuen, 1984.

Hichberger, J.W.M., *Images of the Army. The Military in British Art, 1815–1914*, Manchester, Manchester University Press, 1988.

Hirsch, Marianne and Fox Keller, Evelyn, *Conflicts in Feminism*, London, Routledge, 1990.

Hobsbawm, E.J., *Industry and Empire*, Harmondsworth, Penguin, 1968.

——, *Age of Capital 1848–1875*, London, Weidenfeld and Nicolson, 1975.

——, *Age of Empire 1875–1914*, London, Penguin, 1987.

Hochman, Baruch, '*Daniel Deronda*: The Zionist Plot and the Problematic of George Eliot's Art', in Shalvi 1976.

Holmes, Colin, *Anti-Semitism in British Society 1876–1939*, London, Edward Arnold, 1979.

Holmstrom, John and Lerner, Laurence (eds), *George Eliot and Her Readers. A Selection of Contemporary Reviews*, London, The Bodley Head, 1966.

Holt, Elizabeth Gilmore, *The Art of All Nations 1850–73: the Emerging Role of Exhibitions and Critics*, Princeton, Princeton University Press, 1982.

Hook, Phillip and Poltimore, M., *Popular Nineteenth-Century Painting. A Dictionary of European Genre Painters*, Woodbridge, Antique Collectors' Club, Suffolk, 1986.

hooks, bell, *Black Looks: Race and Representation*, London, Turnaround, 1992.

Horkheimer, Max, 'Sociological Background of the Psychoanalytic Approach', in Simmel 1946.

Houghton, Walter E., 'Periodical Literature and the Articulate Classes', in Shattock and Wolff 1982.

Irwin, Robert, 'Writing About Islam and the Arabs', in *Ideology and Consciousness*, vol. 9, Winter 1981/2.

Jacobs, Sylvia M. 'Give a Thought to Africa: Black Women Missionaries in Southern Africa', in Chaudhuri and Strobel 1992.

Jacobus, Mary, 'The Buried Letter: Feminism and Romanticism in *Villette*', in Jacobus 1979.

——, (ed.), *Women Writing and Writing About Women*, London, Croom Helm, 1979.

Jameson, Fredric, 'Modernism and Imperialism', in Eagleton, Jameson and Said 1990.

JanMohamed, Abdul R., 'The Economy of Manichean Allegory: The Function of Racial Difference in Colonialist Literature', in *Critical Inquiry*, vol. 12, Autumn 1985.

Johnson, Pam, 'Edith Simcox and Heterosexism in Biography: a Lesbian-Feminist Exploration', in Lesbian History Group 1989.

Kabbani, Rani, *Europe's Myths of Orient*, London, Macmillan, 1986.

Kamuf, Peggy and Miller, Nancy K., 'Parisian Letters: Between Feminism and Deconstruction', in Hirsch and Fox Keller 1990.

Kaplan, Cora, 'Pandora's Box: Subjectivity, Class and Sexuality in Socialist Feminist Criticism', in Kaplan 1986.

——, *Sea Changes: Essays on Culture and Feminism*, London, Verso, 1986.

Katz, Jacob, *From Prejudice to Destruction: Anti-Semitism, 1700–1933*, Cambridge, MA., Harvard University Press, 1980.

Kent, Christopher, 'Periodical Critics of Drama, Music and Art 1830–1914: A Preliminary List', in *Victorian Periodicals Review*, vol. 13, nos. 1 and 2, Spring and Summer 1980.

——, 'More Critics of Drama, Music and Art', in *Victorian Periodicals Review*, vol. 19, no. 3, Fall 1986.

——, 'Victorian Periodicals and the Construction of Victorian Reality', in Vann and Van Arsdel 1989.

Kiernan, V.G., *The Lords of Human Kind. European Attitudes Towards the Outside World in the Imperial Age*, London, Weidenfeld and Nicolson, 1969.

Klancher, Jon, P., *The Making of English Reading Audiences, 1790–1832*, Madison, University of Wisconsin Press, 1987.

Kovel, Joel, *White Racism: a Psychohistory*, third edition, London, Free Association Books, 1988.

Laplanche, J. and Pontalis, J.-B., 'Fantasy and the Origins of Sexuality', in *International Journal of Psychoanalysis*, 49, part 1, 1968.

——, *The Language of Psychoanalysis*, London, 1973.

de Lauretis, Teresa (ed.), *Feminist Studies/Critical Studies*, Basingstoke, Macmillan, 1986.

——, 'Aesthetic and Feminist Theory: Rethinking Women's Cinema', in Pribram 1989.

Leavis, F.R., *The Great Tradition*, second edition, Harmondsworth, Penguin, 1980.

Leeks, Wendy, 'Ingres Other-Wise', in *Oxford Art Journal*, vol. 9, no. 1, 1986.

Lesbian History Group (eds), *Not a Passing Phase: Reclaiming Lesbians in History 1840–1985*, London, The Women's Press, 1989.

Levine, George, 'Determinism and Responsibility in the Works of George Eliot', in *PMLA*, vol. 77, 1962.

Levy, Anita, *Other Women: The Writing of Class, Race and Gender, 1832–1898*, Princeton, Princeton University Press, 1991.

Lewis, Bernard, *Race and Slavery in the Middle East: an Historical Enquiry*, New York, OUP, 1990.

Lewis, Reina, 'The Death of the Author and the Resurrection of the Dyke', in Munt 1992.

——, 'Women Orientalist Artists: Diversity, Ethnography, Interpretation', in *Women: A Cultural Review*, vol. 6, no. 1, 1995.

Lipman, V.D., *Social History of the Jews in England 1850–1950*, London, Watts, 1954.

Llewellyn, Briony, *The Orient Observed: Images of the Middle East From the Searight Collection*, London, Victoria and Albert Musuem, 1989.

Loomba, Ania, *Gender, Race, Renaissance Drama*, Manchester, Manchester University Press, 1989.

Low, Gail Ching-Liang, 'White Skins/Black Masks: the Pleasures and Politics of Imperialism', in *New Formations*, no. 9, Winter 1989.

Lowe, Lisa, 'Nationalism and Exoticism: Nineteenth-Century Others in Flaubert's *Salammbô* and *L'Éducation sentimentale*', in Arac and Ritvo 1991.

——, *Critical Terrains: French and British Orientalisms*, Ithaca, Cornell University Press, 1991.

Maas, Jeremy, *Gambart. Prince of the Victorian Art World*, London, Barrie and Jenkins, 1975.

Macleod, Dianne Sachko, 'Art Collecting and Victorian Middle-Class Taste', in *Art History*, vol. 10, no. 3, September 1987.

McNay, Lois, *Foucault and Feminism: Power, Gender and the Self*, Cambridge, Polity Press, 1992.

Mainardi, Patricia, *Art and Politics of the Second Empire: The Universal Expositions of 1855 and 1867*, New Haven, Yale University Press, 1987.

Mangan, J.A. (ed.), *Making Imperial Mentalities: Socialization and British Imperialism*, Manchester, Manchester University Press, 1990.

Mani, Lata, 'Multiple Mediations: Feminist Scholarship in the Age of Multinational Receptions', in *Inscriptions*, no. 5, 1989.

—— and Frankenberg, Ruth, 'The Challenge of *Orientalism*', in *Economy and Society*, vol. 14, 1985.

Mannsaker, Frances, 'Early Attitudes to Empire', in B. Moore-Gilbert 1983.

Marchand, Leslie A., *The Athenaeum: A Mirror of Victorian Culture*, Chapel Hill, 1941.

Marsh, Jan, *Pre-Raphaelite Women: Images of Femininity in Pre-Raphaelite Art*, London, Weidenfeld and Nicolson, 1987.

Martin, Biddy, 'Feminism, Criticism and Foucault', in Diamond and Quinby 1988.

Martin, Carol A., 'George Eliot: A Feminist Critic', in *Victorian Newsletter*, no. 65, Spring 1984.

Marxist-Feminist-Literature-Collective, the, 'Women's Writing: *Jane Eyre, Shirley, Villette, Aurora Leigh*', in *Ideology and Consciousness*, no. 3, Spring 1978.

Melman, Billie, *Women's Orients: English Women and the Middle East, 1718–1918, Sexuality, Religion and Work*, Basingstoke, Macmillan, 1992.

Mercer, Kobena, 'Welcome to the Jungle: Identity and Diversity in Postmodern Politics', in Rutherford 1990.

Meyer, Susan L., 'Colonialism and the Figurative Strategy of *Jane Eyre*', in *Victorian Studies*, vol. 33, no. 2, 1989.

Miller, Jane, *Seductions: Studies in Reading and Culture*, London, Virago, 1990.

Miller, Nancy K., 'Changing the Subject: Authorship, Writing, and the Reader', in de Lauretis 1986.

—— , *Subject to Change: Reading Feminist Writing*, New York, Columbia University Press, 1988.

—— , 'The Text's Heroine: A Feminist Critic and her Fictions', in Hirsch and Fox Keller 1990.

Mills, Sara, 'Discourses of Difference', in *Cultural Studies*, vol. 4, no. 2, May 1990.

—— , *Discourse of Difference: An Analysis of Women's Travel Writing and Colonialism*, London, Routledge, 1991.

Mishra, Vijay and Hodge, Bob, 'What is Post(-)Colonialism?', in *Textual Practice*, vol. 5, no. 3, Winter 1991.

Mitchell, Juliet, *Psychoanalysis and Feminism*, Harmondsworth, Penguin, 1974.

—— and Oakley, Ann (eds), *The Rights and Wrongs of Women*, Harmondsworth, Penguin, 1983.

—— and Rose, Jacqueline, *Feminine Sexuality: Jacques Lacan and the École Freudienne*, London, Macmillan, 1982.

Modder, Montagu Frank, *The Jew in the Literature of England: To the End of the Nineteenth Century*, Philadelphia, The Jewish Publication Society of America, 1939.

Modleski, Tania, 'Feminism and the Power of Interpretation: Some Critical Readings', in de Lauretis 1986.

Mohanty, Chandra, 'Under Western Eyes: Feminist Scholarship and Colonial Discourses', in *Feminist Review*, no. 30, Autumn 1988.

Mohanty, Satya P., 'The Epistemic Status of Cultural Identity: On *Beloved* and the Postcolonial Condition', in *Cultural Critique*, Spring 1993.

Moi, Toril, *Sexual/Textual Politics: Feminist Literary Theory*, London, Methuen, 1985.

Moore-Gilbert, B. (ed.), *Literature and Imperialism*, London, Roehampton Institute of Higher Education, 1983.

Morgan, Thaïs E., 'Male Lesbian Bodies: the Construction of Alternative Masculinities in Courbet, Baudelaire, and Swinburne', in *Genders*, no. 15, Winter 1992.

Mosse, George L., 'Nationalism and Respectability: Normal and Abnormal Sexuality in the Nineteenth Century', in *Journal of Contemporary History*, vol. 17, no. 2, 1982.

Mulvey, Laura, 'Visual Pleasure and Narrative Cinema', in *Screen*, vol. 16, no. 3, Autumn 1975.

——, 'On *Duel in the Sun*: Afterthoughts on Visual Pleasure and Narrative Cinema', in *Framework*, nos. 15–17, 1981.

Munt, Sally (ed.), *New Lesbian Criticism: Literary and Cultural Readings*, Hemel Hempstead, Harvester Wheatsheaf, 1992.

Nandy, Ashis, *The Intimate Enemy: Loss and Recovery of Self Under Colonialism*, (1983) second edition, Delhi, Oxford University Press, 1988.

Nead, Lynda, *Myths of Sexuality: Representations of Women in Victorian Britain*, Oxford, Blackwell, 1988.

Newton, Judith, '*Villette*', in Newton and Rosenfelt 1985.

——, 'History as Usual?: Feminism and the "New Historicism", in *Cultural Critique*, no. 9, Spring 1988.

—— and Rosenfelt, Deborah (eds), *Feminist Criticism and Social Change: Sex, Class and Race in Literature and Culture*, London, Methuen, 1985.

Nochlin, Linda, *Realism*, Harmondsworth, Penguin, 1978.

——, 'The Imaginary Orient', in *Art in America*, May 1983.

——, *Women, Art and Power and Other Essays*, London, Thames and Hudson, 1988.

Nunn, Pamela Gerrish, *Canvassing. Recollections by Six Victorian Women Artists*, London, Camden Press, 1986.

——, *Victorian Women Artists*, London, The Women's Press, 1987.

Olmstead, John Charles, *Victorian Painting. Essays and Reviews*, New York, Garland, 1983.

Ong, Aihwa, 'Colonialism and Modernity: Feminist Re-Presentations of Women in Non-Western Societies', in *Inscriptions*, vol. 3, no. 4, 1988.

Orel, Harold, *Victorian Literary Critics: George Henry Lewes, Walter Bagehot, Richard Holt Hutton, Leslie Stephen, Andrew Lang, George Saintsbury and Edmund Gosse*, London, Macmillan, 1984.

Orton, Fred and Pollock, Griselda, 'Les Données Bretonnantes: La Prairie de Représentation', in *Art History*, vol. 3, no. 3, September 1980.

Orwicz, Michael, 'Criticism and Representations of Brittany in the Early Third Republic', in *Art Journal*, vol. 46, no. 4, Winter 1987.

Parker, Andrew, Russo, Mary, Sommer, Doris and Yaeger, Patricia (eds), *Nationalisms and Sexualities*, London, Routledge, 1992.

Parsons, Christopher and Ward, Martha, *A Bibliography of Salon Criticism in Second Empire Paris*, Cambridge, Cambridge University Press, 1986.

Pathak, Zakia, Sengupta, Saswati and Purkayastha, Sharmila, 'The Prisonhouse of Orientalism', in *Textual Practice*, vol. 5, no. 2, Summer 1991.

Paxton, Nancy L., 'Feminism Under the Raj: Complicity and Resistance in the Writings of Flora Annie Steel and Annie Besant', in *Women's Studies International Forum*, vol. 13, no. 4, 1990.

——, 'Mobilizing Chivalry: Rape in British Novels about the Indian Uprising of 1857', in *Victorian Studies*, vol. 36, no. 1, Fall 1992.

Penzer, N.M., *The Harem: an Account of the Institution as it Existed in the Palace of the Turkish Sultans With a History of the Grand Seraglio From its Foundations to Modern Time*, London, Spring Books, 1936.

Perkin, J. Russell, *A Reception-History of George Eliot's Fiction*, Ann Arbor, Mich., UMI Research Press, 1990.

Petteys, Chris, *Dictionary of Women Artists. An International Dictionary of Women Artists Born Before 1900*, Boston, G.K. Hall, 1985.

Pick, Daniel, *Faces of Degeneration: A European Disorder c.1848–1918*, Cambridge, Cambridge University Press, 1989.

Pinney, Thomas (ed.), *Essays of George Eliot*, London, Routledge, 1968.

Pollock, Griselda, 'Modernity and the Spaces of Femininity', in Pollock 1987.

—— , *Vision and Difference: Femininity, Feminism and Histories of Art*, London, Routledge, 1987.

—— , 'Van Gogh and the Poor Slaves: Images of Rural Labour as Modern Art', in *Art History*, vol. 11, no. 3, September 1988.

—— , 'Agency and the Avant-garde: Studies in Authorship and History by Way of Van Gogh', in *Block*, no. 15, 1989.

Poovey, Mary, *Uneven Developments. The Ideological Work of Gender in Mid-Victorian England*, London, Virago, 1989.

Porter, Dennis, '*Orientalism* and its Problems', in Francis Barker *et al.* (eds), *The Politics of Theory*, Colchester, University of Essex, 1982.

Pribram, Deirdre (ed.), *Female Spectators: Looking at Film and Television*, London, Verso, 1989.

Pudney, John, *The Thomas Cook Story*, London, The Non-Fiction Book Co., 1954.

Pykett, Lyn, 'Reading the Periodical Press: Text and Context', in *Victorian Periodicals Review*, Special Issue *Theory*, vol. 22, no. 3, Fall 1989.

Ragussis, Michael, 'Representation, Conversion, and Literary Form: *Harrington* and the Novel of Jewish Identity', in *Critical Inquiry*, vol. 16, no. 1, Autumn 1989.

al-Raheb, Hani, *The Zionist Character in the English Novel*, London, Zed Books, 1985.

Raider, Ruth, ' "The Flash of Fervour": *Daniel Deronda*', in Gregor 1980.

Rich, Adrienne, 'Towards a Politics of Location', in Rich 1987.

—— , *Blood, Bread and Poetry: Selected Prose 1979–1985*, London, Virago, 1987.

Richon, Olivier, 'Representation, the Harem and the Despot', in *Block*, no. 10, 1985.

Riley, Denise, *'Am I That Name?' Feminism and the Category of 'Women' in History*, Basingstoke, Macmillan, 1988.

Roberts, Diane, *The Myth of Aunt Jemima: Representations of Race and Region*, London, Routledge, 1994.

Roberts, Helene E., 'Exhibition and Review: the Periodical Press and the Victorian Art Exhibition System', in Shattock and Wolff 1982.

—— , 'Periodicals and Art History', in Vann and Van Arsdel 1989.

Robinson, Jane, *Wayward Women: A Guide to Women Travellers*, Oxford, Oxford University Press, 1990.

Rooke, Patricia, 'Slavery, Social Death and Imperialism: the Formation of a Christian Black Elite in the West Indies 1800–1845', in Mangan 1990.
Rose, Jacqueline, 'George Eliot and the Spectacle of Woman', in Rose 1986.
—— , Sexuality in the Field of Vision, London, Verso, 1986.
Rosenman, Ellen, 'The House and the Home: Money, Women and the Family in the Bankers' Magazine and Daniel Deronda', in Women's Studies, vol. 17, nos. 3–4, 1990.
Roth, Cecil, A History of the Jews in England, Oxford, The Clarendon Press, 1941.
Rowell, Geoffrey, The Vision Glorious: Themes and Personalities of the Catholic Revival in Anglicanism, Oxford, Oxford University Press, 1983.
Rutherford, Jonathan (ed.), Identity: Community, Culture, Difference, London, Lawrence and Wishart, 1990.
Said, Edward W., Orientalism, Harmondsworth, Penguin, 1978.
—— , 'Zionism From the Standpoint of Its Victims', in Social Text, vol. 1, 1978.
—— , Covering Islam: How the Media and the Experts Determine How We See the Rest of the World, London, Routledge, 1981.
—— , The World, the Text, and the Critic, Massachusetts, Harvard University Press, 1983.
—— , 'Orientalism Reconsidered', in Race and Class, vol. 27, no. 2, 1985.
—— , 'Representing the Colonized: Anthropology's Interlocutors', in Critical Inquiry, Winter 1989.
—— , 'Yeats and Decolonization', in Eagleton, Jameson and Said 1990.
—— , Culture and Imperialism, New York, Alfred A. Knopf, 1993.
Salbstein, M.C.N., The Emancipation of the Jews in Britain: The Question of the Admission of the Jews to Parliament, 1825–1860, Rutherford, NJ, Fairleigh Dickinson University Press, 1982.
Sarup, Madan, Jacques Lacan, Hemel Hempstead, Harvester Wheatsheaf, 1992.
Scarce, Jennifer, Women's Costume of the Near and Middle East, London, Unwin Hyman, 1987.
Schneider, William H., An Empire for the Masses. The French Popular Image of Africa, 1870–1900, Westport, Conn., Greenwood Press, 1982.
Scholem, Gershom G., Major Trends in Jewish Mysticism, third edition, London, Thames and Hudson, 1955.
Scott, David, 'The Literary Orient', in Thompson 1988.
Sedgwick, Eve Kosofsky, 'Nationalisms and Sexualities in the Age of Wilde', in Parker et al. 1992.
Shalvi, Alice (ed.), Daniel Deronda: a Centenary Symposium, Jerusalem, Jerusalem Academic Press, 1976.
Sharpe, Jenny, Allegories of Empire: The Figure of Woman in the Colonial Text, Minneapolis, University of Minnesota Press, 1993.
Shattock, Joanne and Wolff, Michael (eds), The Victorian Periodical Press: Samplings and Soundings, Leicester, Leicester University Press, 1982.
Showalter, Elaine, 'The Greening of Sister George', in Nineteenth-Century Fiction, no. 35, 1980.

——, *A Literature of Their Own: From Charlotte Brontë to Doris Lessing*, (1977) second edition, London, Virago, 1982.

——, 'Looking Forward: American Feminist, Victorian Sages', in *Victorian Newsletter*, no. 65, Spring 1984.

Shuttleworth, Sally, *George Eliot and Nineteenth-Century Science. The Make-Believe of a Beginning*, Cambridge, Cambridge University Press, 1984.

Simmel, Ernst, 'Anti-Semitism and Mass Psychopathology', in Simmel 1946.

—— (ed.), *Anti-Semitism: a Social Disease*, New York, International Universities Press, 1946.

Sloane, Joseph C., *French Painting Between the Past and the Present. Artists, Critics and Traditions From 1848–1870*, Princeton, Princeton University Press, 1951.

Smith, Anne (ed.), *George Eliot: Centenary Essays and an Unpublished Fragment*, London, Vision, 1980.

Snell, Robert, *Théophile Gautier: a Romantic Critic of the Visual Arts*, Oxford, The Clarendon Press, 1982.

Spillers, Hortense J., 'Mama's Baby, Papa's Maybe: An American Grammar Book', in *Diacritics*, vol. 17, no. 2, Summer 1987.

Spivak, Gayatri Chakravorty, 'Three Women's Texts and a Critique of Imperialism', in *Critical Inquiry*, 12, Autumn 1985.

——, 'Can the Subaltern Speak? Speculations on Widow Sacrifice', in *Wedge*, nos 7/8, Winter/Spring 1985.

——, 'French Feminisms in an International Frame', in Spivak 1988.

——, 'Subaltern Studies: Deconstructing Historiography', in Spivak 1988.

——, *In Other Worlds: Essays in Cultural Politics*, London, Routledge, 1988.

Stacey, Jackie, 'Desperately Seeking Difference', in Gamman and Marshment 1988.

Stanley, Liz (ed.), *The Diaries of Hannah Cullwick: Victorian Maidservant*, London, Virago, 1983.

Stevens, Mary (ed.), *The Orientalists: Delacroix to Matisse. European Painters in North Africa and the Near East*, London, Royal Academy, 1984.

Street, Brian, *The Savage in Literature: the Representation of 'Primitive' Society in English Fiction, 1858–1920*, London, Routledge, 1975.

Summers, Anne, 'Pride and Prejudice: Ladies and Nurses in the Crimean War', in *History Workshop Journal*, no. 16, Autumn 1983.

——, *Angels and Citizens: British Women as Military Nurses 1854–1914*, London, Routledge, 1988.

Suvin, Darko, 'The Social Addressees of Victorian Fiction: a Preliminary Enquiry', in *Literature and History*, vol. 8, no. 1, Spring 1982.

Sweetman, John, *The Oriental Obsession: Islamic Inspiration in British and American Art and Architecture 1500–1920'*, Cambridge, Cambridge University Press, 1988.

Tawardos, Çeylan, 'Foreign Bodies: Art History and the Discourse of Nineteenth-Century Orientalist Art', in *Third Text*, nos. 3/4, Spring/Summer 1988.

Thompson, James, 'Mapping the Mind: the Quest for Eastern Metaphors and Meaning', in Thompson 1988.

—— (ed.), *The East Imagined, Experienced, Remembered: Orientalist Nineteenth-Century Painting*, the National Gallery of Ireland and National Musuems and Galleries on Merseyside, 1988.

Thornton, Lynn, *The Orientalists: Painter Travellers 1828–1908*, Paris, ACR Edition, 1983.

——, *Women as Portrayed in Orientalist Painting*, Paris, ACR Edition, 1985.

Tickner, Lisa, 'Feminism, Art History and Sexual Difference', in *Genders*, no. 3, Fall 1988.

Tomlinson, John, *Cultural Imperialism: a Critical Introduction*, London, Pinter, 1991.

Tuchman, Gaye with Nina E. Fortin, *Edging Women Out: Victorian Novelists, Publishers and Social Change*, London, Routledge, 1989.

Usherwood, Paul and Spencer-Smith, Jenny, *Lady Butler. Battle Artist 1846–1933*, London, National Army Museum, 1987.

Vann, J. Don, *Victorian Novels in Serial*, New York, Modern Language Association of America, 1985.

—— and Van Arsdel, Rosemary T. (eds), *Victorian Periodicals. A Guide to Research*, vol. 1, New York, Modern Language Association of America, 1978.

—— and Van Arsdel, Rosemary T. (eds), *Victorian Periodicals: A Guide to Research*, vol. 2, New York, Modern Language Association of America, 1989.

Vicinus, Martha, *Independent Women. Work and Community for Single Women: 1850–1920*, London, Virago, 1985.

Voeltz, Richard, '. . . A Good Jew and a Good Englishman: The Jewish Lads' Brigade, 1894–1922', in *Journal of Contemporary History*, vol. 23, no. 1, January 1988.

Ware, Vron, *Beyond the Pale: White Women, Racism and History*, London, Verso, 1992.

Warner, Malcolm, 'The Question of Faith: Orientalism, Christianity and Islam', in Stevens 1984.

Watt, Ian, *The Rise of the Novel*, (1957), London, The Hogarth Press, 1993.

Weeks, Jeffrey, *Sex, Politics and Society: the Regulation of Sexuality Since 1800*, Harlow, Longman, 1981.

Werses, Shmuel, 'The Jewish Reception of *Daniel Deronda*', in Shalvi 1976.

Williams, Raymond, *Culture and Society 1780–1950*, second edition, Harmondsworth, Penguin, 1963.

Wolff, Janet, 'The Invisible Flâneuse; Women and the Literature of Modernity', in *Theory, Culture and Society*, vol. 2, 1983–5.

——, 'Excess and Inhibition: Interdisciplinarity in the Study of Art', in Grossberg *et al.* 1992.

Wolff, Michael, North, John S. and Deering, Dorothy, *The Waterloo Directory of Victorian Periodicals 1824–1900, Phase 1*, Waterloo (Ontario), Wilfred Laurier University Press, 1977.

Wood, Christopher, *The Dictionary of Victorian Painters*, second edition, Woodbridge, Antique Collectors' Club, 1978.

Woodhull, Winifred, 'Unveiling Algeria', in *Genders*, no. 10, Spring 1991.

Yeldham, Charlotte, *Women Artists in Nineteenth-Century France and England. Their Art Education, Exhibition Opportunities and Membership of Exhibiting Societies and Academies, with an Assessment of the Subject Matter of their Work and Summary Biographies*, New York, Garland, 1984.

Young, Robert, *White Mythologies: Writing History and the West*, London, Routledge, 1990.

Zatlin, Linda Gertlin, 'High Tea and Matza Balls: Religion in the Victorian Jewish Novel', in *Victorian Newsletter*, Spring 1979.

Zeldin, Theodore, *France 1848–1945, Vol. 2: Intellect, Taste and Anxiety*, Oxford, The Clarendon Press, 1977.

Zimmerman, Bonnie, 'Gwendolen Harleth and "The Girl of the Period" ', in Smith 1980.

Zonana, Joyce, 'The Sultan and the Slave: Feminist Orientalism and the Structure of *Jane Eyre*', in *Signs*, vol. 18, no. 3, Spring 1993.

Index

accomplishment art 56–7, 58, 77
adaptation 213
Adler, H. 207
adulthood 177
affective ties 227
agency 20–1, 27–8, 34
Allom, Thomas 111
Almah 173–4, 189
alterity *see* other
amateur artists 115–16
amateur writers 81
Anderson, B. 13
Anderson, Sophie 119–20, 176;
  Guess Again 176, Plate 40; *In
  the Harem* 120, Plate 27;
  Portrait of Toklihili, 120, Plate
  28
Anglo-Catholic Revival 89–90;
  see also Christianity, Roman
  Catholicism
Anglo-Jewish identity 201–7
Anglo-Jewish press 232
anti-Semitism 205–7, 216, 233;
  and assimilation 205; avarice
  223–4; repressed 206–7;
  uncanniness of Jews 222
Apter, E. 180–1, 190
aristocracy 211
art 56; accomplishment 56–7, 58,
  77; amateur 115–16; battle
  63–4; degeneracy, evolution
  and 102–3; International
  Exhibitions 74, 83; labour and
  98–100; national differences

74–6; opportunities for women
  56–67; Orientalism 2–3, 109–21;
  prints 78–9; professional women
  artists 117 18; *see also* Browne,
  and under other artists
art buyers 65–6
art education 57–9
art féminin 61
Art Journal 66, 92; Browne 131
  (as naturalist 93–4; *Sisters of
  Charity* 88–9, 107); Gérôme 114
  (*Phryne* 75); Jerichau-Baumann
  119, 167–8; national differences
  74, 75
Artiste, L' 94
Ashkenazim 202
assimilationism 205, 208, 233
ateliers 59
Athenaeum 66, 92; Browne 86–7,
  131 (*Rhodian Girl* 171; *Sisters
  of Charity* 87, 88, 89)
Austria-Hungary 202
authenticity: Browne 138–41, 142,
  148; George Eliot 203–4;
  'Orient' in Orientalism 16–17
author, 'death of' 22–30; *see also*
  writing
authority of female Orientalist
  gaze 178–84
avarice 223–4
aversive racist 198–9

Barrell, J. 178
Barthes, R. 23–4, 28